# The Family of Sir Stamford Raffles

Captain Benjamin Raffles (1739–1811),
father of Sir Stamford Raffles
*Private collection*

# The Family of
# Sir Stamford Raffles

John Bastin

Julie Weizenegger

© 2016 National Library Board, Singapore, and John Sturgus Bastin
Design and layout © 2016 Marshall Cavendish International (Asia) Pte Ltd

Published by

National Library Board, Singapore
100 Victoria Street, #14-01, National Library Building, Singapore 188064
Tel: +65 6332 3255 | Email: ref@library.nlb.gov.sg | www.nlb.gov.sg

and

Marshall Cavendish Editions
An imprint of Marshall Cavendish International
1 New Industrial Road, Singapore 536196
Tel: +65 6213 9300 | Email: genref@sg.marshallcavendish.com

Editorial Team
National Library Board: Francis Dorai, Veronica Chee
Marshall Cavendish Editions: Justin Lau, Benson Tan, Glenn Wray

National Library Board, Singapore Cataloguing-in-Publication Data:

Name(s): Bastin, John Sturgus, 1927- author. | Weizenegger, Julie, author.

Description: The family of Sir Stamford Raffles / John Bastin, Julie Weizenegger. | Singapore :
Marshall Cavendish Editions and National Library Board, Singapore, [2016]

Identifiers: OCN922433063 | ISBN 978-981-47-2176-9 (hardcover)

Subject(s): Raffles, Thomas Stamford, Sir, 1781-1826 -- Family. | Raffles, Olivia Mariamne,
1771-1814. | Raffles, Sophia, Lady, 1786-1858. | Colonial administrators -- Singapore |
Colonial administrators -- Great Britain.

Classification: LC Classification DS646.26.R3 | DDC 959.57030922--dc23


Printed in Singapore by Markono Print Media Pte Lrd

*For*
*Lucy*

# Contents

# List of Illustrations

# Foreword

SIR STAMFORD RAFFLES, the founder of modern Singapore, is one of the most significant figures in our history. The subject of Raffles has been thoroughly studied and written about over the past two centuries; his letters and documents have been meticulously scrutinised, and his legacy is the source of frequent debate.

But while we know much about Raffles, we know much less about his family. This is why *The Family of Sir Stamford Raffles* is such an important addition to the canon of Raffles scholarship.

The research of Dr John Bastin and Julie Weizenegger casts new light on personages in the Raffles story who were previously only part of the supporting cast. We learn of Raffles's father, Captain Benjamin Raffles, who died in poverty despite a once-successful seafaring career; we are given insight into Raffles's relationships with his mother, his siblings, and his children; and we learn more about Raffles's two wives, Olivia Mariamne Devenish and Sophia Hull, including what happened to the latter after the death of her husband.

This book plays an important role in drawing out what is known of the people closest to Raffles throughout his life – people who played a crucial part in shaping the character of Singapore's founder, and in a sense contributing to the larger history of Singapore.

**Elaine Ng**
Chief Executive Officer
National Library Board, Singapore

# Preface

THIS SOMEWHAT DISCURSIVE WORK on the family of Sir Stamford Raffles corrects and extends information on the subject published in *Letters and Books of Sir Stamford Raffles and Lady Raffles: The Tang Holdings Collection of Autograph Letters and Books of Sir Stamford Raffles and Lady Raffles* (Editions Didier Millet, Singapore, 2009). The new material comes largely from birth and death registers, parish and insurance records, and also from the Slebech Papers in the National Library of Wales Collection, Aberystwyth; the Abinger Collection in the Bodleian Library, University of Oxford; and the Raffles Family Collection in the British Library, London. It represents a considerable addition to what is at present known about the family of Sir Stamford Raffles.

This work began in response to erroneous statements made in a recently published biography of Raffles, and elsewhere, suggesting that Sir Stamford Raffles's father, Captain Benjamin Raffles, was engaged in the West India slave trade and that the decline in his family's fortunes was probably due to his gambling.[1] Both statements have no basis in fact, but we realise that unless they are contradicted by detailed and documentary evidence they are colourful enough to enter and confound future Raffles scholarship. We have therefore traced details of all Captain Raffles's ships and voyages to the West Indies in order to demonstrate that he was, as correctly assumed by his earlier biographers,[2] engaged in the traditional 'direct' trade between London and Jamaica, carrying so-called 'dry goods', such as English manufactures and Irish agricultural produce, with return shipments of West India sugar and rum.

There will be found in this book a good deal of new information on Raffles's first wife, Olivia Mariamne Devenish, but for details of her life in Penang and Java we have drawn on material from the biography, *Olivia Mariamne Raffles* (Landmark Books, Singapore, 2002). The account of Raffles's second wife, Sophia Hull, is similarly based on the biography, *Sophia Raffles* (Landmark Books, Singapore, 2002).

We wish to thank Sir Edward Dashwood as the copyright holder and the National Library of Wales for permission to quote from the Slebech Papers in the National Library of Wales Collection; Microform Academic Publishers Ltd. for similar permission, including information from the Kenneth Morgan (2004) introduction to the Jamaican material in the Slebech Papers; Rhianydd Davies of the National Library of Wales for her invaluable assistance; David Sarsfield, a representative of Microform Academic Publishers Ltd., for his assistance; Isaiah Levy for the photograph of the grave of Ann Raffles, mother of Sir Stamford Raffles, in St. Mary's Old Church Stoke Newington, and for information from the Hackney Council Archives; Mark Perrett of St. Mary's Church Stoke Newington for additional information on the subject of her grave; Mr. Ed Lyon, Archives Assistant, Hackney Archives, for his assistance; Mary Green, Parish Archivist of St. Mary's Church Teddington, Middlesex, for her assistance; Mr. B. Glen Chandler for the photograph of St. Margaret's Church Westminster; West Surrey Family History Society for permission to use information from the burial records of St. Mary's Church Wimbledon, Surrey; the City of Westminster Archives Centre, London, for permission to use information from the Westminster Rate Books and from the Westminster baptism, marriage and burial records; Clifford Jones, an 'Old Blue' and volunteer Archivist of Christ's Hospital, for information on Benjamin Raffles and other members of his family who were pupils of the school; the National Archives, Kew, for the record of the clandestine marriage of Thomas Raffles and Jane Gibson; Cliff Webb for the record of the burial of Jane Raffles (née Gibson); Marcus Langdon for information on the early history of Penang; the Burney Collection of 17th–18th-century newspapers, courtesy of Gale Digital Collections, Cengage Learning, accessed through State Library e-services, for shipping information; Louise Sanger, Information Centre Deputy Manager, Group Communications, of Lloyd's Register Group Limited for information from Lloyd's Register, London; Jeremy Smith of the London Metropolitan Archives, City of London, for permission to use information from baptism, marriage, burial and Land Tax records, and for permission to reproduce the marriage record of Benjamin Raffles and Ann Lyde; Surrey History Centre for information on Surrey Land Tax records relating to Captain Benjamin Raffles and Thomas Stamford Raffles; the Tate Enterprises Limited, London, for permission to reproduce the portrait of William Godwin by J.W. Chandler, and David Thompson, Sales and Rights Executive from Tate Images for his assistance; Legacies of British Slave-ownership for information on Leonora Carter's slave compensation; Findmypast Australia and UK for permission to use information from records relating to India; the National Maritime Museum, Greenwich, for permission to reproduce the image of the ship *Pitt*; Darryl Lundy of The Peerage for information on birth, death and marriage dates; Sharon Howard of the Humanities Research Institute, University of Sheffield, for permission to quote from the Old Bailey Online transcript of the trial involving Olivia Mariamne Fancourt; Dr. Bruce Barker-Benfield, Senior Assistant Librarian, the Bodleian Library, University of Oxford, for his generous assistance, and the Bodleian Library for permission to quote from the letters and Diary of William Godwin in the Abinger Archive and the online editors, Victoria Myers, David O'Shaughnessy and Mark Philp; the British Library Board for permission to quote from material in the Raffles Family Collection and to reproduce the images of Rayakottai Fort and St. Mary's Church, Madras; and the Dr. Williams's Library, University of London, for permission to quote from the fragment of Thomas Raffles's autobiography.

We should also like to thank Francis Dorai, Assistant Director/Publishing, National Library, Singapore; Justin Lau, Editor at Marshall Cavendish Editions, Singapore; and Veronica Chee, Senior Librarian, National Library, Singapore.

# The Family of
# Sir Stamford Raffles

# CHAPTER ONE
## Sir Stamford Raffles's Father and Grandfather

Beverley with St. Mary's Church
*Contemporary print*

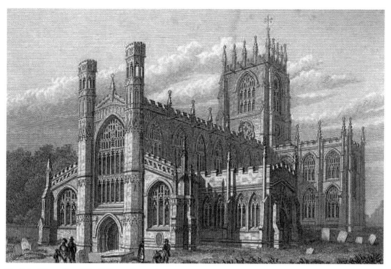

Parish Church of St. Mary, Beverley
*Thomas Allen,* A New and Complete History of the County of York *(London, 1831)*

THE FAMILY OF Sir Thomas Stamford Raffles originally came from Beverley in the East Riding of Yorkshire, where the name in variant spellings appears in the registers of the Minister Church of St. John the Evangelist and the parish Church of St. Mary. A Robert Raffles is recorded in 1513–14 as the Keeper or Governor of Beverley, a position he held in subsequent years even though the post was not sought after as it carried no remuneration. There was a Robert Raffles who was a member of the Beverley Common Council in 1543, and also a 'braseer' (brazier) named Robert Raffulles in 1553. John Raffles or Raffellis was an alderman of the bakers in 1536, and among the 16th-century mayors of Beverley a certain John Raffles was one of the 12 Governors of the town in 1577, who died during his mayoralty in January 1583.[1] John and William Raffles are recorded at the time of the latter's death in 1590 as 'pewtherers' (pewterers), suggesting that the Raffles family was well established as brass and pewter makers in the town. There is also a reference to a knight banneret during the reign of James I named Sir Benjamin Raffles.[2] According to tradition, the family moved from Beverley to Berwick-upon-Tweed, Northumberland,[3] possibly due to the ravages of the plague in the early 17th century, particularly in 1610 when many of the inhabitants left the town. It is interesting, in this connection, that there is a reference to Thomas, son of 'Tho: Raffels', in the baptismal records of Berwick-upon-Tweed as early as 1619, whereas the name disappears entirely from the second volume of the Registers of St. Mary's Church Beverley after 1637.

There were a number of people named Raffles living in Berwick-upon-Tweed during the 17th century,[4] but at the end of the century, or shortly afterwards, Sir Stamford Raffles's family moved to London. This was said to have occurred during the time of his great-grandfather,[5] Thomas Raffles, who may have been the person recorded in the Westminster Rate Book for 1717 as a resident in Strutton Ground, a street which ran up to Tothill-fields,[6] and also in the subsequent Rate Books as a resident in nearby New Pye Street and Duck Lane in the parish of St. Margaret's Westminster, one of the worst slum areas in Westminster in the 18th century, later described by Dickens as the 'Devil's Acre'. It is possible, but not certain, that he was the 'Thomas Raffles, late of St. Margaret's Westminster', who is described as a 'Taylor' in the *London Gazette* of 2 January 1730, and as one of the persons 'being Fugitives for Debt, and beyond the Seas on and before the 1st of February 1728, and having surrendered themselves to the Warden of the Fleet Prison, … intend to take the Benefit of

St. Margaret's Church, Westminster
*Photograph by B. Glenn Chandler, Texas*

the late Act for the Relief of Insolvent Debtors, at the next General or Quarter Sessions of the Peace to be held for the City of London …',[7] the connection resting on the common factor of residence in the parish of St. Margaret's Westminster.[8] Thomas Raffles, at any rate, married Elizabeth (maiden name unknown) and by her had at least three children: Thomas Raffles, who was born on 17 August and baptised in St. Margaret's Church Westminster on 27 August 1710;[9] Anne,[10] who was born on 27 May 1716 and baptised in St. Margaret's Church Westminster two days later; and Mary,[11] who was born on 4 August 1718 and baptised in the same church on 15 August.

The eldest of these three children, Thomas Raffles, was Sir Stamford Raffles's grandfather. He married Susannah (maiden name unknown)[12] probably in 1731, and their first child, James, was born on 25 July 1732 and baptised in St. Margaret's Church Westminster on 17 August 1732. A second child, Elizabeth,[13] was born on 23 February 1734 and baptised on 10 March 1734 in St. Margaret's Church Westminster, and a second daughter, Mary,[14] was born on 16 March and baptised in the same church on 26 March 1736. A second son, Thomas, was born on 3 December and baptised on 18 December 1737 in St. Margaret's Church Westminster, followed by Benjamin, father of Sir Stamford Raffles, who was baptised in St. Ann's Church Blackfriars on 29 July 1739. Then came Henry, who was baptised on 19 April 1741 in St. Ann's Church Blackfriars and buried three months later in the graveyard of St. Margaret's Church Westminster on 15 July 1741. Another Henry was baptised in St. Ann's Church Blackfriars on 27 June 1742, followed by John Raffles, who was baptised on 18 November 1744 in St. Ann's Church Blackfriars and buried at St. Margaret's Church Westminster on 3 August 1746. Next came a daughter named Susannah Julia Raffles,[15] who was baptised in St. Ann's Church Blackfriars on 6 April 1746. Following this succession of births and deaths, Thomas Raffles's wife, Susannah, died and was buried on 2 October 1747 in the graveyard of St. Margaret's Church Westminster,[16] leaving in his care seven surviving children: James, Elizabeth, Mary, Thomas, Benjamin, Henry and Susannah. He was described later by his son Thomas Raffles as 'a Good Moral Man', who loved his children but who brought them up with some strictness.[17]

On 5 October 1750, three years after the death of his first wife, Thomas Raffles married Jane Gibson of St. Ann's Blackfriars in Alexander Keith's New

The Prerogative Office, Doctors' Commons, London,
where Sir Stamford Raffles's grandfather Thomas Raffles was
employed as one of the principal clerks for nearly 40 years
*W. Thornbury and E. Walford,* Old and New London *(London, 1879–85)*

The Writing School, Christ's Hospital
*Aquatint by J. Stadler after F. Mackenzie*

Little Chapel Mayfair. He had four children by her: John, who was born on 26 December 1750[18] and baptised on 30 December 1750 in St. Michael's Church Queenhithe, London; William, who was born in 1751 and baptised on 1 January 1752 in St. Ann's Church Blackfriars;[19] Daniel, who was baptised on 22 April 1753 and buried on 6 July 1755 in the graveyard of St. Ann's Church Blackfriars, and Margaret, who was baptised on 1 November 1754 in St. Ann's Church Blackfriars.[20] Thomas Raffles's second wife, Jane, died in November 1756 from unknown causes and was buried at the Church of the Holy Trinity Clapham, Surrey, on the 16th of that month, leaving him with eight living children.[21] Having earlier been designated as a records clerk, without any indication of his employer, he is described in July 1751 as a 'record-keeper's clerk' and Keeper of Wills in the Prerogative Office of Doctors' Commons, an Inn of Court for lay judges and advocates of the ecclesiastic and admiralty courts situated to the south of St. Paul's-churchyard and the River Thames.[22] In 1757 he was still living in the parish of St. Ann's Blackfriars, but in January 1762, when his son William was admitted as a scholar to St. Paul's School, his address was Cartwright Square, Rosemary Lane (later Royal Mint Street), at the southern end of Cartwright Street leading to the middle of Upper East, Smithfield. On his death on 28 November 1784, aged 74, he was buried in the graveyard of St. Mary's Church Islington, a brief obituary notice in *The Gentleman's Magazine* stating that he had been employed as 'one of the principal clerks' in the Prerogative Office of Doctors' Commons for 'near 40 years'.[23] If this statement is correct, then it would appear that he was already employed in the post before the death of his first wife, and that he resigned his position temporarily to look after his children.

The second son, Thomas Raffles, was accepted by the preparatory school of Christ's Hospital at Hertford in April 1748, afterwards transferring to the senior school at Newgate Street in the City of London. Christ's Hospital, the 'Blue Coat' School, was a royal charitable foundation for the education of children of families in social or financial need, and Thomas was presented by the donation governor Robert Cary, one of the many benefactors of the school, who would not necessarily have been known to his family. Thomas subsequently recorded that the education he received at the school in reading and writing was sufficient to be 'useful in a Merchant's Counting house', and

The Mathematical School, Christ's Hospital, where Captain Benjamin
Raffles was a pupil
*W. Thornbury and E. Walford,* Old and New London *(London, 1879–85)*

The Cloisters, Christ's Hospital
*W. Thornbury and E. Walford,* Old and New London *(London, 1879–85)*

that at school he 'observed sometimes an application for Apprentices to go to the West Indies in the Mercantile way', and that 'from the first moment [he] was predetermined to adventure in such a Station'.[24] On leaving Christ's Hospital on 22 January 1754, he was accepted as an apprentice by Alexander Grant of London, who specifically served Captain George Johnston, a merchant sailing to Jamaica.

He was followed at Christ's Hospital by his brother Benjamin,[25] father of Sir Stamford Raffles, who entered the preparatory school at Hertford in April 1749 aged nine and transferred to the senior school in London two years later, his donation governor being Dr. John Bettesworth. He became a pupil of the Royal Mathematical School, a department of Christ's Hospital founded by Charles II in 1673 to teach navigation to boys destined for service at sea.[26] He was taught, among others, by James Hodgson (1672–1755), F.R.S., a former apprentice of John Flamsteed (1646–1719), the first Astronomer Royal, whose *Atlas Cœlestis* (London, 1729) he helped to edit. Hodgson was also the author of a number of other works, including *The Theory of Navigation* (London, 1706) and the elaborate two-volume work, *A System of the Mathematics, containing the Euclidean Geometry, Plain and Spherical Geometry, the Projection of the Sphere, both Orthographic and Stereographic, Astronomy, the Use of Globes and Navigation* (London, 1723), which was especially prepared for pupils of the Royal Mathematical School at Christ's Hospital. Benjamin obviously proved himself a highly accomplished pupil since his ciphering book on navigation, now in the Phillips Library, Peabody Essex Museum, Salem, Massachusetts,[27] has been acclaimed, with seven others, as exhibiting 'extraordinary penmanship and calligraphy, and an impressively high level of mathematics'.[28]

# CHAPTER TWO

## Captain Benjamin Raffles and the West India Trade

Captain Benjamin Raffles (1739–1811), father of Sir Stamford Raffles
*Private collection*

BENJAMIN RAFFLES LEFT SCHOOL when he was 16, and on 12 July 1755 he was assigned for seven years as an apprentice to George Hooper, master of the *Martin*, a ship of some 220 tons built in the previous year on the Thames and armed with six six-pounders.[1] The ship's Lieutenant was Stephen Hooper and her owners included the London merchants, George Hooper Sr., and Jude and William Hooper, so the management of the ship was something of a family affair. The *Martin* was engaged in the 'direct' West India trade out of the port of London, and Benjamin joined the ship a month after her return from Antigua in June 1755. For the next nine years the ship made an annual voyage from London to Antigua, where her cargo consisted of sugar from the plantations of the ship owners, Richard Oliver & Co., one of some 90 London firms operating as sugar factors in the period between 1740 and 1775.[2] In February 1765 the *Martin* diverted for a single voyage to Jamaica,[3] the largest of the British colonies in the Caribbean, but it is unknown if Benjamin was still on board as his apprenticeship had ended two years earlier.

On 1 November 1764 he appears for the first time as master of the ship *Morant* sailing from Deal for Jamaica, his seafaring career now conforming to Conrad's 'rhythmical swing' of a seaman's life, with departures from England late in each year carrying iron ware and items of British manufacture, landfalls at Cork in Ireland to collect supplies of linen, butter, cheese and other foodstuffs, and arrivals at the free trade ports of Kingston or Port Morant in March or April before reloading with West India sugar and rum for the homeward passage. The *Morant* was a vessel of 180 or 190 tons, built in Boston in 1763 and owned by Lawrence Cole & Thomas Bingley Sr., insurance brokers of Exchange Alley, Cornhill, later of 21 Birchin Lane, Cornhill, London.[4] The ship was in Jamaica in March 1765 and sailed on her homeward voyage in April with a cargo of 50 hogsheads of sugar and two puncheons of rum from the plantation of the absentee plantation owner Chaloner Arcedekne,[5] arriving at Dover on 24–26 June 1765. On her next outward voyage she sailed for Cork on 14 September 1765[6] and then to Jamaica on 5 November 1765 before arriving back at Dover on 16 July 1766[7] and Gravesend four days later. In March and April 1767[8] the ship was in Jamaica, where Captain Raffles was held responsible for the loss of part of her cargo of sugar due to the negligence of his crew.[9] She sailed from Jamaica in May 1767 carrying 50 hogsheads of sugar from the Arcedekne plantation,[10] and arrived at Deal on 10 July 1767.[11] On 25 October 1767 the ship was again at Deal and was still anchored there on 3 November before sailing for Jamaica. On her homeward passage she was reported off Cowes on 5 July 1768, and on 17 August of the following year she was off Portsmouth on her return voyage from Jamaica.[12]

Then, possibly as a result of Lawrence Cole's death early in 1769, and the subsequent sale of the ship, Captain Raffles was recorded four months later, in December 1769, as master of the *Caesar*, outward bound for Jamaica, where she arrived in April 1770. On 23 July, on the homeward passage, the ship struck the leeward reef coming out of Port Morant[13] due to the negligence of the pilot, resulting in her total loss. A report of 28 July from Kingston, Jamaica, citing an extract from a letter from Port Morant,[14] laid the blame entirely on the pilot:

> I doubt not but you have heard before this reaches you, of the unhappy Misfortune Capt. Raffles has met with, in the total Loss of the ship Cæsar, which now lies a Wreck on the Leeward Reef, and it is feared no Part of her Cargo can be saved. It was entirely owing to the Unskillfulness of the Pilot (belonging to Mr. Fleming, of Port Royal). Captain Raffles and Captain Dallton's Mate were on board; they both repeatedly told him, he was too near the Reef, but he being mule-headed and obstinate, still persisted. Capt. Raffles was afraid to take the Charge from him on Account of the Insurance. – Thus went as fine a Ship as ever came to the West-Indies.

This was also the conclusion of Captain Raffles's friend and Jamaican plantation owner, Nathaniel Phillips,[15] who wrote to the ship's London owners, Hibbert, Purrier & Horton, on 9 August 1770: 'I am very sorry to acquaint you that the Caesar Cap[t]. Raffles's ship was stranded going out of the Harbour the 23[d] last Month, owing entirely to the obstinacy & unskilfulness of the Pilot, who ran her on the Lee spit when she was just clear of the Channel. The ship is gone to Pieces, about 60 or 70 Pun[s]. Rum, 2 or 3 hhds Sugar & some Mahog[y]. Planks, all that is saved of the Cargo'.[16]

Captain Raffles's brother Thomas, who at this time was working as a merchant at Port Morant, also recorded details of the incident:

> I had a Brother who commanded a Ship which loaded annually at the Harbour where I lived. [H]aving completed his Loading he set sail I think on the 22 June [*sic*] [and] on going through the Channel which leads out into the open Sea & which is very narrow & Dangerous, [h]is Ship solely through the unskilfulness of the Pilot struck upon a rock & in Two hours was bulged & lost all hope of recovery. [T]he lives of the Crew were saved but the Cargo was lost except the Captain's Cabin furniture which in a few Days after was brought on Shore & lodged in my House[,] amongst other things was a Desk & Bookcase the latter of which contained several Religious Books.[17]

The remaining cargo and wreck of the *Caesar*, except for 20 puncheons of rum, were sold at public auction, and Captain Raffles left Port Morant for Liverpool in August 1770 carrying the documents necessary to satisfy the consignees and underwriters for a settlement of the insurance claim.

As no blame could be attached to him in the loss of the *Caesar*, Captain Raffles was restored in 1771 to the command of the *Morant*, now owned by Clarke & Co., London. Subsequent shipping reports place the *Morant* at Jamaica in July 1771 and at Dover in September 1771. She sailed again for Jamaica in December 1771 and arrived at Port Morant in April 1772. On 25 June 1772 the ship passed Gravesend on her homeward passage from Jamaica and two days later entered the port of London. It was her last voyage under Captain Raffles's command, as the ship was advertised for sale in the *Public Ledger*, London, on 25 July 1772:

> For SALE by CANDLE. At NEW LLOYD'S Coffee House, in Pope's Head Alley, Lombard Street. On Wednesday, the 19th July, at One o'Clock in the Afternoon The Good ship MORANT, Plantation built Burthen One Hundred and Eighty Tons, more or less, is sheathed, and remarkably well sound in all Manner

of Stores, one suit of Sails, almost new, Cables ditto, and is of very proper Dimensions for the Grenada, or Windward Islands, Carolina, Newfoundland, or Streights Trade, now lying at Battle Bridge, Benjamin Raffles, Commander. Inventories to be had on board, at the Place of Sale, and of PET M'TAGGART, Broker, At the Jamaica Coffee House …

Efforts by the house of Hibbert, Purrier & Horton to secure Captain Raffles a better command seem indicated by the statement in a letter from Nathaniel Phillips to Thomas Hibbert Jr. in Kingston, Jamaica, dated 16 April 1772:

Cap^t. Raffles whom I recommended to you before I left the Island, has been countenanced by your House, & they have agreed to hold a share in a Ship to be purchased for him when he returns, provided he can find friends to fill up the other shares. My Name is on the list, and I hope M^r. Taylor and some of the other Shippers at Port Morant may be persuaded to take a part in her. If Raffles succeeds, he is to be sent annually to Ireland, so that you would then have three ships employed in the most advantageous way …[18]

Phillips wrote to the overseer William Thomson in Jamaica on 1 July 1772 that 'Raffles may be able to get a good ship with the particular assistance of Mess^rs. Hibbert & C^o.',[19] and subsequently, on 10 October 1773, that 'We are building a ship for Cap^t. Raffles, which is to be launched in the next Summer to be ready for the crop [of 17]75'.[20] Phillips's own personal commitment was to take a 1/16th share in the ship by making regular payments of £25 for a total of £260.8s.9d. to the ship-builders during the course of construction in 1773–4,[21] and it would appear that Captain Raffles himself took an equal share, presumably with outside financial help.

The ship was built by Edward Greaves and George Colson Smith at their yard in Limehouse, London, and was named *Port Morant*. Her first voyage to Jamaica under Captain Raffles's command was in 1774, with the homeward voyage to London by way of Gravesend in mid-September of that year. At the end of January and early February 1775 the ship was at Port Morant, and after loading 600 hogsheads of sugar and several puncheons of rum she began her homeward voyage, when, on 28 May 1775, under full sail, she struck the Hog Styes in the windward passage with a total loss of the ship and its cargo. According to the *Morning Chronicle and London Advertiser*, the 'Captain, crew, and several passengers were saved by taking to the boats, and lived on a rock for ten days, with nothing to eat but some raw beef and pork that they saved out of the ship, and were afterwards taken up by a small vessel, and carried to Providence, and put on board the Charlotte, Green, who has brought them home'.[22]

Captain Raffles's elder brother Thomas was on board the ship, returning to England after working for 16 years in Jamaica, and he later recorded details of the incident:

> In the year 1775 it pleased God after removing unsurmountable [*sic*] difficulties which lay in my way to make the way plain for my return to my Native Country & accordingly on 17th May in that same year I embarqued on Board a Ship of my Brothers aforementioned. We sailed in the morning & were soon out at Sea … & pursued our voyage with good success for 11 Days but in the night of the 28th May or rather in the morning about ½ past one … to the no small Consternation of the Captn & all on Board our Ship in a moment struck upon a Rock & stuck fast & the more to our surprise because we did not deem ourselves to be near Land. We were sailing with a good breeze & the ship I think was going 7 knots an Hour [*sic*] so that the force drove her about the Length of the Ship fast upon a rock which lay just below the surface of the water. We knew not where we were & longed much for Daylight which soon appeared & then to our great grief we found the ship bulged which cut off any prospect of our getting her off & that the place was the Hogilies, a rock [?] about 18 miles round in the form of a Horn with two Rocky Keys … [T]he passengers Eleven in all including children were put into the little boat with the Two Cabin boys to conduct them as not one of the sailors nor Captain could then leave the Ship. [I]t was a merciful providence that I

could steer the Boat ... [Supplies were taken from the wreck] until in 8 days, after a Vessel came to our Relief bound to the Island of Providence so you see the providence of a God of providence was with us every step of our way & brought us through such great and imminent dangers until in his goodness, & mercy He conducted us safe & in three days were we all safe landed in this Island of Providence ... We remained here 18 days & may humbly say that God turned the heart of a Mr Duniscome ... who rec[eive]d us courteously into his own house & provided every necessary until we were embarked to provide for ourselves, & he having a Ship ready to sail for London we embarqued on the 27th June & set sail ... [W]e all arrived safe at Gravesend the first of August following to the great Joy of all our friends & relations.[23]

The loss of the *Port Morant* represented a devastating blow to Captain Raffles even though it seems that the ship and cargo were fully insured.[24] However, it does not appear to have occasioned any loss of confidence in his professional standing with the ship's principal owners, Hibbert, Purrier & Horton of Mincing Lane, London, since he was given immediate command of the *Ann*, a copper-sheathed ship of 260 tons, built in Scotland in 1765.[25] She sailed from Deal for Jamaica in mid-February 1776 and arrived at Kingston in May 1776, as Nathaniel Phillips informed Hibbert & Co. on the 19th of that month: 'Cap$^t$. Raffles, who arrived here a few days ago; he is to be despatched the next after Wate, so that I think he may get away [at] the beginning of July. I would hope the Wheel of Fortune is now turned in his favor, & that he may yet do well under your Wing'.[26]

The *Ann* returned to Gravesend on 9 November 1776 and then to the port of London. Shortly afterwards, on 21 November, Captain Raffles of the parish of St. Botolph, Aldgate, married Ann Lyde, a 21-year-old spinster of the parish of St. Mary Somerset in the City of London, daughter of Edward Lyde, an oilman and purveyor of soap, candles and glue, and his wife, Ann Salter.[27] The ceremony was performed at the now-demolished 17th-century church of St. Mary Somerset in Upper Thames Street by Ann Lyde's brother-in-law, the Revd. John Lindeman,[28] the witnesses being Captain Raffles's father, Thomas

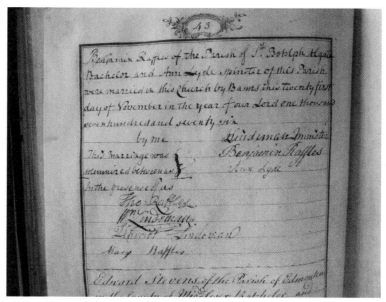

Marriage register of the Church of St. Mary Somerset, London, recording the
marriage of Captain Benjamin Raffles and Ann Lyde on 21 November 1776
*Reproduced by courtesy of the London Metropolitan Archives, City of London*

Raffles, his sister or great aunt, Mary Raffles,[29] William Lindeman, father of
the Revd. John Lindeman, and the latter's wife, Harriot Lindeman, sister of
Ann Lyde.

Two months after the wedding, in early February 1777, possibly with his
new bride on board, Captain Raffles sailed in the *Ann* for Jamaica, returning to
Deal on 15 August and to the Thames three days later. The ship left Deal again
for Jamaica on 1 November 1777 under convoy of HMS *Aurora* and arrived at
Port Morant sometime before April 1778. She returned to the Thames in July
1778 and sailed again for Jamaica in November, clearing Port Morant on her
homeward passage in late May or early June 1779[30] and arriving at Deal on 17
November. She was outward bound for Jamaica soon afterwards, and returned
to Portsmouth on 23 July 1780 in the company of 82 ships of a large convoy of
130 ships escorted by HMS *Salisbury* which had fallen in with a Spanish ship
of 60 guns during the previous week. The *Ann* was off Deal on 1 August 1780
and sailed for the Thames shortly afterwards. She loaded again for Jamaica and
arrived with the outward-bound London fleet in April 1781, being accompanied
with the other ships into Port Royal harbour by HMS *Suffolk* (74 guns).

Three months later, on 5 July 1781, when the *Ann* was at Port Morant, Ann Raffles gave birth to a son, Thomas Stamford Bingley Raffles, who was named after his father's friend, the plantation overseer of the Harbourhead Estate in Jamaica, Thomas Stamford.[31] He was christened 20 days later when the ship was anchored in Port Royal harbour by Thomas Davis, chaplain of HMS *Princess Royal*, one of the ships assigned to convoy the fleet of merchantmen preparing to sail for England. On 1 August a violent hurricane struck Jamaica, causing great damage to the plantations in the west of the island and driving some 97 ships ashore in Port Royal harbour, including the *Ann*, though she was later reported to be safely anchored. The homeward-bound ships eventually sailed in three divisions between 19 and 23 August accompanied by HMS *Princess Royal* (90 guns), HMS *Ruby* (74 guns), HMS *Janus* (44 guns), HMS *Torbay* and HMS *Albion* (74 guns), commanded by the commodore of the convoy, Captain (later Admiral) (Sir) George Bowyer (1740–1800). The *Ann* arrived safely at Plymouth on 22 November, Portsmouth on 2 January 1782, and Gravesend 12 days later.

Shortly afterwards, Captain Raffles took command of the *West Indian*, a three-deck ship of 400 tons built in France in 1776 and owned by Hibbert, Purrier & Co. of London. Judging by an entry in the account book of Nathaniel Phillips with Hibbert, Purrier & Co. dated 30 April 1783, it would seem that Captain Raffles sold his share in the *Ann* shortly after taking command of the *West Indian*: 'By final Division for his 1/12th of Sale of the ship *Ann* Capt. Raffles … £167.9.9'.[32] The *West Indian* joined the London fleet of about 32 ships under the protection of HMS *Preston* (Captain Leslie) which sailed from Spithead on 27 April 1782. She arrived at St. Lucia on 7 July 1782, and subsequently sailed on to Kingston, where her cargo of goods was advertised for sale in *The Royal Gazette* by Rutherford and Bryce at their store in Port Royal Street. These included Irish and printed linens, cottons, men's shoes and white silk stockings, ladies' shoes with 'common heels' or 'French heels', and Morocco and kid shoes with French heels, broadcloth, men's 'fashionable cocked black beaver hats', brown riding hats, superfine Hyson tea, raisins, currants, cinnamon, cloves, mace, nutmegs, boxes of Polish starch, onions and Yorkshire hams.[33] These were some of the items, together with food and wine, that made the London–West India trade at the time, and during the next 10

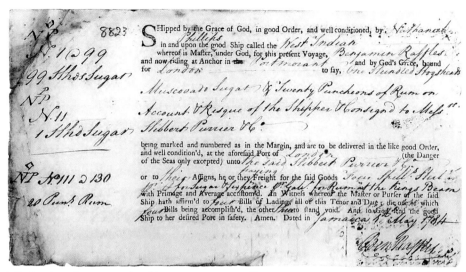

Bill of Lading ship *West Indian* (Captain Benjamin Raffles) Port Morant, Jamaica, 1 May 1784
*Image © Microform Academic Publishers with permission of the National Library of Wales*

years, one of the most important branches of English overseas commerce, with many more ships engaged in the trade than with the East Indies.

The *West Indian* sailed from Port Morant to Kingston in November 1782 to join a returning convoy of ships under the protection of HMS *Torbay*, HMS *Preston*, and the sloop-of-war HMS *Badger*,[34] and arrived at Dover early in March 1783.[35] In November 1783 she again sailed from Deal to Jamaica, returning to Gravesend in June 1784. She cleared Deal on 8 November 1784 for Jamaica and returned to Deal in April 1785. In November 1785 she was off the Downs waiting to sail with other ships for Jamaica, and in August 1786 she was 'spoke to' by Captain Foster of *Duckenfield Hall* on her passage to London from Jamaica clear of the windward passage. In mid-December 1786 the *West Indian* again sailed for Jamaica and arrived safely in April 1787. In June 1787 Captain Raffles was reported to have seen a large three-deck ship with yellow sides on the southern part of Acklin's Key in the windward passage from Jamaica, the crew having pitched a tent on the shore of the South Keys with a schooner lying nearby.[36] In November 1787 the *West Indian* was at Deal waiting with other ships to sail for Jamaica, where she arrived in March 1788. On her return passage she passed Deal on 25 June 1788, and was at Gravesend two days later. At the end of October 1788 she sailed from Gravesend for Jamaica, and returned

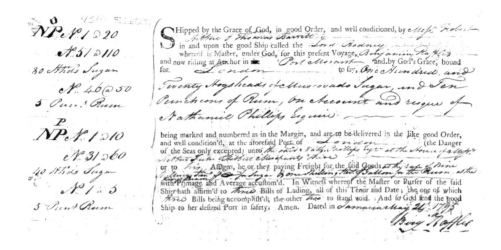

Bill of Lading ship *Lord Rodney* (Captain Benjamin Raffles) Port Morant, Jamaica, 26 May 1795
*Image © 2008 Microform Academic Publishers with permission of the National Library of Wales*

later in 1789. In that year, Captain Raffles was given command of a new ship of 334 tons, also named *West Indian*, which had been built on the Thames for Hibbert & Co. The ship sailed in November 1789 and arrived at Jamaica in March 1790. On 28 May the *West Indian* was off Plymouth on her homeward voyage from Jamaica, *Lloyd's List* recording her at Dover on 1 June 1790.

This was Captain Raffles's last voyage in the *West Indian* before taking command of a Hibbert, Fuhr & Hibbert ship[37], the *Lord Rodney*, a three-deck copper-sheathed ship of 440 tons and 34 guns which had been launched in September 1782 from the Wells yard at Greenwich. On 12 November 1790, with Captain Raffles as master, she sailed from the Downs[38] and arrived at Jamaica in March 1791.[39] She left Jamaica on 29 March and, after passing Lands End on 23 May, and beating against strong easterly winds, she was off the Isle of Wight in early June (having 'on the 4th of April spoke the Sandwich Packet from Falmouth, 20 leagues to windward of Jamaica'),[40] and arrived at Deal shortly afterwards. She sailed again from there with the outward-bound London fleet in October 1791,[41] and arrived at Jamaica in early February 1792. On the homeward passage she was at Plymouth on 3 June 1792[42] and Deal six days later.[43] She sailed again from Deal for Jamaica in October 1792,[44] passing Gravesend on the 30th of that month, and remained at Deal during early November.[45] She made Port Morant in February 1793, when she was able to send her launch to the assistance of HMS *Providence*, commanded by Captain William Bligh, who was engaged in distributing bread-fruit plants in the island.[46] The *Lord Rodney* returned to Deal on 4 September 1793 and sailed for the Thames a few days later. During the course of the voyage a quantity of rum was lost on board, which Thomas Barritt alluded to in a letter to Nathaniel Phillips on 18 January 1794: 'I am much surprised at the loss of Rum on board the Lord Rodney, as the puncheons were as I thought in high order, I wish they have not been spil[l]ed, as I saw some of them on the deck where the Cables & Sailors lay.'[47] The *Lord Rodney* again sailed for Jamaica from Gravesend in mid-December 1793[48] and returned to Deal on 24 July 1794[49] and to Gravesend three days later.[50] She sailed from Deal for Jamaica in November 1794[51] and returned to Gravesend in August 1795.[52]

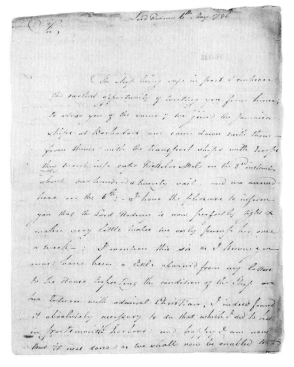

Letter of Captain Benjamin Raffles to Nathaniel Phillips written on board the *Lord Rodney* at Port Morant, Jamaica, on 6 May 1796, relating to the repairs of the ship
*Image © 2008 Microform Academic Publishers with permission of the National Library of Wales*

This was a difficult time for masters and owners of ships trading with the West Indies, not only because of the war with France, and the increase in duties on sugar, but also because of the high wages paid to seamen as a consequence of the ravages of yellow fever ('yellow jack') in Jamaica and the other islands during the 1790s.[53] Added to these additional costs and difficulties, Captain Raffles's next voyage to Jamaica in the *Lord Rodney* was to prove particularly expensive for the owners. After leaving Deal early in December 1795 with the outward-bound fleet, the *Lord Rodney* was found to be 'among the Leakey Ships',[54] and Captain Raffles decided to put into Portsmouth for a refit. He made the decision himself, and because of the heavy expenditure involved he was at pains to explain his action in a letter to Nathaniel Phillips immediately on his arrival at Port Morant on 6 May 1796:[55]

Lord Rodney 6<sup>th</sup> May 1796

Sir,

The ship being safe in port I embrace this earliest opportunity of writing you from hence; to advise you of the same; we joined the Jamaican ships at Barbadoes and came down with them from hence with the transport ships with troops[;] *they* went into cape Nicholas Malo on the 3rd instant about one hundred & twenty sail and we arrived here on the 6th. – I have the pleasure to inform you that the Lord Rodney is now perfectly tight & makes very little water[,] we only pump her once a week: I mention this sir as I know you must have been a little alarmed from my letters to the House respecting the condition of the Ship on her return with admiral Christian;[4] I indeed found it absolutely necessary to do that which I did to her in Portsmouth harbour: and happy I am now that it was done as we shall now be enabled to take the quantity of sugar proposed, or any quantity that M<sup>r</sup> Barratt [*sic*] may think proper to put on board. I had this point particularly in mind before I went into the Harbour for after being strained in the manner she was, something was necessary to be done to her, either in England or here; and as we had still a Winter passage to contend with I thought it most prudent to do it there, as in doing it here would have been attended with disagreeable consequences and probably not have been in time to sail with the Convoy – It might have appeared singular to you and the gentlemen of the house that the Lord Rodney alone should have occasion to have gone into refit at Portsmouth but I do assure you sir not one of the ships that did return with admiral Christian and sailed again with us but wish they had done as I did as the most of them have kept their pumps going all the way out.[56]

I have been thus particular in mentioning the above circumstances that you may not have the worst of opinion of the Lord Rodney[.] I shall think myself perfectly safe in coming home in her even if we should not get away before the 26<sup>th</sup> July. I am going to Town tomorrow and there learn of any Convoy is appointed that we can be in time for, and shall write the house by first packet.

I most sincerely hope that this will find you in good health and
am with due respect

Sir
Your most obliged and
Hbl Servant
Ben[jamin] Raffles

PS I send this down by a person going to Town. I hope he will be
in time for the Packet.

On her return passage, the *Lord Rodney*, 'fully loaded', sailed from Port
Morant on 13 July 1796 to join the convoy at Port Royal. Thomas Barritt
reported to Nathaniel Phillips two days later: 'Captain Raffles and his Ship's
men have exerted themselves in landing the Supplies, and loading the Ship
in good time. He has 190 Hogsheads of your Sugar, and 10 Pun⁵. Rum …
Captain Raffles will deliver … a box of Sweet meats, and as his Ship was
very tight, I hope he will arrive safe.'[57] The *Lord Rodney* managed to join the
London-bound ships under convoy of HMS *Intrepid* and *Malabar* before they
sailed on 26 July 1796,[58] and anchored in the Thames in mid-October 1796.[59]
This proved to be Captain Raffles's last voyage in the ship because although
the owners were inclined to allow him to remain as master, his age and lack of
energy were beginning to show, George Hibbert noting rather ominously in
a letter to Nathaniel Phillips on 8 October 1796 that he would 'not see large
dividends from poor Raffles' ships'.[60]

A year later, Captain Raffles managed to secure command of the *Catherine*,
a three-flush-decked square-sterned vessel of 334 tons built on the Thames,
which had been advertised for sale in 1791.[61] She sailed for Jamaica on 20
November 1797 and arrived late in February 1798, as stated by Thomas Barritt
in a letter to Nathaniel Phillips dated 26 March 1798:

Captain Raffles arrived abᵗ. four weeks ago in Kingston with the
Cork fleet, and has been now ten days in Port Morant harbour. He
has landed most of the Cork Supplies[,] all of which seems to be in
good order! I have mention'd to him that he will get one hundred

Hogsheads of your Sugar, and requests he would use every exertion to get loaded by the 10th. of May, the time appointed for the first convoy, but I am rather afraid he will not be ready by that day, having no Shallop [light open boat], only a 6 Hogshead boat to bring his Sugar from the out ports to the Ship. – Every assistance in my power shall be given him –.[62]

Barritt wrote further on 12 June 1798 reporting that after making 'a shift to get the 120 Hogsheads of Sugar & 10 Puns. Rum down in time for Captain Raffles',[63] the *Catherine* only managed to leave Port Morant with two other ships on 9 June. She was able to join the London fleet off Barbados, and arrived safely at Gravesend on 16 August 1798, but by now Barritt's patience with Captain Raffles was exhausted. In a letter to Phillips on 10 August 1798 he expressed the hope that he would not 'be plagued wth. Captain Raffles another year. He is a good meaning man, & an old Servant, but I conceive him too old & weak a one for the profession he follows.'[64] On 26 October 1798 he wrote further: 'I was glad to see Captain Raffles's health at last enabled him to go home in his Ship – When I applied to him to take some more of your Sugar, he said he could not, on account of his Mate having badly stowed the Ship. He was obliged to leave out some Sugar that was already engaged.'[65] A month later, on 22 November 1798, Barritt again wrote: 'I suppose Captn. Raffles has made his last trip to Jamaica. Poor man, his Health is too much shattered to allow him to take the conduct of a vessel with that sort of activity which he once possessed!'[66]

This gloomy prediction proved false, because after securing the safe arrival of the *Catherine* to the Thames in August 1798, Captain Raffles managed to get command of the *Uxbridge*, a copper-sheathed ship of 346 tons and 10 mounted guns built nine years earlier and owned by J. Kenyon.[67] According to *Lloyd's List*, the ship sailed from Gravesend for Jamaica on 7 November 1798, and her arrival in early March was reported by Thomas Barritt in a letter to Nathaniel Phillips dated 10 April 1799: 'The … *Uxbridge* Raffles came with the Cork fleet about 5 weeks ago. … [He] passed by the Harbour [of Port Morant] with his Ship to Kingston, and is not yet come up. – By her I received Bills of Lading, and Invoices for our Irish Supplies, which we are in want of …'[68] He hoped that Raffles might be able to return to England in the Second Fleet, but the season was already advancing fast and 'he has not the Spirit and activity now to load a Ship, he once possessed. He shall have every possible assistance from me to get him away in time –.'[69] On 15 May 1799 he informed Phillips that the fleet had sailed from Port Antonio five days earlier and 'the next is appointed to go from thence the 30 of June and Captain Raffles is now loading fast, so that there is no doubt but he will be then pretty loaded. He takes Home 100 Hogsheads of your Sugar and 10 Puncheons Rum a part of which he has on board & we give him every assistance in our power. – He has landed the Irish Provisions in good order –.'[70] On 5 June 1799 he reported that 'Captain Raffles of the Uxbridge is two thirds loaded, and will be ready in good time to sail with the next Convoy appointed to go from Port Antonio the 30th Ult°. – He has not yet all the 100 Hogsheads Sugar, and 10 Puncheons of rum on board …'[71]

The ship apparently sailed in time but was the subject of an alarming report by Barritt to Phillips on 11 July 1799 that 'Raffles of the Uxbridge with three others of the South Side Ships were captured by a Privateer when going round the East end to join the Convoy …'[72] The report was untrue, and he was able to confirm 'Captain Raffles's safety' in a further letter to Phillips dated 2 August 1799 and of Raffles's own confirmation of 'his Ship & Crew being all well' and of his having 'joined [the] Convoy at Port Antonio …'[73]

The safe return of the *Uxbridge* to England at the close of 1799 should have brought an end to Captain Raffles's seafaring career, but the matter was confounded by a report received by Thomas Barritt from Leonora Sophia Carter, widow of Ambrose Carter,[74] dated 16 November 1800: 'I have just learnt that Mrs. Carter has received a letter from Captain Raffles saying he is coming out in the first fleet in a Ship called the Milton to load in our Port. If this be true … I think we shall be better of[f] for Ships next year in Port Morant and Harbour than we have been for several years past …'[75] The report, as it turned out, was incorrect, as was also the listing of Captain Raffles's name as master of the *Uxbridge* in *Lloyd's Register* during the years 1800 to 1805, since there is no record in the shipping reports or *Lloyd's List* of any voyage made by him to the West Indies during those years. Lloyd's has confirmed that details of a ship could have been carried over in each of these years if no specific information had been received,[76] and this seems to have been the case with the *Uxbridge*.

# CHAPTER THREE
## Captain Benjamin Raffles and his Family

Ann Raffles (née Lyde) (1755–1824), mother of Sir Stamford Raffles
*Private collection*

Thomas Stamford Raffles (1781–1826)
*Engraving by C. Thomson after a miniature portrait in the possession of his mother*

THE END OF Captain Raffles's involvement in the West India trade in 1800 resulted in considerable financial hardship for his family,[1] for his wife Ann Raffles, his 19-year-old son, Thomas Stamford Raffles,[2] and his four daughters – 16-year-old Harriot Raffles,[3] 15-year-old Leonora Raffles,[4] 11-year-old Mary Anne Raffles,[5] and 7-year-old Ann Raffles.[6] Judging by an advertisement in *The Times* on 10 May 1800, the first consequence of his retirement was the sale of the leasehold of the family home at No. 10 Camden Street, Islington, described as 'A Genteel, Substantial DWELLING-HOUSE, pleasantly situate, … containing two rooms on each floor, a neat garden, offices, and arched cellaring, lett to Captain Raffles, tenant at will, at a net rent of 25£. per annum, held for 63 years, at a low ground rent'. The house seems to have been occupied by the family during the previous couple of years, and although it is difficult to determine precisely the times and places of Captain Raffles's residence in London, the birth dates of his children provide some clues. Thus

Islington, London, about the time when Sir Stamford Raffles was living with his family at No. 10 Camden Street
*W. Thornbury and E. Walford,* Old and New London *(London, 1879–85)*

Church of St. Dunstan in the East, London, where Captain Benjamin Raffles's second child, Ann, was baptised in September 1779
*W. Thornbury and E. Walford,* Old and New London *(London, 1879–85)*

The Church of St. Benet Fink, London, where Captain Raffles's daughter Elizabeth was baptised in 1787
*W. Thornbury and E. Walford,* Old and New London *(London, 1879–85)*

when his second child, Ann, who was born on 27 August and baptised on 26 September 1779, was buried in the following year at St. Dunstan in the East, a parish church on St. Dunstan's Hill, halfway between London Bridge and the Tower of London, his nearby residence was No. 149 Fenchurch Street, where he is recorded in that year as having taken out insurance. On 4 June 1783, and also in June of the following year, when his son Thomas Stamford Raffles was three years old, he was assessed for land tax in the parish of Hornsey, Middlesex, a district of Haringey in north-west London, some six miles from Charing Cross. Two years later, in 1786, there is another insurance record showing that he was living at No. 17 Throgmorton Street, London, with a similar record of 22 October of the following year confirming his place of residence and his occupation as a 'Mariner'. Moreover, in March of that year his daughter Elizabeth was baptised at the nearby Church of St. Benet Fink in Threadneedle Street. He moved from there some time afterwards, as he was visited by Nathaniel Phillips during the first half of 1789 at his new address of Walcott Place (later New Road), Lambeth,[7] the baptism of his daughter Mary Anne in June 1789 at St. Mary's Church Lambeth, and the death of his daughter Elizabeth at this address on 3 March 1791, confirming the fact.

Church of St. Michael and All Angels at Eaton Bishop, where Sir Stamford Raffles was re-baptised on 4 July 1784
*Reproduced by permission of Jonathan Billinger, UK Beach Guide*

Mary Anne Raffles (1789–1837), sister of Sir Stamford Raffles
*Miniature portrait by E. Nash (?)*

The house at Walcott Place in Lambeth provided a relatively long period of residence for Captain Raffles's family since it was from this address on 9 March

East Lane, Walworth, London
*Contemporary print*

Burial ground in the Old Newington Churchyard where Sir Stamford Raffles's
mother was buried in 1824
*W. Thornbury and E. Walford,* Old and New London *(London, 1879–85)*

1791 that the body of his daughter Elizabeth was taken for burial at St. Mary's Church, and where, on 12 May two years later, his daughter Ann was baptised. He was still paying rent at Lambeth in 1796, but in the following year he seems to have moved with his family to a house in East Lane, Walworth, which is referred to in the 'Reminiscences' of the Revd. Dr. Thomas Raffles, who recounts having flown his 'kyte' with his cousin Thomas Stamford Raffles in the nearby fields. The Walworth house can only have been occupied by the family for a year or so because Captain Raffles was paying rent or land tax between 1798 and 1800 on a leasehold property in St. Mary's Islington, namely No. 10 Camden Street, already referred to. Following the sale of the leasehold on this property in 1800, the Raffles family moved in the following year to Apollo Buildings in the parish of Newington St. Mary in the borough of Southwark, situated along East Street and off Walworth Road, to the north of Walworth Fields. Curiously, the property remained registered in Captain Raffles's name until his death in 1811.

The regular changes of his family's places of residence clearly indicate that Captain Raffles was under financial pressure even before his seafaring career came to an end. In 1795 a shortage of funds led to the removal of his 13-year-old son from the Mansion House Boarding School, Hammersmith,[8] for employment as a clerk in the East India Company, and a similar factor led in 1800 to the sale of the leasehold of No. 10 Camden Street, Islington,[9] in favour of cheaper accommodation across the Thames at Newington. His son later complained of his father's inability to meet his rising debts, and he described his family at this

Fees from mid-Summer to Christmas 1793 and to mid-Summer 1794 charged by Dr. James Anderson of the Mansion House Boarding School, Hammersmith, London, for the education of Richard Wynter, son of Nathaniel Phillips. Similar fees would have been paid by Captain Raffles for the education of his son, Thomas Stamford Raffles, at the school.
*Slebech Papers, Accounts, item 5377, image 59, courtesy of Microform Academic Publishers with permission of the National Library of Wales*

East India House, Leadenhall Street, London
*Engraving of 1799 showing the East India House with its new classical façade*

time as living 'in obscurity and distress', and his being reprimanded by his mother for 'extravagance' in burning a candle in his room.[10] 'My earnings', he wrote, 'went to their relief, but it was insufficient. Long-standing debts, and a want of the means to prevent still further involvement, caused me many a bitter moment.'[11]

Raffles's employment as an 'extra clerk' in the Secretary's Office of the East India Company in Leadenhall Street provided him with a salary of £50 a year, the sum specified by Charles Lamb in describing 'extra clerks' in a letter to Robert Southey in 1798: '[T]here are in the India house what are called *Extra Clerks*, not on the Establishment, … but employed in Extra business, by-jobs – these get about £50 a year, or rather more, but never rise –'.[12] This was not the case with Raffles, who by application and hard work, and with the support of the Secretary, William Ramsay,[13] was appointed a junior clerk on the permanent establishment on 16 July 1800 on a salary of £70 per annum.[14] On 7 April of the following year he was paid a gratuity of £20, which included arrears from the previous mid-summer, and in 1802 he received £98, including a gratuity

Trinity House, London, where Captain Benjamin Raffles lodged his Petition to become a
Pensioner of the Corporation of Trinity House at Deptford
*W. Thornbury and E. Walford*, Old and New London *(London, 1879–85)*

of £30 paid on 21 July, possibly for extra hours worked. In 1803 his salary
amounted to £100 and in 1804 to £110, part of which had to be allocated for
the upkeep of his family, but it appears that his appointment to a permanent
post on the establishment of the East India Company, and specifically the
payment to him of a gratuity of £20 in April 1801, provided him with the
necessary spur to leave his family and take up residence on his own. Between
June and November 1801 he is recorded as a 20-year-old 'Established' clerk
in the Secretary's Office on a salary of £20 (obviously the gratuity paid in his
new post) residing at No. 7 East Place, Lambeth, a relatively new house erected
in 1786 at the same time as East Street (now Lollard Street) was developed.[15]
On 18 November 1801 he took out insurance on the house with the Sun Fire
Office, and he remained at this address until some time between June 1803
and June 1804, when he moved to an unknown address in Bloomsbury. He
appears to have resided in Bloomsbury until his appointment in March 1805 as
Assistant Secretary of the new Presidency government of Prince of Wales Island
on a salary of £1,500 a year.[16]

This promotion represented a godsend to his family, and it is not without interest that within three months of his son's sailing from England to take up his new post Captain Raffles petitioned Trinity House Corporation at Deptford for admission as a pensioner. The Corporation, officially known as 'The Master, Wardens, and Assistants, of the Guild, or Fraternity, of the most glorious and undivided Trinity, and of St. Clement, in the parish of Deptford Strond, in the county of Kent', had been founded in 1515 by Henry VIII for the promotion of commerce and navigation by the regulation and licensing of pilots and the erection of beacons, lighthouses and buoys for the safety of shipping. Under the direction of a Master, four Wardens, eight Assistants and 18 Elder Brethren, who were selected from commanders of the Navy and merchant service, the Corporation generated substantial revenues from its licensing and regulatory activities, and these revenues, supplemented by charitable donations, were used mainly for the relief of poor and disabled seamen, and for their widows and orphans. Petitions for assistance, like that of Captain Raffles, were submitted directly to the offices of Trinity House on the northern side of Great Tower Hill in London, where the business of the Corporation was conducted for the parent house at Deptford.[17]

His Petition was made on a standard printed form filled in by the applicant:[18]

Captain Raffles's Petition to Trinity House Deptford

To the Honourable the Master, Wardens, *and* Assistants
*of the* CORPORATION *of* TRINITY-HOUSE, *of*
Deptford-Strond.
The Humble Petition of
<u>Benj$^n$. Raffles</u>

Sheweth,

THAT your Petitioner <u>Benj$^n$. Raffles</u> was bred to the Sea, and
served there as a <u>Seaman & Commander of several Vessels for</u>
<u>upwards of Forty Years, the last Ship of which he was Commander</u>
<u>was the Lord Rodney, has a wife & 4 Child$^n$. all female of the age</u>
<u>of 20 years & under</u>

That your Petitioner is not now able to support <u>him</u> self <u>& family</u>
without the Charity of this CORPORATION, having no Pension
or Relief from any other Public Charity or Company, except
[blank]

Your Petitioner therefore most humbly prays, that <u>He</u> may be
admitted a Pensioner of this CORPORATION, at the usual
Allowance.

*Your Petitioner will ever pray, &c.*
<u>Benj. Raffles</u>

We whose Names are hereunder subscribed, know the Petitioner,
and Circumstances, or have received such Information concerning
<u>him</u> may be fully relied on, so that believing the Contents of this
Petition to be true, and that the Petitioner is a Person of good
Character and Reputation, We recommend <u>him</u> as a proper Object
of the Corporation's Charity.

As Witness our Hands, the [blank] Day of [blank]
*This to be signed by*
Younger Brethren,
*Or others well known*
to the Corporation.                    [six signatures in ink]

Whatever charitable sums Captain Raffles drew as a Petitioner of Trinity House at Deptford, they were sufficient only for his own subsistence, leaving his wife and daughters to be provided for by his son, who seems to have borrowed money for this purpose before leaving England. He subsequently remitted funds to his mother from Prince of Wales Island through the attorney Richard Stephens Taylor of Field Court, Gray's Inn,[19] and later through his London agent, John Tayler of the East India Agency House of Edmund Boehm & John Tayler of Bishopsgate Church-yard.[20] He further relieved pressure on her by taking with him to Penang his sister Mary Anne, and arranging shortly afterwards for his sisters Leonora and Harriot to follow him. This left his mother and youngest sister Ann to be provided for, and he later arranged for the sum of £400 to be paid annually to his mother for their support. Captain Raffles, in the meantime, eked out the last six years of his life in the company of other seafaring companions at Deptford, where he died and was buried in Trinity Ground at the Church of St. Nicholas, Deptford, on 23 November 1811, the event eliciting from Raffles a letter to his Uncle William thanking him for his assistance on the occasion of the burial.[21]

St. Nicholas Church, Deptford
*W. Thornbury and E. Walford,* Old and New London *(London, 1879–85)*

William Raffles (1751–1825), brother of Captain Benjamin
Raffles and uncle of Sir Stamford Raffles
*Private collection*

# CHAPTER FOUR

## Sir Stamford Raffles's First Wife: Olivia Mariamne Devenish

Olivia Mariamne Raffles (1771–1814)
*Miniature portrait by Andrew Plimer, London, 1805*

RAFFLES'S APPOINTMENT AS Assistant Secretary of the Prince of Wales Island government was officially announced on 8 March 1805, and six days later he was married at the parish Church of St. George, Bloomsbury, to a widow named Olivia Mariamne Fancourt, who was nearly 10 years older than him. She was born on 16 February 1771, the illegitimate daughter of George or Godfrey Devenish[1] of Casheltauna Four Mile House,[2] County Roscommon, by an unknown Circassian woman. Although she grew up in Ireland, she was probably born at Madras in India, but there is no record of her birth or of her father having lived there. In a letter to the Scottish poet and orientalist John Leyden in August 1808, she refers to a brother,[3] who is assumed to have been Lieutenant Christopher Devenish, who was born in 1757–8. He studied at Trinity College Dublin from 1 November 1774 and was appointed a Cadet in the Bengal Army six years later.[4] He died at Madras in 1783 and probate on his Will was granted on 11 March 1784, but the name of his father is recorded as William Devenish of Roscommon, not George or Godfrey, so the mystery surrounding Olivia's birth remains unresolved.

According to her great-granddaughter, Charlotte Louisa Hawkins Dempster (1835–1913),[5] Olivia as 'a young girl' went 'to join some relations in India', and sailed on board the East Indiaman *Rose*, possibly on the ship's maiden voyage in February 1787,[6] though her name is not among the passengers nor is there any record in the Court Minutes of the East India Company of her having been granted official permission to proceed to India. The ship was commanded by John Hamilton Dempster (1750–1800),[7] a younger half-brother of George Dempster (1732–1818), laird of Dunnichen in Angus, Scotland, and a long-serving Member of Parliament for the Fife and Forfar Burghs.[8] Captain Dempster was then 37 years old, and was married to Jean Fergusson (1766–98),

Charlotte Louisa Hawkins Dempster (1835–1913), principal informant on the early life of Olivia Mariamne Raffles
*C.L. Hawkins Dempster,* The Manners of My Time *(London, 1920)*

Harriet Dempster, the illegitimate daughter of
Sir Stamford Raffles's first wife, Olivia
*Miniature portrait by Andrew Plimer, London, 1805*

daughter of Charles Fergusson (1740–1804) of London.[9] Although more than twice her age, Captain John Hamilton Dempster is said by Charlotte Louisa Hawkins Dempster to have become intimate with Olivia during the voyage, which 'resulted ere long in the birth of a little girl, Harriet Milton Dempster'.[10]

The *Rose* arrived at Madras on 2 June 1787, so that if the story is true, Olivia must have given birth to her child later that year or early in the following year. The birth is not recorded in the Madras records and Olivia is not listed among the Madras inhabitants, though the early manuscript lists of the names of this period do not include those of widows or unmarried women. Five years later, on what was expected to be his final homeward voyage from India, Dempster may have taken the child with him when the *Rose* sailed from Madras for London on 4 March 1793 since Charlotte Louisa Hawkins Dempster records that he had her expensively educated at a school at Musselburgh, near Edinburgh, and brought her up as his ward.[11] Following his death in October 1800, when his ship *Earl Talbot* was lost in the South China Sea,[12] and the death of his only son George on 17 April 1801, Harriet inherited the estates of Skibo, Over Skibo and Pulrossie in Sutherland in which he had invested, with his brother,

St. Mary's Church, Fort St. George, Madras, where Olivia Devenish married
Assistant Surgeon Jacob Cassivelaun Fancourt in 1793
*Coloured aquatint by J.W. Gantz, 1841, reproduced by permission of © The British Library Board, P708*

his profits from the India and China trade. Before that, in the expectation of
securing marriage for his natural daughter, Dempster had taken Harriet with
him on the *Earl Talbot* as far as Bombay, where, not yet 14, she married on 17
January 1801 William John Soper (baptised on 8 December 1763), a 37-year-
old senior merchant in the service of the East India Company, who was Marine
Paymaster and Commissioner of Customs at the port of Surat.[13] Subsequently,
Soper added by Royal Licence the name of Dempster to his own when his wife
inherited the Scottish estates.[14]

After parting from her daughter, Olivia married at Madras on 26 May 1793
an Assistant Surgeon on the East India Company's medical establishment
named Jacob Cassivelaun Fancourt. The marriage took place in St. Mary's
Church before witnesses whose names are not given in the official transcript
from the church records. He had earlier married a widow named Ann Carlos
in St. Michael's Church, Crooked Lane, London, on 28 August 1785, but she
died on 3 March 1790. Two and a half years later, on 11 August 1792, he was
appointed, on the nomination of the Chairman of the East India Company, Sir
Francis Baring (1740–1810), as Assistant Surgeon at Madras, with assignment

The East Indiaman *Pitt* (John Gerrard), 775 tons, in which Olivia Fancourt sailed from Madras to London in 1798
*Based on a painting by Dominic Serres, 1787, reproduced by permission © National Maritime Museum, Greenwich, London*

by General Orders of the Government of Fort St. George on 21 January 1793 to the 8th Regiment of Madras Native Infantry. The *Calcutta Gazette* of 30 May 1793, printing news from Madras dated 3 May, reported that 'Mr. Jacob Casivilaun [*sic*] Fancourt, having arrived from Europe, with Indentures from the Honorable Court of Directors, is admitted as Assistant Surgeon on this establishment, and stationed at the presidency General Hospital'. As he married Olivia on 26 May,[15] only three weeks after his arrival at Madras on 29 April 1793, one must assume that there was a whirlwind romance or that they had known each other earlier. Of Olivia's life at Madras during the following five years nothing is known, but on 24 January 1798, by General Orders of the Madras Government, Fancourt was 'appointed to do duty with the 8th Regiment Native Infantry', as part of the build-up of British military forces against Tipu Sultan and his French allies. With growing political and military uncertainty in Madras, and for other unknown reasons, Olivia took passage for London early in 1798 aboard the 775-ton former convict ship *Pitt* (John Gerrard).[16]

The *Pitt* had sailed from Saugor (Sagar) Island at the eastern entrance of the Hugli River in company with the East India Company ships *General Goddard* (Thomas Graham), *Sir Stephen Lushington* (George Gooch), and *Friendship* (John Newman) late in December 1797. At Madras they were joined by the East Indiamen *Lord Hawkesbury* (John Price) and *Lord Macartney* (James Hay) to form a convoy under the protection of the frigate HMS *Heroine* (Captain Murray), carrying to England the retiring Governor of Fort St. George, Lord Hobart (1760–1816), and his staff.[17] The ships left Madras on 21 February 1798 and arrived at the Cape on 23 April 1798, where one of the passengers on the *Pitt*, Mrs. Charlotte Maule, who was accompanying her niece and nephew to England, made a Will which assigned to Olivia's care the 10-year-old Charles Edward Clayton and his seven-year-old sister, Emma Maria Clayton, children of Captain (later Lieutenant-Colonel) Thomas William Clayton (1763/4–1804) of the 18th Bengal Native Infantry and his deceased wife, Emma Maria (née Jenkins). Mrs. Maule died on 1 May before the *Pitt* sailed from the Cape so Captain Gerrard became executor of the Will and Olivia assumed responsibility for the two children during the voyage to England. The *Pitt* and the other ships, together with the East Indiaman *Sullivan* (Sampson Hall), now under the protection of HMS *Isis* (Sir Edward Hughes), called at St. Helena on 25–26 May and arrived off the Downs on 2 August. The passengers disembarked the following day, including Olivia with her two young charges, who were presumably handed over to their family.[18]

Shortly after her arrival in London, Olivia rented rooms at No. 9 Golden Square East, St. James, Piccadilly, in the house of Mr. John Hayman, a purveyor of 'Maredant Antiscorbutic Drops', supposed to be 'a certain cure for the sea and land scurvy' and for 'all eruptions of the Skin'. According to a newspaper advertisement, he had for many years 'made Scorbutic Complaints his particular Study', and had during that time 'witnessed the universally

Golden Square, London, where Olivia Fancourt resided after she returned from India in 1798
*W. Thornbury and E. Walford,* Old and New London *(London, 1879–85)*

beneficial effects of the above-mentioned Medicine, both during the practice of the late Surgeon Norton, and since he succeeded him in his profession ...' The drops had been invented by John Norton of Golden Square and on his death in 1783 they continued to be sold by his wife, who was in turn succeeded by Hayman, a long-time resident at different addresses in Golden Square. He had been subject to bankruptcy proceedings in 1796,[19] which may explain why he was taking lodgers in his house, although Dickens noted later in *Nicholas Nickleby* that Golden Square had gone down in the world and had 'taken to letting lodgings'.

Soon after Olivia's arrival, Hayman was called upon to give evidence in an extraordinary trial at the Old Bailey in a case brought by Olivia against her servant Mary Goring for stealing a number of handkerchiefs and a petticoat. The case was heard before Mr. Justice Grose and a jury at the Old Bailey in December 1798 and was deemed of sufficient importance for it to be reported in the newspapers. Mary Goring, who was employed by Olivia as a cook and a washer of her morning dresses, was indicted on a charge of stealing 'four muslin neck handkerchiefs, value 3s. two muslin pocket handkerchiefs, value 12d. a cotton petticoat, value 3s. and a wooden pen case, value 4d.', the property, in accordance with the law, of Olivia's husband, Jacob Cassivelaun Fancourt. The jury heard that on 9 November several items were found missing in the house and a search was made of the prisoner's box, which 'was opened by her with apparent reluctance'. A petticoat was found which Olivia claimed to be her property, a fact admitted by the prisoner, who stated that Olivia's black servant had given it to her to wash and that she had put it in her box for safekeeping. However, other articles belonging to Olivia were found, which were identified in Court as 'being made under her own inspection at Madras', and for which the servant was unable to give an account. In her defence, Mary Goring said that all the items were given to her by the black girl to wash, and that Olivia had given her the pen-case as a present, which was denied. The jury enquired why the black servant was not called to give evidence and were told that it was not considered necessary as she was unable to speak English. This circumstance seems to have influenced the jury in deciding on an acquittal, which surprised the judge, who observed that 'he never saw a clearer case in his life'.

The official Old Bailey record contains some instances of Olivia's testimony under cross-examination:[20]

> Mrs. OLIVIA FANCOURT *sworn.* – I lodge at Mr. Hayman's; I was present when the things were found in the prisoner's box; they are in the custody of one of the officers.
>
> CHARLES HEAD *sworn.* – I am lanthorn bearer and beadle's assistant in St. James's watch-house (*produces some handkerchiefs, a pillow-case, and a petticoat*); they were delivered to me when the prisoner was taken into custody.
>
> *Mrs. Fancourt.* These are my property, I have wore them repeatedly, I have got others at home like them.
>
> JAMES KENNEDY *sworn.* I am a constable. (*Produces a pen-case.*)
>
> *Q.* (*To Mrs. Fancourt.*) What is your husband's name? – *A.* Jacob Cassivilan [*sic*] Fancourt; this pen-case is mine; the things were all found in a box of the prisoner's, she was my servant.
>
> *Kennedy.* I searched the box a second time, and found this pen-case in it.
>
> *Mr. Knapp.* (*To Mrs. Fancourt.*) *Q.* These things that are produced, you say are like several that you have? – *A.* Yes.
>
> *Q.* Therefore you do not mean absolutely to swear to their being your property, but that they are like your's? – *A.* I mean to swear that they are mine.
>
> *Q.* A great many others of the same quality come from India? – *A.* Yes; they were made under my inspection.
>
> *Q.* What is there about this pen-case that makes you suppose it to be your's? – *A.* I bought it at Madras, and I never saw any like it besides.
>
> *Q.* You have a black servant, I believe? – *A.* Yes.
>
> *Q.* Is she here? – *A.* No.
>
> *Q.* She was employed by the prisoner to wash? – *A.* Yes, she was.
>
> *Q.* In what capacity was the prisoner? *A.* As my cook, and to wash my morning gowns.

*Q.* Whether that black girl might give her these things to wash without your knowledge, you cannot say? – *A.* I cannot swear that, but I should think it impossible.

------- HAYMAN *sworn.* – I live in Golden-square, Mrs. Fancourt lodges at my house, I was present at the opening of the prisoner's box, when these things were found.

*Q.* Was that box under lock and key of the prisoner? – *A.* Yes, I saw her open it.

*Q.* Had she been, previous to that, charged with taking any property of Mrs. Fancourt's? –

*A.* No. On the 9th of November my servant complained that she had lost several articles of her own wearing-apparel, and upon hearing that, with Mrs. Fancourt's leave, I called all the servants together, and the prisoner's box was the first thing that was opened, upon it being opened, Mrs. Fancourt found these things belonging to her; the watchman was called in, and we gave charge of her, with the property, to the watchman; some of my servant's things were found in the room, but not in the box.

*Cross-examined by Mr. Knapp. Q.* There were other persons in the house who had access to that room besides her? – *A.* I understood it always to be kept locked.

*Q.* It was not till after you had challenged all the servants in the house, that you went up and found these things in the box? – *A.* No, it was not.

*Q.* The prisoner was acquainted that her box was to be searched? – *A.* Yes, with the other servants.

*Q.* And she then gave you the key, and opened the box? – *A.* She hesitated very much before she did it.

*Q.* Did she not at that time say, that she had received them from the black girl? – *A.* She did not acknowledge to have received all of them from the black girl; the petticoat was the first thing taken out; she said she had that from the black girl to wash; with respect to the handkerchiefs, she said they were things not fit to be looked at, implying that they were foul linen, but they were not.

ISAAC THOMPSON *sworn.* – I am a watchman; I was called in to Mr. Hayman's in Golden-square, to take charge of the prisoner and the property, which I did, Mr. Hayman went with us to the watch-house.

*Prisoner's defence.* That pen-case my mistress gave me, and the other things I had to wash, but had not had time.

The prisoner called two gentlemen, with whom she had lived [as a] servant, and who gave her an excellent character.

Q. (*To Mrs. Fancourt.*) Did you ever give the prisoner that pen-case? – *A.* No.

*Jury. Q.* Is there any particular reason why the black girl was not produced? – *A.* None upon earth, she cannot speak English.

NOT GUILTY

The report of the case in the London *Evening Mail* of 5–7 December 1798 makes clear that the question about the absence of the black servant was put by the Jury directly to Olivia: 'The Jury, after consulting for some time, asked Mrs. Fancourt why the black servant was not produced? To which she replied, that she did not think her presence was necessary, particularly as she could not speak English; but that if the prisoner thought her testimony could be of any use, she might have procured her attendance'. It is clear from this that the black servant was in Olivia's employ and that in all likelihood she was a Tamil servant who had accompanied her from Madras and was able to converse with her in Tamil.

Olivia's lodging with John Hayman in Golden Square East resulted in an early acquaintance with the artist, poet and musician John Westbrooke Chandler (1762–1807), who resided two doors away at No. 7. The natural son of Francis Greville, 1st Earl of Warwick, also known as Lord Brooke (1719–73), Chandler had exhibited 10 portraits at the Royal Academy between 1787 and 1791, and between January and May 1798 he was engaged in painting the portrait of the radical political philosopher and novelist, William Godwin (1756–1836).[21] In December 1798 Chandler seems to have introduced Olivia to Godwin, whose wife Mary Wollstonecraft (1759–1797), author of *A Vindication of the Rights of Woman* (1792), had died after childbirth in September of the previous year.[22]

Portrait in oils of William Godwin by J.W. Chandler,
1798
*Reproduced by permission: Tate Collection © Tate, London 2015. Tate Images*
*Millbank, London*

Godwin found Olivia sufficiently interesting and intelligent to have dined
or taken tea with her on a number of occasions during the next three and a
half years, initially in the company of Chandler. Unfortunately, the entries in
Godwin's manuscript Diary simply record the date of the engagement, without
giving details,[23] an exception being an entry on 31 January 1799 which states:
'Mrs F.[ancourt] affirms, that the subjects of the Mahometan princes in India
are all Moors, & the subjects of the Hindoo princes all Hindoos'. An entry of
22 June 1799 records his taking tea at Olivia's with Chandler and Mrs. Delany
and meeting the heraldic draughtsman to the College of Arms, Ange Denis
MacQuin (1756–1823),[24] before going on with Olivia and Chandler to the
New Royal Circus near the turnpike in Blackfriar's Road, St. George's Fields,
to see 'Almoran & Hamet or, The Fair Circassian', followed by the comic
pantomime 'The Seasons' – an interesting reference, considering Olivia's own
supposed Circassian origins from the north-western region of the Caucasus.
A further entry in Godwin's Diary of 1 January 1800 records his presence at
a New Year's Day dinner party at Olivia's attended by Chandler, MacQuin,

James Northcote (1746–1831)
*Engraving by W.H. Worthington after a painting by George Henry Harlow*

the portrait painter James Northcote (1746–1831),[25] the actor John Litchfield (1774–1858), Mrs. Maria Gurney, daughter of William Hawes (1736–1808), founder of the Royal Humane Society, and wife of the lawyer (Sir) John Gurney (1768–1845), who may have been involved in Olivia's court case in 1798, and four people named Hutchinson.

There is a similar entry in Godwin's Diary five days later, on 6 January 1800, recording another dinner at Olivia's with Northcote, MacQuin and Chandler, the last time Chandler is mentioned in the Diary. This may have been due to a letter Chandler wrote to Godwin on 18 January 1800 relating to what he considered to have been extravagance on Olivia's part in giving so many parties, attended, so it would seem, by various guests introduced by Godwin himself:

> You have long known the interest I take in M[rs]. Fancourt's happiness and you are not I believe wholly unacquainted with the state of her pecuniary resources[.] [Y]ou cannot wonder then that every party she has had since new year's-day was without my

approbation even then I was much displeased at the introduction of so many unexpected ladies – When [with] an eye to our mutual pleasure I form'd the small party of yourself Northcote & Macquin I did not think it would have led to such unwarrantable extravagance to which however I had determin'd to put an end before I knew of the last appointments – It was not till the evening on which the apology you need was written that I understood the nature or intended numbers of the party or that M$^r$. Fuzeli's name had been mention'd – Northcote who in terms not much like his own told you that apology was in consequence of a [word missing] of my economical prudence (a virtue for which I am not distinguished) and have told you also I was much surprized that you knowing the nature of my friendship for M$^{rs}$. Fancourt should without previously hinting it to me propose to introduce any person however distinguished to her acquaintance (Indeed the authority I have exercised in not suffering her as you call it to fulfil her engagements seems to indicate [that] I might have expected as much) He [must] have told you likewise which is very gratifying to me that she thought I acted like her true friend & that she highly approved my conduct.[26]

The letter is far from clear, and another of a similar nature which followed on 20 January 1800, containing the interesting statement that Olivia's house 'for ought I know like Aspasia's of old might have become the resort of all the wits of Athens',[27] is equally obscure, though it possibly reflects Chandler's displeasure at the introduction to her circle of the Swiss painter and Royal Academician, Johann Heinrich Füssli (1741–1825), known as Henry Fuseli, and described by 'Peter Pindar' (John Wolcott, 1738–1819) as the 'hobgoblin painter in ordinary to the Devil'. Chandler's own proprietary interest in her is evident, but the relationship, whatever it was, ended early in 1801,[28] when he left London for Aberdeen, where he received commissions to paint a number of portraits. He subsequently moved to Edinburgh, where he was reported, variously, to have indulged in free thinking and melancholic speculations, to have unsuccessfully tried to kill himself, and to have died in one of the city's lunatic asylums. In fact, after living for some years in Stroud in Gloucestershire, he died at Stafford, aged 45, sometime before 9 May 1807, when the *Staffordshire Advertiser* of that date announced its intention to publish 'Lines to the memory of J. W. Chandler, by Q', but never did so. An obituary notice in another publication referred to his 'urbanity of manners, and excellence of heart', and in June 1823 the *Apollo Magazine* suggested that the 'romantic singularity' and other irregularities of his conduct were 'caused by a disappointment in love': 'he was a very proud man, who would have felt acutely

Rayakottai in Tamil Nadu (Madras), where Olivia Fancourt's first husband was killed
*Coloured aquatint 'Ryacotta in the Barramah' (1802) from Thomas Daniell's* Oriental Scenery *(1802), reproduced by permission of © The British Library Board, X432/3(12)*

any ill-success in pursuit of the divinity he worshipped, whether metaphysical or mortal'. While there is no direct evidence to suggest in this context that Olivia was the cause of his unhappiness, his letters to Godwin point to a strong emotional attachment to her. His leaving London to visit Scotland must have coincided with her learning that she had become a widow by the death of her husband on 5 April 1800 at Rayakottai in the Salem district bordering the Presidency of Madras while serving with the 8th Regiment of Madras Native Infantry and the 4th Regiment of Native Cavalry during the Mysore War.[29]

Sometime after Chandler's departure for Scotland early in 1801, Olivia moved to No. 9 Charles Street, Marylebone, where she paid rates of 6s.8d. for the year of 1802. Godwin called on her on 11 May 1802, 16 months after his previous visit, when her name appears in his Diary for the last time, presumably reflecting his connection with Mary Jane Clairmont (1766–1841) from May of the previous year, and his marriage to her on 21 December 1802.[30] Chandler's place, in the meantime, had been taken by the young Irish poet, Thomas Moore (1779–1852),[31] who had arrived in England from Dublin at the close of 1800 and achieved meteoric fame in the following year with the publication of his mildly erotic *Odes of Anacreon*. In a letter to his mother dated 6 June 1801 he alludes to his poems being 'very much admired' and goes

Thomas Moore (1779–1852)
*Engraving by W. Finding after a portrait by Sir Thomas Lawrence*

on to report that he and his friend Captain Joseph Atkinson 'dined together yesterday at Mrs. Fancourt's', the first reference he makes to her, at least by her married name.[32] It is possible that Moore and Olivia had met earlier in Ireland, and certainly the way he alludes to her in his letter seems to suppose that his mother knew to whom he was referring. A further reference to Olivia is contained in another letter to his mother dated 3 June 1802 in which he describes having accompanied her to the Union Masquerade on 31 May: 'The Union Masquerade on Monday was rather a Bartholomew Fair business, though tickets sold for *fifteen* guineas each. Mrs. Fancourt, as *Wowski*, was the best dressed and supported character I ever saw. I accompanied her as Trudge. The Morning Post of to-day, I see, speaks of her, though they do not know her by name, and says she was attended by '*Anacreon Moor*.'[33] The account in *The Morning Post* reads: 'A beautiful *Wouski* was allowed to be one of the best supported as well as dressed characters in the rooms, at the Union Masquerade. She had on a profusion of fine pearls, diamonds, and valuable coloured gems,

Grosvenor Square near Green Street, London, where Olivia Fancourt was living when she met Raffles in 1804

*W. Thornbury and Edward Walford,* Old and New London *(London, 1879–85)*

and was accompanied by Anacreon Moore, as *Trudge*'.[34] Wowski and Trudge were two of the popular characters in the comic opera, *Inkle and Yarico*, which was set in the West Indies. With tickets at such a price Olivia was clearly living up to her reputation for extravagance, and, indeed, also to Lord Minto's later description of her as a 'rather showy person'.

The extent of her income at this time is unknown as it is uncertain if she derived any advantage from her husband's Will, which was proved for probate at Madras and St. Marylebone, London, in June 1802, the administration of his goods having been completed by July of the previous year. As the wife of a military officer on the Madras establishment, she was entitled to apply for a widow's pension from the compassionate Clive Fund of the East India Company, so named because its funds originally derived from the moneys granted by Mir Jaffar to Lord Clive. Her husband's death was reported in the *Asiatic Annual Register, for the Year 1801* (London, 1802), but it was not until 5 September 1804, when she was living in Green Street, Grosvenor Square, London, that she submitted her application for a pension, the delay presumably being due to difficulty in obtaining the necessary legal papers from India. Demetrius Boulger in his *Life of Sir Stamford Raffles* suggests that the application of this 'tall, distinguished-looking lady, with flashing black Italian eyes' may have been handled in the Secretary's Office of the East India Company by the young Raffles, thus accounting for their meeting,[35] but there is no evidence to support this romantic story apart from the circumstance that it must have been about this time that they first met.

While we have Boulger's account of the impression Olivia may have made on Raffles, we have no idea how he appeared to her. According to his Malay scribe Munsyi Abdullah, he was of medium build with light-brown hair and a good complexion. His left eye watered slightly from a cast and he walked with a slight stoop.[36] He was by universal account extremely amiable, Abdullah recording the fact that he spoke in smiles. Even so, one would hardly suppose that he would have had much appeal to her in any physical sense, and certainly not as a prospective husband on a clerk's salary of £100 a year. This all changed on 8 March of the following year when he was appointed to the post of Assistant Secretary in the new Presidency government of Prince of Wales Island on a salary of £1500, with seemingly unlimited prospects for advancement in the service of the East India Company. He later recorded the reasons for his proposing marriage to Olivia:

> 'My Resolution to proceed to India and my app[t]. to Prince of Wales Island were made before the marriage took place; and when I was about to quit all other ties and affections it was natural that I should secure one bosom friend, one companion on my journey who would soothe the adverse blasts of misfortune and gladden the sunshine of prosperity –'.

But he also added that the marriage gave him 'no new connections – no wealth, but on the contrary a load of debt, which I had to clear off – it increased my difficulties & thus encreased my energies, it gave me domestic enjoyment and thus contributed to my happiness, but in no way can my advancement in life be accounted owing to that connection –'.[37] While his proposal of marriage was

St. George's Church, Bloomsbury, London
*Engraving by W. Deeble*

thus inspired by strong emotional needs and genuine affection, her acceptance, leaving aside her personal feelings, are perhaps more easily surmised. She was a 34-year-old widow with a somewhat colourful past and an entirely uncertain future, with expensive tastes and mounting debts, and a pension of only one shilling and three pence a day. The prospect of a return to Asia with a husband 10 years her junior must have been extremely appealing. It would be wrong, all the same, to dismiss her personal emotions and affection for Raffles, judging by the depth of feeling she later expressed in one of her surviving letters when she wrote of 'my beloved and *every way worthy husband*'.[38]

The marriage was celebrated on 14 March 1805 at St. George's Church, Bloomsbury, by the Revd. A.P. Poston, the entry in the marriage register, no.

64, reading: 'Thomas Raffles Esquire to Olivia Mariamne Fancourt, Widow, both of this Parish, by License, on the fourteenth day of March one thousand eight hundred and five (1805) by Revd. Poston, Curate. Witnesses Richard S. Taylor, Charles Hamond, Marianne Etherington, Maria Walthen'. Apart from Raffles's uncle, Charles Hamond, tea merchant of Milk Street, Cheapside,[39] little is known about the witnesses. Richard S. Taylor is referred to by Raffles in a letter he wrote from Penang in 1809 as 'my friend M$^r$ R S Taylor of Gray's Inn',[40] the context seeming to imply that he had some charge over his funds in London. Maria Walthen was probably the mother of the young man who engaged to accompany Raffles to Bengkulu in 1817, but who deserted the ship *Lady Raffles* at Falmouth to return to his family. Of Marianne Etherington nothing is known apart from the confusion caused by Boulger in his *Life of Sir Stamford Raffles* by rendering her first name as 'Mariamne' and setting off a chain of speculation that she might in some manner be related to Olivia.[41] Her name was, in fact, 'Marianne', as clearly appears in the marriage register.

During the six weeks between her marriage and departure for Penang, Olivia seems to have been reunited briefly with her daughter Harriet in London in 1805, when they had their miniature portraits painted by Andrew Plimer (1763–1837) at his studio at No. 8 Golden Square, Olivia's next door neighbour when she was living there.[42] The miniatures were inherited by Harriet's granddaughter, Katharine Hawkins Dempster, later Lady Metcalfe,[43] the eldest sister of Charlotte Louisa Hawkins Dempster, who recorded the interesting particulars about Olivia's early life. At that time, and subsequently, the miniatures were attributed to Andrew's brother, Nathaniel Plimer,[44] but their attribution has increasingly gone in favour of Andrew.[45] The miniatures were clearly painted as a pair, strongly suggesting that the two subjects were together in Plimer's studio. They depict a remarkable likeness between mother and daughter, with the qualification, expressed by Graham Reynolds, that as Plimer was not good at catching a likeness, he gave all his sitters 'a large, long nose, wide-open eyes and a gipsy complexion', with the result that 'his portraits, of women especially, look very much the same'.[46]

In late April 1805 Olivia and Raffles, accompanied by Raffles's sister Mary Anne, joined the numerous officials of the new Presidency government of Prince of Wales Island at Portsmouth, where a large fleet of between 18 and 22

Philip Dundas (1762–1807), Governor of Prince of
Wales Island
*Reproduced by permission of Mrs. A. Dundas-Bekker, Arniston House,
Scotland*

East Indiamen was preparing to sail under the protection of HMS *Blenheim*,
74 guns (Austin Bissel), carrying the flag of the new commander of the East
Indies station, Rear-Admiral Sir Thomas Troubridge (1758–1807). With so
many ships and such a number of passengers, including military personnel of
the 53rd, 56th and 67th Regiments, 'the confusion was beyond description',
resulting in several passengers having to pay 100 guineas to the boatmen to be
taken out to the ships. The Prince of Wales Island officials and their families
sailed in the East Indiamen, *Cumberland* (William Farrer), *Warley* (Henry
Wilson), *Hope* (James Pendergrass), *Dorsetshire* (Robert Brown), and *Ganges*
(Thomas Harrington). The Governor, Philip Dundas, with his wife Margaret
and child, and her sister Jean Wedderburn, together with John Hope Oliphant
(Second in Council), John James Erskine (Assistant Superintendent of Marine
and Storekeeper), William Dick (Head Surgeon), Quintin Dick Thompson
(Sub-Warehouse Keeper) and James Finlay (Clerk to the Governor) all sailed in
the 1,260-ton *Cumberland*, while Raffles, Olivia, Mary Anne, Alexander Gray
(Third in Council), and the Writers, Arthur Tegart, Robert Ibbetson, John
Curson Lawrence and William Armstrong Clubley, were all taken on board the

*Ganges*, a three-deck ship of 1,502 tons, built by Wells in 1797 and principally owned by William Moffat, who had commanded the ship in the previous year when she was second in line of the fleet of 16 East Indiamen and 11 Country ships under the command of Commodore Nathaniel Dance (1748–1827) which faced down a squadron of five French ships, including the 42-gun frigate *La Belle Poule* and the 74-gun *Marengo* flying the flag of Rear-Admiral C.A.L. Durand de Linois, off Pulau Aur in the Straits of Melaka.[47] The new commander of the *Ganges* for the 1805 voyage, Thomas Talbot Harrington, was a 26-year-old Wiltshireman, who later became a friend and partner of the Singapore merchant Alexander Guthrie.

The convoy sailed from Portsmouth on 24/25 April 1805 and enjoyed an uneventful voyage until 22 July, when a severe gale in Latitude 39° South resulted in the *Coutts* and the *Warley* losing their fore top-sails and parting company. Two weeks later, on 6 August, at four o'clock in the afternoon, in Latitude 19°5 South and Longitude 81°22 East, the convoy had the misfortune to run into Linois's *Marengo* and *Belle Poule*, with the captured East Indiaman *Brunswick* in tow. Running under the lee quarter of the *Cumberland*, the *Marengo*, with *La Belle Poule* behind, managed to put a shot into her. The heavily armed East Indiamen in the convoy commenced a return of fire when HMS *Blenheim* hove into view and began firing her main and quarter-deck guns, the heavy sea preventing the lower-deck guns from operating.[48] The French ships immediately withdrew,[49] but the next morning they were still about four leagues to the westward, and Troubridge placed himself between them and the convoy under easy sail in the hope of inducing de Linois to re-engage. The French ships continued to follow the convoy but disappeared during the night. The engagement had been relatively short and little damage was done, but one passenger in HMS *Blenheim* was killed, and a soldier in the *Ganges* was killed by a 9lb. shot, which must have made the event somewhat harrowing for Olivia, Mary Anne and Raffles.

After a passage of 17 weeks the convoy arrived off Madras on 23 August 1805. The *Ganges* was redeployed to Calcutta, so Raffles and his party had to join Captain Henry Wilson in the 1,200-ton *Warley*,[50] which had arrived at Madras a few days after the main convoy. Rear-Admiral Troubridge in HMS *Blenheim* now escorted the China-bound East Indiamen *Cumberland*, *Hope*,

*Coutts*, *Exeter* and *Warley* to Prince of Wales Island, where they arrived on 18 September to a salute of 15 guns from Fort Cornwallis. Troubridge and Governor Dundas with their respective officers and officials landed early the following morning at the new wharf, where they were ceremoniously greeted by the Secretary to the Lieutenant-Governor, William Edward Phillips, the officer commanding the troops, Major George Dick, together with the principal local officials, and conducted to Government House through lines of troops and the fifes playing 'Rule Britannia' in the Admiral's honour.[51] On 20 September the commissions of the Governor and Commander of the Troops, Colonel Norman Macalister, were read to the general assemblage, and the officials of the new Presidency government were installed in their respective posts. As Sunday was the anniversary of the coronation of George III, the royal standard was flown on HMS *Blenheim* at sunrise with accompanying salutes fired by the ships and the guns of Fort Cornwallis.

The *Ganges* East Indiaman
*Contemporary print*

# CHAPTER FIVE

## Olivia Mariamne Raffles in Penang, Melaka and Java

Fort Cornwallis, Penang
*Aquatint by J. Havell from Colonel James Welsh,* Military Reminiscences *(London, 1830)*

View from George Town to the Kedah Coast
*Aquatint from James Wathen,* Voyage to Madras and China *(London, 1814)*

WITH SUCH POMP AND CEREMONY Olivia was introduced to her new
life in an island with a small European and Asian population, very different
from her experience of living in India with her first husband. She had barely
recovered from the long voyage from England when she was required to nurse
a recently arrived invalid who had been found in dire circumstances by her
husband. The newcomer was the Scottish poet and orientalist, Dr. John Leyden
(1775–1811), who had landed at Penang with three servants on 22 October
1805 aboard a Parsee brig from Quillon in south India with the intention of
studying Malay and recovering his health. He had arrived 'terribly ill', and
had taken accommodation in a naval tavern, 'ringing with the vociferation of
tarpaulins, the hoarse bawling of sea-oaths, and the rattling of the dice-box',[1]
where his condition attracted the sympathy of Raffles, who took him home to
be cared for by Olivia. The three quickly forged bonds of the most intimate
friendship and affection, leading Raffles to declare later that Leyden was 'my
dearest friend, and I may truly say that while I looked up to him with all the
admiration and respect which his wonderful Talents and glowing Virtues were
calculated to command … I felt towards him the most brotherly affection –'.[2]

Strawberry Hill, Penang
*Aquatint by W. Daniell after Captain Robert Smith (1821)*

Leyden was a product of the Scottish Enlightenment, a friend of Francis Horner, Thomas Campbell, Richard Heber, Alexander Murray and (Sir) Walter Scott, with whom he had collaborated in the compilation of the *Minstrelsy of the Scottish Border* (Kelso, Edinburgh, 1802–3). He had also published in his own name *A Historical & Philosophical Sketch of the Discoveries & Settlements of the Europeans in Northern & Western Africa, at the Close of the Eighteenth Century* (Edinburgh, 1799), inspired by the adventures of his fellow Borderer, Mungo Park (1771–1806), and *Scottish Descriptive Poems; with some Illustrations of Scottish Literary Antiquities* (Edinburgh, 1803), as well as his popular poem, *Scenes of Infancy: Descriptive of Teviotdale* (Edinburgh, 1803). After obtaining a medical diploma from the Royal College of Surgeons of Edinburgh, and the degrees of A.M. and M.D. from the University of St. Andrews, he was appointed by the East India Company to the medical establishment at Madras, where he worked for a year from August 1803 in the General Hospital before serving as medical assistant and naturalist on the Commission to survey the Mysore provinces.[3] Leyden's principal interest was in Indian and Oriental languages, and it was his desire to investigate Malay and the Indo-Chinese

Dr. John Leyden (1775–1811)
*Lithograph by W. & A. Johnston after a sketch by the*
*Hon. George Elliot on board HMS* Modeste *in 1811*

Sir Gilbert Elliot (1751–1814), 1st Earl of Minto
*Engraving by W.J. Edwards after a painting by George Chinnery*

languages that drew him to Penang. His scholarly example and encouragement served as the spur for Raffles to pursue more seriously his own study of Malay, which helped ensure his future promotion. His translation of the Maritime Code of the Malays, which was published in Calcutta in volume XII of the *Asiatick Researches*, was the direct result of Leyden's encouragement.[4]

Leyden proved to be a welcome guest for Olivia while he remained in her care, providing agreeable and intelligent conversation of a kind not found in the limited society of Penang. He was closer to her age than her husband was, but he was not physically attractive, with wild dark staring eyes, a pointed nose, and sandy-coloured hair. His broad Scottish accent and loud grating voice, which rose when he became excited into shrill 'saw-tones', was not pleasant on the ear, and he talked endlessly, leading the Governor-General Lord Minto to declare, 'I do not believe that so great a reader was ever so great a talker before'.[5] He was boastful of his own achievements, and was offensive to strangers. His manners, Sir Walter Scott wrote, 'revolted the fastidious and alarmed the delicate',[6] but Scott also noted that despite his lack of social graces he seemed to find particular favour with the female sex, including Jane, Duchess of Gordon

(1749–1812), and Lady Charlotte Campbell (1775–1861), both leaders of fashionable society in Edinburgh at the end of the 18th century. Olivia became deeply attached to him, feeling, as she wrote, 'an affection … such as I feel for my only and beloved Brother'.[7] His feelings for her bordered on love.

Before leaving Penang, Leyden addressed to her one of his best-known poems, 'Dirge of the Departed Year', which was dated 'Penang Jany 1, 1806' and subsequently printed in the *Prince of Wales Island Gazette* on 22 March 1806, the text varying slightly from a manuscript copy in the National Library of Scotland (MS 971, fols. 113–14). The poem consists of 17 stanzas, including:

> *Olivia! ah! forgive the Bard*
> *If sprightly strains alone are dear*
> *His notes are sad for he has heard*
> *The footsteps of the parting year*
>
> *…*
>
> *But chief that in this Eastern isle*
> *Girt by the green and glistening wave*
> *Olivia's kind bewitching smile*
> *Seemed to recall me from the grave*
>
> *When far beyond Malaya's sea*
> *I trace dark Soonda's forests drear*
> *Olivia I shall think of thee; –*
> *And bless thy steps, Departed year!*
>
> *Each Morn or Evening spent with thee*
> *Fancy shall mid the wilds restore*
> *In all their charms, and they shall be*
> *Sweet days that shall return no more*
>
> *Still may'st thou live in bliss secure*
> *Beneath that Friend's protecting care*
> *And may his cherished life endure*
> *Long long thy holy love to share.*

Leyden and Olivia exchanged a number of letters, his first being dated 7 January 1806, the night of his departure from Penang on board the Portuguese ship *Santo Antonio*. In this, he writes of 'all the pleasant recollections' he had 'hoarded up … in the society of you and your amiable husband', and asks her (as 'my dear sister Olivia') to think of him kindly 'and never to believe any evil you may hear of me till you have it under my own hand'.[8] In another letter dated 6 March 1806, written some time after his arrival at Calcutta, he ends by 'telling my dear amiable Olivia again how much I *love* her. Don't start now at the term for I repeat it[.] I love you with a true brotherly affection, and never think of you without the kindest emotions as indeed I ought to do.' He then somewhat qualifies matters by referring to her as 'my dear good matronly sister', clearly floundering to express his emotions for her.[9] When Olivia received this letter early in April 1806 she was recovering from a serious illness, caused, as Raffles explained to Leyden, by 'a fall in dancing', which ruptured some blood vessels near or in her liver and led to 'a violent hemorrage [*sic*]'.[10] She lost weight and was reduced to a mere skeleton. That she recovered at all was due entirely to the care and attention of 'a good & worthy friend', a surgeon on HMS *Blenheim* named Thomas Quin from Hambledon, who died at Penang on 12 November 1806 following a short illness.

Her reply to a letter from Leyden dated 10 May 1808, in which he informed her that he had sponsored Raffles's election as a member of the Asiatic Society of Bengal, and had secured for him a favourable notice of his Malay studies in Lord Minto's Annual Address to the College of Fort William,[11] is her only surviving letter to him:[12]

> Penang – Aug[st]. 3[d]. 1808 –
>
> My very dear D[r]. Leyden, if you knew the real heart-felt joy I experienced on reading your dear kind letter you would be convinced how tenderly you are remember'd by me – I feel an affection for you such as I feel for my only and beloved Brother – and when I heard you were dangerously ill I felt such a sudden pang as assured me of the sincerity of my regard – you cannot then blame me for having been unhappy when I imagined you had forgotten me when I knew you were well and yet thought not

of me so far as to write and tell me so – for I have never received more than your first delightful letter and that which you sent by M[r]. Beureau [Captain A.W. Burreau] – I have written many many – but a truce with complainings, I am remember'd & happy –

You will believe I rejoice most sincerely that your super eminent abilities have not been overlooked at Bengal, any others than *blind stupid* or *envious* men would have rewarded them long ago – I thank God you are settled at last for many reasons, though I think you have a vast deal too much on your mind and hands for your health['s] sake – I only hope you will have a little more care for it now than you have hitherto had – will you not? Yes – then I will love you dearly –

Who but you could, who but your dear self would have remember'd my beloved and *every way worthy husband* in the elegant and honourable manner in which we saw his name – ah my dear friend, I shed many grateful tears on the paper, so did your friend – The little paltry wretches here were astonished and nearly maddened by envy – for after some battles your friend has succeeded in keeping them all at bay – they may bark as a dog does at the Moon, and with as much effect – his old enemy M[r]. [John] Dickens[13] is going to Calcutta with his heart full of rancour and his mouth full of scurrility against him – for what Olivia? [Be]cause he has proved himself *almost* as learned in the Law as himself – *"Great Judge and M."* [be]cause he has saved the Government (bad as it is) from his insolent and unmerited attacks – [be]cause he has proved himself above him in all things and has persevered in politeness to him – and last of all [be]cause he would not allow an address from some of the Wapping Pedlars voting him a piece of plate, and a reply from him, to be published as it reflected on the Government in a very severe manner[,] but I dare say you will see it as a copy is to be sent to the secretary at Calcutta – he says he will publish it there in spite of their teeth – he is really the most *impudent, ignorant,* affected, *envious* ungrateful *old Jay* I ever heard of – he came to this Island seven years ago in debt – he leaves it now worth forty thousand pounds – most part of which has been torn from the poor Malays, Chinese &c &c &c under the title of *fees*! tho' he received a salary of three thousand pounds a year, with a House &c – yet *he* calls himself *an honest man* – he wished much to have been appointed Registrar and told Sir Edmond Stanley[14] that he would never be able to get through a cause without *him* or some such great and able personage – however Sir E. and the Governor & Council conjured Mr. Raffles to act as Registrar, and you will see that everything is going on perfectly correct – a cause of some consequence has been tried and gain'd for the plaintiff to the satisfaction of all – you know what a public spirit your friend has – he has taken the enormous task of Registrar and without *fee* or present reward – Secretary without an assistant, or any one who can afford him the least possible assistance – the consequence begins to shew itself very soon – he is ill and quite worn [out] – and I dread another long lingering fit of illness such as he had last, which was brought on by intense labour of mind and body – all here is dull stupidity – Mary Anne has a beautiful little Girl two months old yesterday and has been living on the Hill for the last month[15] – M^r. R. is building a pretty brick house on the Beach which I hope will be finished in eight or ten weeks – did I tell you about *our* Hill? If not, I will describe it in my next – and now that you have taken me again to your liking I shall not be miserable as I used to be, if you should not write as often as I wish, knowing all that you have to do – as I have said before I wish quantity may make up for quality in your eyes – May all that's good attend you ever – and you see you are not the worse for the prayers of your cummer, for she did pray for you, and foretold that if you lived you would be the greatest Man in India – and so you are & so you will be, and I trust I shall live to hear it[,] ay[e] and see your *greatness* too – once more God bless you –

Your affectionate Sister
Olivia Mariamne R –

She added a postscript:

*Oh thou whom ne'er my constant heart*
*One moment hath forgot*
*Tho fate severe hath bid us part*
*Yet still forget me not –*

*Yet let not distance from thy breast*
*My image ever blot*
*Let our fond friendship bear this test,*
*Absent, forget me not –*

Now don't be like a Great Big larned [*sic*] Pundit in finding a thousand and fifty faults in my poor unrefined & incorrect scrawl – I know about as much of fine writing as I do about Greek – but you will understand me –

Leyden's reply to this letter was written sometime in September or October 1808[16] and is important in revealing a closer connection between Olivia and Thomas Moore than is suggested by the few references to her in his correspondence. In her own letter to Leyden, Olivia had not thought it necessary to state that her poem was in imitation of Moore's style, as she had clearly informed him in Penang that she was the 'Nona' of Moore's love poetry. Leyden's reply to her letter is intelligible only on this supposition:

You are wrong for once Mrs Olivia for as much as you are accustomed to be in the right – The Verses in spite of a little incorrectness especially in the second Stanza, are an exceeding good imitation of Moore's manner, and I thank you for them heartily Mrs Olivia for to tell you a secret I don't like *Nona* at all at all. Indeed I am perfectly certain that I am not a little jealous or so of Moore and his everlasting Nona[.] Certain it is at all events that you shall never be-Nonaed by me – The last Stanza has all the enthusiasm of real feeling but why don't you say "Informed by genius all divine" [?] I would ask a dozen of pardons for taking the liberty of suggesting it, only I never ask pardon unless when I mean an *insult*[,] aye an iron insult[.]

> *Oer Nona's grave to Nona's shade*
> *Tom Moore funeral rites has paid*
> *But I beneath Malayan skies*
> *Shall bid her like the phoenix rise*
> *In grace & sweetness all the same*
> *But let Olivia be her name*
> *Let Greek Anacreon claim the West*
> *Here Persian Hafez reigns confest.*

That Olivia had identified herself as 'Nona' to Leyden is clear from another poem he had addressed to her in December 1805 before he left Penang. It is entitled 'Christmas in Penang':[17]

> *Dear Nona, Christmas comes from far*
> *To seek us near the eastern star*
> *But brings not to the Orient clime*
> *Her wintry wreaths & ancient thyme*
> *What wreaths then shall we weave for thee*
> *For glossy bay & rosemary*
>
> *Champaca flowers for thee we strew*
> *To drink the merry Christmas dew*
> *Though hailed in each Malayan grove*
> *The saffron-tinted flower of love,*
> *Of none more loved amid the fair*
> *Her tulip-buds adorn the hair*
>
> *Banana leaves their ample screen*
> *Shall spread to match the holly green.*
> *Well may their glossy softness please*
> *Sweet emblem of the soul at ease*

*The heart expanding frank and free*
*Like the still-green Banana tree*

*Nona, may all the woodland powers*
*That stud Malaya's clime of flowers*
*Or on the breeze their fragrance fling*
*Around thee form an angel ring*
*To guard thee ever gay & free*
*Beneath thy green Banana tree.*

Leyden was almost certainly the one responsible for informing Lord Minto of the connection between Olivia and Moore for after meeting her at Melaka the Governor-General wrote to his wife on 31 May 1811: 'I have heard, but am not sure of the fact, that she was one of the beauties to whom Anacreontic Moore addressed many of his amatory elegies.'[18] Rumours about her being the subject of Moore's love poetry were already current in Penang, as is shown by the recollections of a young midshipman who visited the island at this time: 'This [Penang] was one of poor Sir Stamford Raffles' pet spots; and here I recollect right well his coming on board, with a rather elderly lady, dressed rather fantastically, a good and clever creature, and one already celebrated in song – "Rosa" – of a certain little bard. Ye gods! Well, anything but Rosa! How well your poetic flights thus point to a discrepancy'.[19]

The ungallant writer confuses 'Rosa' with 'Nona', who was the subject of only one of Moore's juvenile poems, 'The Natal Genius. A Dream', which was dedicated 'To –, The Morning of Her Birth-day'. It appeared in *The Poetical Works of the Late Thomas Little, Esq.*, a small volume published anonymously in London by Moore in 1801:

*In witching slumbers of the night,*
*I dream'd I was the airy sprite*
*That on thy natal moment smil'd;*
*And thought I wafted on my wing*
*Those flow'rs which in Elysium spring,*
*To crown my lovely mortal child.*

*With olive-branch I bound thy head,*
*Heart's-ease along the path I shed,*
*Which was to bloom through all thy years;*
*Nor yet did I forget to bind*
*Love's roses, which his myrtle twin'd,*
*And dew'd by sympathetic tears.*

*Such was the wild but precious boon,*
*Which Fancy, at her magic noon,*
*Bade me to Nona's image pay —*
*Oh! Were I, love, thus doom'd to be*
*Thy little guardian deity,*
*How blest around thy steps I'd play!*

*Thy life should softly steal along,*
*Calm as some lonely shepherd's song*
*That's heard at distance in the grove;*
*No cloud should ever shade thy sky,*
*No thorns along thy pathway lie,*
*But all be sunshine, peace, and love!*

*The wing of time should never brush*
*Thy dewy lip's luxuriant flush,*
*To bid its roses with'ring die;*
*Nor age itself, though dim and dark,*
*Should ever quench a single spark*
*That flashes from my Nona's eye!*

There is nothing in the poem that directly connects 'Nona' with Olivia but she herself reported the connection to other people, and given the fact that she knew Moore well when the poem was published in the summer of 1801, one must accept that it was written to celebrate her birthday on 16 February of that year. There is only one surviving book belonging to her, but unfortunately it is not *The Poetical Works of the Late Thomas Little, Esq.*, in

The Revd. Dr. Thomas Raffles (1788–1863), cousin of Sir
Stamford Raffles
*Engraving by J. Thomson after a portrait by A. Mosses, London, 1822*

which the 'Nona' poem appears, but a copy of his later work, *Epistles, Odes, and
Other Poems* (London, 1806), which bears an ownership inscription in her own
hand, 'O.M.R. March. The 6th. 1810'.[20] Raffles himself was a friend of Moore,
and it is certain that she was responsible for introducing them after Moore had
returned to London from the West Indies in November 1804. He refers to 'my
friend Mr Moore' in a letter to his cousin, the Revd. Dr. Thomas Raffles, dated
16 January 1817,[21] but gives no indication when they first met. Moore himself
in his Journal states that he was served bird's-nest soup at a dinner given by
Raffles in London in 1816 or 1817,[22] and in a later reference he records having
met 'my old friend Sir Stamford Raffles' at Bowood House in Wiltshire, the
seat of Lord Lansdowne, on 29–30 October 1824.[23]

There are a few references to Olivia and Raffles's life together in Penang,
one of them being in the letter she wrote to Leyden on 3 August 1808 in which

she referred to her husband building 'a pretty brick house on the Beach', later Northam Road.[24] This was one of a number of houses then being constructed along the north beach by various government officials and was not completed until early 1809 when it was designated 'Runnymede'. One of those officials, William Robinson,[25] was a neighbour and close friend of Raffles and Olivia, and in November 1809 the *Prince of Wales Island Gazette* described a dinner party he gave to 'a select party of friends … at his Mansion on the North Beach'.[26] This was followed in the evening by 'a most elegant fête', arranged by two young Writers, William Clubley and John Lyon Phipps, and attended by the Governor and 'the beauty and fashion of the Island'. The ball commenced between eight and nine and Clubley had 'the honour to lead Mrs Raffles down the first Dance to the tune of "Off She Goes"'. At 12 o'clock the supper rooms were thrown open with tables 'covered in every delicacy which India could produce', with wines 'of the most delicious quality'. Later, several ladies and gentlemen entertained the guests with songs, 'displaying on the one part the most true delicacies of taste and on the other true original comicality'.[27]

Olivia's sister-in-law, Mary Anne, had a particularly beautiful voice but it is not certain if she was present on the occasion as her husband Quintin Dick Thompson, Sub-Warehouse Keeper and Deputy Paymaster, had died less than five months earlier. He had travelled out to Penang aboard the *Cumberland* in the suite of the Governor Philip Dundas and so presumably met his future wife only after her arrival in the island on 19 September 1805 since she sailed in the *Ganges* to Madras and from there to Penang in the *Warley*. His death at the age of 26 years on 29 June 1809, after an illness of only two days, was 'Deeply and deservedly lamented', according to the inscription on the tombstone.[28] As a widow, Mary Anne was left with three children, Olivia becoming especially attached to Charlotte Raffles Drury Thompson, named after Raffles and her god-father, Vice-Admiral William O'Bryen Drury, Commander-in-Chief on the East Indies Station. Quintin Dick Thompson's sister Charlotte was married to James McClelland, Baron of the Court of Exchequer, and Raffles addressed letters to him[29] and Quintin Dick in London[30] concerning the provisions of Thompson's Will and the Marriage Settlement. The estate seems to have amounted to a relatively small sum of between £1,000 and £1,800 and Raffles was obliged to shoulder some of his sister's expenses, though he did manage to

Government House, Calcutta
*Aquatint from J.B. Fraser,* Views of Calcutta and its Environs *(London, 1824–6)*

retain for himself his deceased brother-in-law's position as Naval Agent, which carried no salary but a small commission on disbursements. Baron McClelland and his wife eventually adopted the two surviving children, Acheson and Charlotte, who grew up on the Annaverna estate in County Louth in Ireland.[31]

Following the British naval conquests in the Maluku islands in eastern Indonesia in April 1810, Vice-Admiral Drury suggested to the Governor-General that Raffles should be placed in charge of the captured Dutch possession, but when Raffles arrived at Calcutta aboard the *Union* (A.H. Reid) to press his claim he found that the post had already been assigned to someone else.[32] He was, however, retained in Calcutta by Lord Minto, who appointed him on 1 October 1810 as Agent to the Governor-General with the Malay States, with instructions to proceed to Melaka and make preparations for the British invasion of Java. During his residence of more than four months in Calcutta, Raffles stayed for a time with Leyden,[33] who wrote to Olivia on 22 August informing her of the cordial reception her husband had received in Calcutta,[34] and on 22 October of his own future prospects after the conquest of Java and his determination to be Raffles's Secretary: 'I have ... settled with

R[affles] that the instant he is Governor of Java I am to be his Secretary. That is the only chance you ever have of seeing me. The time fast approaches when I shall proceed to take possession of Borneo & whenever I *proceed*, I am determined to *succeed*.'[35]

After Raffles arrived back at Penang on 17 November aboard HEIC cruiser *Ariel* (Lieutenant D. Macdonald),[36] he made arrangements for the sale of his house 'Runnymede' and also for the East India Company's brig at Penang to take Olivia and his sisters Harriot and Leonora to Melaka, the latter having been married to the Madras surgeon Billington Loftie on 22 November 1810.[37] He followed them in the *Ariel* four days later, and at Melaka arranged for the whole family to be accommodated in a house at Bandar Hilir on the estate of the son of the Chinese Kapitan. Here he also settled his Malay secretariat, which included the 14-year-old Abdullah bin Abdul Kadir, who later in his *Hikayat* recalled his impressions of Olivia:[38]

> I noticed that the character of Mr. Raffles's wife was unlike that of ordinary women. She shared her husband's charm, his modesty and prudence in everything that she did. She spoke in a friendly and courteous manner alike to the rich and the poor. She enjoyed making a thorough study of Malay, and used to ask how the Malays say this and that. All the points that she noted she wrote down on paper. And I observed too that whenever Mr. Raffles wanted to do something, for instance to make a purchase, he always asked his wife first and if she agreed he acted. It was her nature, I noticed, to do all her work with the greatest alacrity, never wasting a moment in idleness, but forever working away at one thing or another … Mrs. Raffles was as active as the cockroach which has no tail, doing one thing after another, after tidying the house she would sew and after sewing she would write letters. May I be blinded if my eyes ever saw her retire or compose herself for rest in the middle of the day. She was up and about all the time. Allah alone knows. Unless I have misunderstood what I saw, this is a sign that she was wise and capable of doing important things. As I saw it, it was her character and industry that fitted her to do her husband's work

Malacca from the sea
*Aquatint by John Clark from James Wathen,* Voyage to Madras and China *(London, 1814)*

Malacca River
*Engraving by George Cooke after E.H. Locker from John Pinkerton,*
Voyages and Travels *(London, 1808–14)*

and to be his helper. For Allah had joined together the pair of
them making them of one mind, like a ruler and his minister, like
a ring and the jewel set in it, like sugar in milk.

Olivia and Raffles spent more than six months together at Melaka but she was
often ill and confined to bed. Raffles reported to Leyden on 15 December 1810
that she was 'in very bad health',[39] but she seems to have gradually recovered
and with the arrival of the first (Bengal) elements of the British invasion force
at the end of April the pace of life in the settlement quickened. Mary Anne had
joined them earlier from Penang, and her beauty soon
attracted the notice of Captain William Lawrence Flint,
commander of HMS *Teignmouth*, and a younger brother
of Sir Charles Flint, private secretary to the Duke of
Wellington.[40] They were married on 2 May 1811, shortly
before the arrival on 18 May of the Governor-General
Lord Minto aboard the frigate *Modeste*, commanded by
his son, the Hon. George Elliot,[41] together with other
members of his staff, including the Military Secretary,
Captain Thomas W. Taylor of HM 24th Dragoons,[42]
Archibald Seton, the new Governor of Prince of Wales
Island,[43] and John Leyden, who had managed to secure
the position of Malay Translator, to assist Raffles in his
correspondence with the Malay and Indonesian rulers.[44]

Captain William Flint, R.N. (1781–
1828), first Master Attendant
of Singapore
*Private collection*

Two days after his arrival, the Governor-General,
together with Captain Taylor and probably Leyden,
breakfasted with Raffles and his family at Bandar Hilir. Minto later wrote to his
wife: 'Mrs Raffles is the great lady, with dark eyes, lively manner, accomplished
and clever. She had a former husband in India; and I have heard, but am not
sure of the fact, that she was one of the beauties to whom Anacreontic Moore
addressed many of his amatory elegies'.[45] To another correspondent he wrote:[46]

Our European society, I mean that which includes the better
half of creation, has hitherto been confined to the family of M^r.
Raffles. – M^rs Raffles, Olivia Mariamne, is a tall & rather showy

person, with dark eyes & the complexion from which I have myself made my choice. Her countenance is lively & spirituelle, & her conversation deserves the same epithets. Upon the whole, my expectations are more than answered, & I am very glad to see Raffles, who really is a very amiable as well as clever man so happy in his interior, for he is a true admirer of his lot. They have no children – Raffles has three sisters here, all very fair, one extremely well-looking, & the other two not the contrary. Their manners are also sensible & gentlewomanlike. The beauty is married to Capt. Flint, a Post Captain in the Navy. Another sister is M^rs. Loftie, lately married to a surgeon of that name.[47] The third has not yet made her choice.[48] We have breakfasted & dined with this family & they have dined with me, which is the honest amount of my confessions on the female chapter.

The King's Birthday on 4 June was celebrated at Melaka with the usual festivities, and a ball in the evening at the Stadhuis was attended by some 150 army and naval officers and the principal Dutch and British residents, including Olivia, Mary Anne and her two sisters. Two days later, the first of the Bengal

Stadhuis Malacca
*Engraving by George Cooke after E.H. Locker from John Pinkerton,* Voyages and Travels *(London, 1808–14)*

contingents of the Java invasion force sailed for Java, and in the succeeding days small divisions of transport ships, escorted by the frigates, followed them. The combined fleet of four ships of the line, 14 frigates, seven sloops, eight Company cruisers and 57 transports, under the command of Commodore William Robert Broughton (1762–1821) in HMS *Illustrious* (Captain Festing), had all sailed by the middle of the month, carrying a mixed European and Asian force of 11,000 troops under the command of Sir Samuel Auchmuty (1756–1822).[49] HMS *Modeste*, with Lord Minto and Raffles on board, sailed last, on 18 June, accompanied by the schooner *Minto*, commanded by Captain Greig, who was to determine the safest route to Java.[50] Also aboard the *Minto* were John Leyden and the Malay writers, while Olivia, Mary Anne, Harriot and Leonora were all accommodated in the East Indiaman *Preston*, commanded by Henry Sturrock.

Sir Samuel Auchmuty (1756–1822)
*Engraving after A. Cardon from the* Military Chronicle *(London, 1811)*

Java Invasion Fleet off Pulau Penembangan, 1811
*Aquatint by Josesph Jeakes from William Thorn,* Conquest of Java *(London, 1815)*

Country house at Weltevreden, Batavia, where Raffles and Lord Minto stayed
during the British hostilities leading to the capture of Java
*Watercolour drawing by James George, 1811, from* Catalogus van Jhr. Mr. P.R. Feith *(Batavia, 1937)*

Government House, Rijswijk, Batavia (Jakarta)
*Watercolour drawing by James George, 1811, from* Catalogus van Jhr. Mr. P.R. Feith *(Batavia, 1937)*

After sailing through the Straits of Singapore and reassembling at Pulau Penembangan, south of Pontianak, the British invasion force sailed by way of Tanjung Sambar in southern Borneo to Cilincing in Java, nine miles east of Batavia, where the troops disembarked. After the capture of Batavia, Lord Minto and his staff occupied a country house near Weltevreden and remained there until after the defeat of the Franco-Dutch forces at Meester Cornelis on 26 August.[51] Two days later, Leyden, who had hurried ashore to examine the Dutch records in a closed library in Batavia, was carried off with a fever and was buried the same day at Tanah Abang in the presence of Lord Minto, Raffles and, almost certainly, Olivia.[52] On 11 September Raffles was appointed Lieutenant-Governor of the island and five weeks later he gave 'a grand dinner and entertainment' in honour of the Governor-General at his official residence at Rijswijk. Two days later, Lord Minto and his officials embarked for Calcutta, having spent the afternoon dining with Raffles and his family, where the mood was funereal. He made a short speech whereupon Olivia and her sisters-in-law burst into tears. Raffles accompanied him to the wharf, from where he was conveyed in a barge to HMS *Modeste*, which sailed the following morning.[53]

When news of Minto's safe arrival at Calcutta reached Java, Olivia addressed a letter to him in which she alluded to Raffles's visits to the courts of Surakarta and Yogyakarta in central Java during the previous month and to the heavy burden of his administration.[54]

Buitenzorg

Jan'y the 28th 1812 –

My dear Lord

I cannot let the present opportunity go by without attempting to say something to your Lordship; to greet you on your escape from hence, and to congratulate you on your safe arrival at Calcutta – but how is it possible for my untutored pen to convey to you the true feelings of my heart, I am sadly deficient in words, and therefore can only assure you in the simple language of the heart that it throbs with affection as dear and as tender for you as ever a child's did for a Father – you my Lord gave me a right to call you so, when at Malacca you desired me to consider myself as your Daughter, *happy me*, and this right, this dear right, I will only resign with my last breath – I am proud and selfish enough, not to make distinctions in favour of those, your Daughters excepted, who now engross you to the exclusion of me from the place you said I should hold in your memory – and while memory lives in my brain, there you shall live, the first and most respected of created beings – I have but one wish, one hope now, and that is to see your Lordship once again before you leave India, and yet that wish makes me sad, for if you do leave India and come here on your way to dear England, when shall I ever see you again? [Y]et I will hope to see you here one day, in *your Country* – This beautiful Java – everything here is beautiful! Sweet, enchanting! "The leaves whisper in the breeze", "the birds sing in the shade", "the river sparkles in the sun, and makes sweet music" and my heart dances to it. The conviction that you, and you only, have been the cause of our enjoying this sweet happiness adds infinitely to my content – and if this letter gains for me an answer, there will be another *bright spot* on my dial – I am happy to have the power to say that my dear husband holds up beyond my thought, and when I consider his very delicate state of health, all that he has done, all that he is doing, the very great fatigue he underwent in his journey to the Eastern Courts I am indeed astonished – I am a loser by all this for I am deprived of the happiness of his company – I never see him now oftener than once in eight or ten days – is not this sad, miserable, but I will not again whine – I own that I have been very naughty, and wept plenty at times, and thought myself neglected, which was, as your Lordship may think, very ungrateful in me, but I promise to be good in future –

According to the Customs of the East, a Letter should be accompanied with a token – Mine humble as it is, a simple Madurese Instrument, untutored in the strains of art – solicits the honor of your acceptance – God bless you my dear Lord and believe me to be with the truest regard

Your grateful and affectionate
Olivia Mariamne Raffles

Government House, Buitenzorg (Bogor)
*Anonymous watercolour drawing of 1812 from M. Archer and J. Bastin,* The Raffles Drawings *(Kuala Lumpur, 1978)*

The unhealthy climate of Batavia led Raffles to live principally at the former Dutch Governor-General's palace at Buitenzorg (Bogor). This essentially became his and Olivia's home during the years they spent together in Java, requiring him to make the 40-mile journey to Batavia for meetings of the Council and other official engagements and for Olivia to make a similar journey to hold her occasional Drawing Rooms for the British and Dutch ladies. The palace, or Government House as it came to be known, was in poor condition when they took up residence, but repairs were made and Raffles and Olivia were able to occupy large rooms in the central part of the building, which also accommodated the principal government offices.[55] The house enjoyed spectacular views of Salak and Gede and was described by Raffles at the time as resembling 'something of the nature of an old English Mansion', with a stud of no fewer than 60 small Indonesian horses required for frequent travel in coaches of four or six.[56] Among the first receptions hosted by Raffles and Olivia at Government House was for the Sultans of Cirebon on 25 March 1812,[57] and the house became the centre of all official and private celebrations during the remaining two-and-a-half years of Olivia's life.

She suffered from long periods of poor health, which often prevented her from travelling in the island. In April 1812 she attended a ball given by the

Major-General Robert Rollo Gillespie
(1766–1814)
*Engraving by H.R. Cook after a miniature by W. Haines, 1814*

military officers at Batavia but, according to the *Java Government Gazette*, she 'did not join in the more light amusement of the dance to which she usually seemed so partial and to partake of with so much spirit and success'.[58] She accompanied Raffles to Semarang and Salatiga during the British military operations at Yogyakarta in June 1812, and she remained at Salatiga until late August, unable to travel because of 'a very severe illness'.[59] She returned to Buitenzorg on 8 September, the *Java Government Gazette* expressing regret four days later that she was 'still extremely weakened and indisposed'.[60] By Christmas she was well enough to take part in the seasonal festivities and to entertain a large number of guests,[61] and she was able to visit Batavia to be present at the Queen's Birthday celebrations at Gunung Sari in January 1813,[62] and to attend, as god-mother, a Lutheran christening service at Government House for Mary Anne's four-month-old child, Stamford Charles Raffles Flint, who was born at Semarang on 16 September.[63] She was also present at another family occasion on 20 April 1813 at Government House, Buitenzorg, for the marriage of her sister-in-law Leonora Raffles (widow of Billington Loftie) to Thomas Campbell Brown, an Assistant Surgeon in the Bengal medical service who had been appointed by Raffles in the previous November to perform the civil duties at Buitenzorg.[64] In early May she and Raffles travelled to Batavia for the King's Birthday celebrations on 4 June, when she was said to have been 'in wonderful health and spirits', and she attended a lavish ball at Gunung Sari which was opened by the Commander of the Forces, Colonel Robert Rollo Gillespie. '[O]ur amiable Lady Governess', the *Java Government Gazette* reported, '… seemed to have recovered her usual health'.[65]

Matters quickly changed, for Raffles informed his friend William Brown Ramsay at the end of June that she had 'lately been severely afflicted with the

Gout in her head and stomach, but on the whole retains her wonted Spirit and animation –'.[66] There was little improvement during the following months, and in mid-September he again wrote to Ramsay stating that neither his health 'or that of M[rs]. Raffles is very good – I begin to feel the effects of a hot climate very sensibly and M[rs]. Raffles will not be able to remain in the Country many years longer –'.[67] A month later the situation was much the same: 'Mrs. Raffles has of late been far from well having had several very severe fits of the Gout in the head & Stomach – she however retains her accustomed Spirits …'[68] She managed in October to host a farewell party at Government House, Rijswijk, for her sisters-in-law, Harriot and Mary Anne, who with Captain Flint were about to sail aboard the *Lord Eldon* (J. Cowles) for London.

Despite her ill-health, Olivia decided in early November 1813 to accompany Raffles on a visit to the Javanese courts of Surakarta and Yogyakarta in central Java. A day before their departure, a Levee was held at Government House, Rijswijk, to welcome Major-General Miles Nightingall (1768–1829), who had replaced Gillespie as Commander of the Forces and Vice-President of the Council.[69] On 2 November Raffles and Olivia sailed aboard HEIC *Malabar* (R. Deane), accompanied by HEIC *Aurora* (D. Macdonald), for Semarang, where they attended a series of dinners, balls and public breakfasts. After other official engagements, Olivia accompanied Raffles on 31 December to the recently opened Salatiga Race Course at Taju, where they watched several races and had 'a most sumptuous style' breakfast on the course.[70] Following their return to Semarang, they set out with civilian officials and a military detachment

Semarang
*Aquatint by Joseph Jeakes from William Thorn,* Conquest of Java *(London, 1815)*

for a week-long visit to Surakarta and Yogyakarta, where they were received by the Susuhunan, Sultan and other members of the Javanese courts.[71] They left Yogyakarta on 12 December for their return journey to Semarang, where they stayed until after Christmas before again boarding HEIC *Aurora* for Jepara and Surabaya. Raffles made a hasty visit to Sumenap on the island of Madura, but because of the need to deal with government despatches he left Olivia at Surabaya and travelled overland to Buitenzorg. She appears to have delayed her return as she did not reach Batavia until the evening of 15 February 1814, but she was well enough to attend a Drawing Room next day for 'most of the English

Bodyguard of the Sultan of Yogyakarta
*Lithograph from Pfyffer zu Neueck*, Skizzen von der Insel Java *(Schaffhausen, 1829)*

and Dutch Ladies of the Settlement'.[72] Raffles joined her on 17 February in order to attend a ball and supper at Gunung Sari given by their friend William Robinson to celebrate her 43rd birthday.[73] Among the guests were Major-General Nightingall and his wife Florentia,[74] by now Raffles and Olivia's most intimate friends.

Olivia remained in good health, and on 14 March a large party assembled at Buitenzorg to celebrate the ninth year of her marriage to Raffles.[75] Ten days later she travelled with her husband to Batavia to attend a ball and supper given by Jacob Andries van Braam, a former President of the Council of the Indies, at his mansion at Rijswijk,[76] which later became the palace of the Dutch Governors-General. They attended another ball and supper at the end of the month given by William Watt, a partner in the agency house of Dalton & Watt, at his house in Rijswijk,[77] and on the eve of the celebrations of the King's Birthday on 4 June they were present at a concert, supper and ball given by Abraham Couperus, a former Dutch Governor of Melaka, at his house in Batavia.[78] Next morning, Raffles held a Levee at Government House, Rijswijk, when news of the liberation of the Netherlands and the restoration of the House of Orange was celebrated, and the Java Auxiliary Bible Society was launched with a subscription list headed by Raffles and Olivia.[79] In the evening, a magnificent ball and supper at the Government House was attended by British military and naval officers as well as European and Indonesian government officials, but during the latter part of the celebrations Olivia became ill. 'We are sorry to add', the *Java Government Gazette* reported, 'that our amiable Lady Governess was attacked with a return of indisposition towards the close of the evening, which has continued, but we are glad to learn by our last accounts from Buitenzorg, that she was recovering'.[80]

She had recovered sufficiently to join her husband and a few friends for a short tour of the Priangan Regencies in July, when they travelled to Cianjur, Cipanas and Cisarua, where the government kept a small farm house. Her health was said to have 'derived much benefit from the excursion',[81] but she was too ill to attend the official welcome given by Raffles at Government House, Rijswijk, to Vice-Admiral Sir Samuel Hood (1762–1814), Commander-in-Chief on the East Indies Station, on 23 July, or the Levee two days later, when Hood was introduced to the principal inhabitants of Batavia.[82] She was also absent, due to an 'indisposition', from a ball and supper given by Jan Samuel Timmerman Thijssen in honour of Hood at his country house at Kampung Melayu on 25 July.[83] Whether or not she was able to attend the evening celebrations on 12 August at Government House, Rijswijk, to mark the birthday of the Prince Regent is uncertain,[84] but she was present at a Public Breakfast given by the Dutch member of Council, W.J. Cranssen, at his house on the Jakatraweg on 24 August to celebrate the birthday of the Prince of Orange.[85] In the evening she and Raffles attended a grand ball and supper at the house in Rijswijk of the President of the Orphan Chamber, Lieve Willem Meijer.[86]

After her return to Buitenzorg, Olivia was hostess at a ball at Government House on

Sir Samuel Hood (1762–1814)
*Engraving by Ridley, Hall & Blood from an original miniature in the possession of Lady Hood*

Harmonie, Rijswijk, Batavia
*Lithograph from C.W.M. van de Velde,* Gezigten *(Amsterdam, 1843–5)*

11 September, but it is uncertain if she was present at a dance and supper given for members of the Batavian Society of Arts and Sciences at the Harmonie building in Rijswijk on 24 September.[87] She was the principal guest at an entertainment hosted by Major-General and Mrs. Nightingall on 14 October at the military cantonment at Weltevreden, which was attended by British military and naval officers, government officials, and Dutch residents of Batavia,[88] and she also attended the grand opening of the Military Bachelors' Theatre at Weltevreden three days later, when George Colman's play *The Heir-at-Law*, with its principal character of Dr. Pangloss, was performed before an enthusiastic audience.[89] The ball on 14 October was probably the last she ever attended. She returned to Buitenzorg in poor health, and was unwell during the following month, when Raffles wrote of her being 'far from well, but in good Spirits'.[90] She died at Buitenzorg on Saturday 26 November 1814, aged 43 years.

Her body was taken to Batavia, where she was buried two days later alongside the grave of John Leyden at the Tanah Abang burial ground (Taman Prasasti). At Buitenzorg, in the Botanical Gardens (Kebun Raya), Raffles had erected in her memory a beautiful marble monument in Byzantine style inscribed with the words:

Tombs of Olivia Raffles and John Leyden at Tanah Abang (Taman Prasasti), Batavia (Jakarta)

*SACRED*
*To the Memory of*
*OLIVIA MARIAMNE*
*Wife of*
*THOMAS STAMFORD RAFFLES*
*Lieutenant-Governor*
*Of Java and its Dependencies*
*Who Died*
*at*
*BUITENZORG*
*On the 26 November 1814*

Below was inscribed a stanza of the short poem she had written to John Leyden in 1808:

*Oh Thou Whom Ne'er My Constant Heart*
*One Moment Hath Forgot!*
*Tho' Fate Severe Hath Bid Us Part*
*Yet Still Forget Me Not*

There are no eye-witness accounts of her burial,[91] but a letter from Caroline Maria Currie (née Laidet), wife of the Assistant Surgeon Claude Neil Currie of the 1st Battalion of the 78th Highlanders (Ross-shire Buffs), to her sister in Scotland, written between 23 and 28 November 1814, contains some interesting comments on the burial and on Olivia herself:

> Mrs Raffles died on the 26th and was buried this morning. Mrs Gregory and I were the only Ladies in the Cantonment [at Weltevreden] that did not attend the funeral, and I am very glad I did not, as I am told they all made themselves very ridiculous by weeping aloud when the Corpse was taken from Government house and when it was put into the grave and all this for a woman whom some of them had never seen above once or twice. I had seen her two or three times, she called here and I returned her visit but I never was in her house except at a ball when she was not present, as she always lived in the Country since we came here but when she came to a ball or a play. People who knew her seemed to like her very much and said she was a very good hearted woman, but she had one great failing and that was being too fond of a glass of Brandy and when she had taken too much of it and got her Aid De Camps about her, I am told that no modest woman could sit in her company – .[92]

Raffles was totally overcome by Olivia's death, and his health was seriously affected. After the funeral he travelled in west Java in the company of a few friends and in January 1815 he and others climbed Gunung Gede. His feelings for her were unquestionably very deep, and he wrote in September of 'the melancholy affliction which … deprived me of almost all that I held dear on earth'.[93] In a farewell letter to his friends, written on his departure for England aboard the ship *Ganges* (P. Falconer) on 30 March 1816, he again wrote of his loss: 'You have been with me in the days of happiness and joy – in the hours that were beguiled away under the enchanting spell of one of whom the recollection awakens feelings which I cannot suppress'.[94]

Buitenzorg (Bogor) depicting the monument erected to Olivia Mariamne Raffles
*Aquatint by W. Daniell after Mary Fendall from Lady Raffles,* Memoir of Sir Thomas Stamford Raffles *(London, 1830)*

Monument erected to Olivia Mariamne Raffles by her husband,
Thomas Stamford Raffles, in the Botanical Gardens (Kebun Raya),
Buitenzorg (Bogor)

# CHAPTER SIX

## Sir Stamford Raffles's Second Wife: Sophia Hull

Lady Raffles (1786–1858)
*Replica of a miniature portrait by A.E. Chalon, 1817*

The Crescent, Cheltenham
*Aquatint by J. Bluck after T. Hulley*

RAFFLES ARRIVED IN LONDON on 16 July 1816 and took up rented accommodation at No. 23 Berners Street, but in August, in order to recover his health, he moved for a time to 'a very capital house' at No. 3 The Crescent in the spa town of Cheltenham with his sister Mary Anne, his aide-de-camp Captain Thomas Otho Travers, and his friend William Brown Ramsay. Shortly after his arrival, he met the 31-year-old Sophia Hull,[1] second eldest of a large family of 15 children of James Watson Hull, a former Factor in the service of the East India Company, and Sophia (née Hollamby),[2] whom he had married in Bombay on 20 November 1783.

By the time he retired in 1786 to Belvidere, Drumbo, near Lisburn in Ireland, Hull had amassed a considerable fortune and was known locally as 'the Nabob'. He served as a Justice of the Peace in the counties of Antrim, Down and Meath, and in 1789 as High Sheriff of County Down. He was a Captain in the Drumbo Independent Volunteer Company, but in 1793 he left Ireland and settled his family at Petergate in York, and later at Great

Captain Thomas Otho Travers
(1785–1844)
*Private collection*

Baddow, near Chelmsford in Essex, where he took an active part in local affairs as a Justice of the Peace, a Captain in the Great Baddow Volunteer Company, and from March 1803 as Deputy Lieutenant of the county. In 1816 he left Great Baddow to settle at No. 349 The High Street, Cheltenham, possibly in order to give his daughters the chance of finding marriageable partners among the hundreds who flocked to the fashionable town every season. Sophia's younger sister, Mary Jane, had already married Peter Auber (1788–1848), Assistant Secretary of the East India Company, at Great Baddow in December 1815,[3] and the move to Cheltenham soon proved successful, as Sophia met Raffles in August 1816 and was married to him six months later, while the second-eldest daughter, Alice Watson Hull, became engaged to Captain (later Lieutenant-Colonel) Richard Zachariah Mudge and was married to him on 1 September 1817.[4] Of the remaining Hull sisters, two remained spinsters,[5] and the seventh, Elizabeth Mary Ann Hull, later married the Revd. Thomas Page of St. Paul's Church Cheltenham.[6]

St. Marylebone Parish Church
*Engraving by W. Wise after J. Coney*

Raffles and Sophia Hull were married on the morning of 22 February 1817 at the New Parish Church, Marylebone, by the Revd. R.H. Chapman in the presence of her father, James Watson Hull, her sister, Alice Watson Hull, and Raffles's sister, Mary Anne Flint, all of whom signed the marriage register. They immediately left for two days at Henley-upon-Thames, from where Raffles addressed a letter to his cousin, the Revd. Dr. Thomas Raffles, informing him of the marriage and assuring him that 'neither Rank fortune or beauty have had weight on the occasion'.[7] Captain Travers described Sophia in his Journal at this time as 'amiable affectionate sensible, personable, tho' not very handsome, with a good figure[,] extremely well brought up and possessing many amiable qualities both of head and heart –',[8] and the British naval surgeon, Dr. Joseph Arnold (1782–1818), somewhat more flatteringly a year later, as 'a very handsome elegant woman, yet … very delicate, and … very subject to fainting fits'.[9] On their return from Henley-upon-Thames the married couple settled to life in Berners Street, with Raffles busily engaged in writing his *History of Java*. The book was dedicated to the Prince Regent, who on 29 May conferred on him the honour of knighthood at a Levee at Carlton House.

Sophia now joined her husband on a seven-week tour of the Continent,[10] accompanied by her brother, William Hollamby Hull,[11] her sister-in-law, Mary Anne Flint,[12] Raffles's cousin, the Revd. Dr. Thomas Raffles,[13] Eliza Ella Torriano,[14] and a maid. They travelled in a carriage accompanied by a courier riding on horseback, the total expenses for the tour, amounting to £1,000, being met by Raffles. They left Brighton on the Dieppe packet in the early hours of 6 June 1817, and after halting briefly at Dieppe they set out for Paris, where they were accommodated at the Hotel Mirabeau in the Rue de la Paix. From there they journeyed to Geneva, where Sophia and Raffles enjoyed fine views across the lake from their hotel, leaving indelible impressions on Sophia, who loved Geneva more than any other city. From Lausanne they set out for Basel and after crossing the Rhine they directed their journey to Frankfurt and on to Cologne, from where they travelled to Aachen, Liege and Brussels. Here Raffles dined with the Dutch Colonial Minister, Anton Reinhard Falck (1777–1843),[15] and two days later with King Willem I. They returned to Ramsgate on 25 July and arrived in London on the following morning, Travers recording in his Journal that he never saw Raffles looking better and Lady Raffles 'also seemed very much improved in appearance –'.[16]

Preparatory to their departure for Bengkulu in west Sumatra, where Raffles was to take up his appointment as Lieutenant-Governor of Fort Marlborough, Sophia joined him in a series of farewell visits to their relations in England and Ireland. On 11 August they left London to visit Raffles's uncle, John Raffles,[17] in Birmingham, and after travelling through the Lake District they stayed for a week with the Revd. Dr. Thomas Raffles and his wife in Liverpool.[18] They then journeyed north to Edinburgh and Glasgow, and visited Archibald, 9th Duke of Hamilton and Brandon (1740–1819), the father of Raffles's friend

Charlotte, Duchess of Somerset (1772–1827)
*Miniature portrait*

William Marsden (1754–1836)
*Etching by Mrs. D. Turner after a painting by T. Phillips*

Charlotte, Duchess of Somerset (1772–1827).[19] From Port Patrick they sailed to northern Ireland and then proceeded south to Dublin,[20] before returning on 5 September to Clifton, near Bristol, where Sophia's parents were staying. Sophia remained with them while Raffles visited the Duke and Duchess of Somerset at Maiden Bradley, near Bath.[21] On 10–11 October, Sophia, Raffles and Mary Anne visited 'Edge Grove' at Aldenham in Hertfordshire, the house of William Marsden (1754–1836), orientalist and author of *The History of Sumatra* (London, 1783–1814),[22] with whom Raffles had corresponded when he was in Penang and Java.[23] Sophia may also have accompanied Raffles to Milton Bryant in Bedfordshire to see the former Deputy Chairman of the East India Company, Sir Hugh Inglis (1744–1820),[24] father of her later friend, Sir Robert Harry Inglis (1786–1855).[25]

For Sophia, who was now five months pregnant, her approaching departure from England filled her with dread and apprehension as she knew that her child was likely to be delivered on board ship before they reached west Sumatra. On 21 October 1817 she wrote a farewell letter from Portsmouth to the Duchess of Somerset in the most sombre terms:

> ... nothing remains but to say farewell, & in doing so I dare not say how sad the future appears – the uncertainty of this world – all

its blessings, & all its pleasures, – strikes & chills me, how then can I say I hope we shall meet again, that I shall again see you as I last saw you, hear you speak as your voice still vibrates on my ear, when you said "God bless you, we shall meet again" – Alas shall we do so? that we may, I will implore as a mercy from Heaven, but if I should be called upon to appear at the Throne of God whilst absent from this dear Land & those dear friends who have hitherto brightened every joy & blessed every hour of my existence, do not, pray do not forget that my heart always yearned towards you, as to one whose soul was so bright & pure … This is such a dismal place, & every time I raise my eyes I am reminded by some object that I am going to part from those near & dear to me, & this with the fear least the sickness I have to encounter should be injurious to that being to whose Birth I look forward with such a mixture of Hope & anxiety makes me feel cowardice stealing upon me, & the longer I stay here the less I fear of a Heroine I shall prove – .[26]

The ship *Lady Raffles* of 647 tons had been named in her honour, and was to be commanded by her owner, Harry J. Auber,[27] brother of Peter Auber,[28] who was married to her sister, Mary Jane. She was also to be accompanied on the voyage by her brother, William Hollamby Hull, who was promised an appointment at Fort Marlborough, and Nurse Mary Grimes,[29] who had been recommended to her by the Duchess of Somerset, and who would remain in her service for the rest of her life.[30]

The *Lady Raffles* got under weigh from Portsmouth on the morning of 23 October, and after a difficult voyage along the Channel was forced by contrary winds to take shelter at Falmouth, from where she sailed nearly a month later. The naval surgeon Dr. Joseph Arnold, who had been engaged by Raffles to accompany him to Bengkulu as a naturalist, was on board the ship and wrote of his distress at seeing 'the formidable effects only three days tossing about, has had upon Lady Raffles; from being a fine, healthy, florid faced woman, she is become so feeble that she cannot even sit upright without fainting; and is as pale as ashes, – I am the more sorry for this, as she is one of the most gentle amiable creatures I ever met with'.[31] Matters improved a good deal in mid-

Dr. Joseph Arnold (1782–1818)
*Miniature portrait, 1817*

Raden Rana Dipura
*Lithograph by J.B.A.M. Jobard after W. Daniell from*
*Fr. J.F. Marschal,* Description de Java *(Brussels, 1824)*

December when the ship entered warmer waters, and although the weather became cooler by the third week of January 1818 it was decided not to put into the Cape of Good Hope but to deal with Sophia's confinement on board ship. On 15 February, after a short labour of less than an hour, with the assistance of Dr. Arnold and Nurse Grimes, she gave birth to a girl, who was christened three days later by Captain Auber as Charlotte Sophia Tunjung Segara, the latter name meaning 'Lotus of the Sea' being suggested by Raden Rana Dipura, who said that the child of a great man of Java should have a name appropriate to the peculiar circumstances of its birth.[32] Sophia thought the idea was 'too simple & beautiful' not to be adopted, but added apprehensively, 'I do hope my dear Baby will realise it –'.[33] The child was named after Charlotte, Duchess of Somerset, to whom Raffles wrote expressing their good fortune in having Dr. Arnold to attend to Sophia, and also Nurse Grimes, who had been 'invaluable, every thing we could wish, active intelligent careful & affectionate –'.[34]

The ship anchored off Pulau Tikus, south-west of Bengkulu, during the afternoon of 19 March 1818, when it was arranged that Raffles and his party would be conveyed ashore in the accommodation boat on the following morning. They landed at about 11 o'clock to a salute of 19 guns, with the troops of the garrison drawn up under the command of Captain Nicholas Manley

(1784–1823).[35] After his Commission as Lieutenant-Governor of Fort Marlborough was read out, and the official reception concluded, Raffles and Sophia were taken to the house of the Acting Resident, William Robert Jennings (1784–1823),[36] who provided them with temporary accommodation as both Government Houses had been badly damaged by earthquakes two days previously, when the tremor had been so severe that it was felt by those on board

Road from Fort Marlborough leading to the Wharf
*Aquatint by J.C. Stadler after S. Andrews, 1799*

the *Lady Raffles* 200 miles out to sea. The shocks continued at Bengkulu at regular intervals until the 22nd of March, leading Raffles to write to Marsden:

> This is, without exception, the most wretched place I ever beheld. I cannot convey to you an adequate idea of the state of ruin and dilapidation which surrounds me. What with natural impediments, bad government, and the awful visitations of Providence which we have recently experienced, in repeated earthquakes, we have scarcely a dwelling in which to lay our heads, or wherewithal to satisfy the cravings of nature. The roads are impassable; the highways in the town overrun with rank grass; the Government-house a den of ravenous dogs and polecats. The natives say that Bencoolen is now *tána mati* (dead land). In truth, I could never have conceived any thing half so bad.[37]

Bengkulu had an equally depressing effect on Sophia, who informed the Duchess of Somerset that it was

> in a miserable state of ruin & desolation, & the poor people appear depressed & wretched ... The Climate is far superior to what I expected[,] the heat not so overpowering – but the Country less beautiful – the view being confined by the ridge of Hills that

divides the Island & the eye is wearied for the want of some opening to meet the power of vision – I am told the interior of the Country is beautiful, but of this I have not been able to judge, tho' Sir Stamford will not long remain stationary, & when he is ready to move I am to wean my Baby that I may accompany him – .[38]

Added to her tribulations, news had awaited her at Bengkulu of the death on 23 December 1817 at Calcutta of her 16-year-old brother, Edward Anthony Hull.[39]

In mid-May 1818 Sophia left Charlotte in the care of Nurse Grimes in order to accompany her husband and Dr. Arnold on a journey to Pasemah ulu Manna in an attempt to conciliate the local people and prevent their incursions into the coastal territories of the East India Company. Dr. Arnold expressed fears about her accompanying them:

Government House and Council House, Bengkulu, west Sumatra
*Aquatint by J.C. Stadler after S. Andrews, 1799*

> Lady Raffles … I believe … would follow Sir Stamford to the world's end. For my part I would not have permitted her to go, for we know nothing of the difficulties we might have to encounter, nor any thing of the disposition of the people we were going to trust ourselves among, except that former reports mentioned that they were treacherous & murderous … In spite of all, however, she would go, & I believe the Governor thought that by taking his wife, the people of Pasummah would be more certain of his coming with a peaceable intention.[40]

The party left Bengkulu on horseback and reached Manna two days later. After resting, they set out for Pasemah ulu Manna on 18 May, accompanied by the Resident, Edward Presgrave (1795–1830), the Pangeran of Manna, a number of Bugis officers, and some 60 porters carrying baggage and provisions. They were warmly received by the Pasemaher people, and on 23 May Raffles signed a formal treaty placing their country under the protection of the East India Company, and granting them freedom of cultivation and permission to settle in the coastal districts.[41] During the journey Dr. Arnold and his Indonesian servants discovered specimens of the giant fleshy flower, measuring a yard across, which was named *Rafflesia arnoldi* by Robert Brown (1773–1858) in honour of its discoverers.[42]

The journey to southern Sumatra gave Sophia a taste for travelling and in the following month she joined her husband, Dr. Arnold, and the American naturalist Dr. Thomas Horsfield (1773–1859), on a journey into the Minangkabau highlands of central Sumatra. They left Bengkulu on 8 July aboard the *Lady Raffles* for Padang, where a formidable party of some 200 Indonesian porters and 50 Sepoys and Bugis soldiers was assembled to accompany them.[43] During the early part of the journey Sophia was on horseback, but thereafter she was forced to walk or, where they encountered difficult terrain, to be carried on the shoulders of the porters. On 24 July they reached Pagarruyung, where Raffles concluded a

Dr. Thomas Horsfield (1773–1859)
*Lithograph by Day and Hage after a portrait by T. Erxleben*

Padang River, Sumatra
*Aquatint from William Marsden,* The History of Sumatra *(London, 1811)*

Padang Hill, Sumatra
*Aquatint from William Marsden,* The History of Sumatra *(London, 1811)*

Village House, Sumatra
*Aquatint from William Marsden,* The History of Sumatra *(London, 1811)*

treaty with the Minangkabau rulers providing for the cession to the East India Company of the coastal districts from Inderapura to Natal.[44] The party set out on the return journey and reached Padang, having travelled some 250 miles, in 14 days.

Raffles sent accounts of their journey to the newspapers in England, where Lady Raffles's exploits created something of a stir. 'I am very unworthy [of] the attention I have excited & which has quite astonished me', she wrote to the Revd. Dr. Thomas Raffles. 'I was influenced by one motive – affection for my Husband – to be parted from him is the only misery my Soul shrinks from – to be united to him in life & death the only bright hope of my existence –'.[45]

After their return to Bengkulu, Raffles decided to visit Calcutta in order to discuss with the Governor-General, the Marquess of Hastings (1754–1826), his ideas on extending British power and influence in Sumatra. Although Sophia was pregnant she resolved to accompany him, and they sailed from Bengkulu on 2 September 1818 on the brig *Udney*, which was infested with centipedes and scorpions and had only a small cabin with a single porthole. The ship lost a mast in the Bay of Bengal, when in the charge of a drunken pilot, and came to grief in the night on a dangerous sand bank at the mouth of the Hugli River.[46] During their stay at Calcutta Raffles had discussions with the Governor-General and members of the Supreme Council about what he perceived to be Dutch threats to British commercial and political influence in Sumatra, but the opinion of Lord Hastings led to a modification of his views in favour of establishing a British trading station at the southern extremity of the Malay Peninsula.[47]

It had been intended that they would return to Bengkulu in time for Sophia's confinement, but they now boarded HEIC *Nearchus* (William

Princess Charlotte Augusta (1796–1817) and Prince Leopold
George Frederick of Saxe-Coburg-Saalfeld (1790–1865)
*Contemporary print*

Maxfield) for Penang, where Sophia remained while Raffles completed his missions to Singapore and Aceh. During her stay at Penang, she gave birth to a son, Leopold Stamford, who was named after Prince Leopold of Saxe-Coburg-Saalfeld (1790–1865), husband of the late Princess Charlotte,[48] and baptised on 12 March by the Chaplain of Prince of Wales Island, the Revd. Joseph R. Henderson.

Raffles and Sophia left Penang on 22 May on board the *Indiana* (James Pearl) for Singapore. After a four-week stay in the new settlement, when Raffles issued regulations for its future administration, they set out for Bengkulu, where Sophia was happily reunited with their daughter, Charlotte. Two months later, the brig *Favourite* brought news of the rumoured death of the Governor of Penang, John Alexander Bannerman (1759–1819), and Raffles decided to proceed immediately to Calcutta to press his claims to succeed him.[49] As there was insufficient space in the ship to accommodate Sophia, she remained behind to care for her two children. Charlotte's second birthday was celebrated on 15 February 1820 with a large party given by Captain Travers,[50]

Ship *Indiana*
*Oil painting reproduced by permission of Antiques of the Orient, Singapore*

William Charles Raffles Flint (1819–1884)
*Miniature portrait, 1825*

and on the 23rd news arrived that Raffles had left Calcutta without securing the governorship of Penang. He arrived at Bengkulu on 3 March on board the *Indiana*, bringing with him his sister Mary Anne, her husband Captain William Flint, and Sophia's brother, Captain Robert Redman Hull (1789–1820) of the 10th Bengal Native Infantry,[51] who was to take the place of her brother William, who had returned to England. Captain Flint departed shortly afterwards for Java, leaving his wife and child, William Charles Raffles Flint (1819–84),[52] at Bengkulu. On 25 May, Sophia gave birth to a son, who was named Stamford Marsden after the historian of Sumatra. He was baptised by the Chaplain, the Revd. Christopher Winter, on 15 June 1820, the baptismal register also recording the name of 'Chaya Bankooloo' or 'Chaya Bankahulu'.

Mary Anne Flint left Bengkulu at the end of August to join her husband in Singapore. Sophia was still nursing her baby when the death occurred of her brother Robert on 24 October, after an illness of only five days.[53] She had cared for him during his illness, assisted by her brother Lawrence Nilson Hull (1799–1845), who had arrived from Calcutta on leave to work as Raffles's secretary.[54]

After a period of mourning, Sophia entered into what was for her and her husband the happiest period of their lives, attending to local and domestic matters and surrounded by their young children. Amidst all these scenes of family happiness, she was constantly reminded by Raffles not to expect to retain 'all the blessings God in his bounty had heaped upon them at this time, but to feel that such happiness once enjoyed ought to shed a bright ray over the future, however dark and trying it might become'.[55] On 25 May 1821, exactly a year after the birth of Stamford Marsden, Sophia gave birth to a daughter, Ella Sophia, who was named after Eliza Ella de Visme (née Torriano), the elder sister of Jane Charlotte Torriano, who later married her brother, William Hollamby Hull.[56] Ella Sophia was to live into early adulthood, the only one of Sophia's children to survive the ravages of sickness and disease in west Sumatra.

Distant View of Sungai Lemau Hills from Bengkulu, west Sumatra
*Aquatint by J.C. Stadler after S. Andrews, 1799*

On 27 June 1821, after a short illness, Leopold died and was buried on the same day by the Chaplain, the Revd. Christopher Winter. He held a special place in Raffles and Sophia's hearts and his death affected them greatly.[57] Sophia took to her couch in a darkened room and, overwhelmed with grief, could not bear the sight of her other children until she was reprimanded by her Indonesian servant.[58] Two weeks later, Captain Harry Auber, commander of the ship that had brought them to Sumatra, also died.[59] During the next six months Sophia and the whole family became seriously ill, and Raffles engaged Captain John Clunies Ross of the private licensed ship *Borneo* to take the remaining three children to England when the vessel returned to Bengkulu in February. Early in the New Year, however, their remaining son Stamford Marsden developed a violent bowel complaint and died on the night of 3 January 1822.[60] A fortnight later, on 14 January, he was followed to the grave by his sister Charlotte, who was buried the following day. 'This blow was almost too much for us', Raffles wrote to his friend Thomas Murdoch (1758–1845) in England, '[b]ut we had still one little one left and [we] embraced the first opportunity of sending her to a safer Climate'.[61]

Government Hill, Singapore
*Aquatint by Langlumé after Deroy from* Album Pittoresque de la Frégate la Thétis et de la Corvette
l'Espérance *(Paris, 1828)*

Ella was hastily bundled on board the *Borneo* when the ship sailed from Bengkulu on 4 March 1822 in the care of Nurse Grimes and a Eurasian servant named J. Rousseau. 'She leaves us in excellent health', Raffles informed his brother-in-law Peter Auber, 'and we indulge the hope that by the strong measure we have taken of sending her to a healthier climate, we may be spared this *one* comfort to solace and enliven our declining days'. Sophia's health, he added, had suffered severely, but she was now improving.[62] To other correspondents, he stated that she was 'miserably reduced and lowered' by her losses, but that his own health had suffered more.

Raffles had already made arrangements to visit his new settlement of Singapore later in the year, and in the meantime they led an entirely retired life. They had hoped to leave Bengkulu on 14 September, but the wind was contrary, and the delay meant that they were able to bury Dr. William Jack, whose death was felt by Raffles as that of a brother.[63] They reached Singapore on 11 October and during the next nine months Raffles introduced new laws and regulations for the administration of the settlement.[64] For long periods of their stay he was unwell, suffering from blinding headaches, and reliant on Sophia's devoted care. 'She is ... a host to me', he wrote to the Duchess of

Lieutenant-Colonel William Farquhar (1770–1839)
*Portrait in oils circa 1825*

Somerset on 30 November 1822, 'and if I do live to see you again it will be entirely owing to her love and affection – Without this I should have been cast away long ago –'.[65]

They lived at first with Mary Anne and her husband Captain William Flint, who had been appointed Master Attendant of Singapore,[66] but in January 1823 they moved to a small wooden bungalow which Raffles had built on Government Hill.[67] They immediately felt the beneficial effects of the change of air, Sophia in particular fully recovering her health and spirits. Having arranged for John Crawfurd (1783–1868) to succeed Lieutenant-Colonel William Farquhar (1770–1839) as Resident,[68] Raffles and Sophia, together with her brother Lawrence Nilson Hull, sailed from Singapore on 9 June 1823 aboard the *Hero of Malown* (James Neish) for Bengkulu, taking with them Mary Anne Flint's eldest son, William Charles Raffles Flint, who was to accompany them to England. Before they left they learned that their daughter Ella had arrived safely in England, which was comforting news for Sophia, as she was five months pregnant, having experienced a miscarriage the previous September.[69]

The *Hero of Malown* arrived at Bengkulu on 17 July 1823 after an uncomfortable passage against adverse north-west winds. Sophia was exhausted from seasickness and had to be carried ashore on a mattress in the bottom of a boat. She was still feeling the effects of her illness on 5 August when they moved to their country house at Pematang Balam, 12 miles from Bengkulu,[70] and it was there on 19 September that she gave birth prematurely to a daughter named Flora. All seemed to go well at first, but a month after the birth Sophia suffered from a severe inflammatory fever and for weeks her life was in danger. Just as she was beginning to recover, her baby died on 28 November, and was buried by the officiating Chaplain and Baptist missionary, the Revd. William Robinson.[71] 'The loss of an infant only a few months old', Raffles wrote to Peter Auber,

> is one of those things which in itself perhaps might soon be got over, knowing how uncertain life is at that period, but this loss of our fourth and only remaining child in India has revived all former afflictions, and been almost too much for us. Fortunately Sophia's fever has not returned since the event, and upon the whole she is in better health than she was preceding, but she has not yet left the house; her spirits as well as my own are completely broken, and most anxious are we to get away from such a charnel-house, but here we are detained for want of an opportunity. How often do we wish the Fame had come out direct – we might have saved this last misfortune – .[72]

There followed a spate of deaths at Bengkulu, including that of their particular friend, the Master Attendant Francis Salmond, on 23 November.[73] A general gloom pervaded the British settlement, and it seemed only a matter of surviving until the East Indiaman *Fame* (Charles Young) arrived. The ship had been especially chartered by the East India Company from its owner Joseph Dowson to take them to England, but the delayed arrival led Raffles in January 1824 to arrange a passage with Captain John Clunies Ross in the small square-sterned 428-ton private ship *Borneo*, which had conveyed Ella to England two years earlier. Before the contract with Ross was concluded, the *Fame* arrived, and while the *Borneo* reached Gravesend safely on 29 May, the *Fame* was consumed by fire shortly after leaving Bengkulu, with the total loss of her

Pematang Balam, west Sumatra
*Watercolour c. 1823 from M. Archer and J. Bastin,* The Raffles Drawings *(Kuala Lumpur, 1978)*

The ship *Fame* on fire off the west coast of Sumatra 1824
*Contemporary print*

cargo, including Raffles's valuable natural history collections. 'Would to God we had started in the Borneo', Raffles wrote to his friend Thomas Macquoid, 'bad as her accommodation was – but we waited for the Fame and have met with such an awful Calamity as will I am sure shock you beyond measure –'.[74]

Raffles and Sophia had embarked on the *Fame* on 2 February with their nephew, William Charles Raffles Flint, Sophia's brother, Lawrence Nilson Hull, the son of one of their Singapore friends, David Scott, and Assistant Surgeon Dr. B. Bell. The ship sailed at daylight in a fair wind, and in the evening after Sophia had gone to bed, and Raffles was in the process of following her, the dread cry of 'Fire, fire' rang out. Within a short time the whole ship was engulfed in flames and the passengers and crew took to the life-boat.[75] They drifted along the coast during the rest of the evening and the following day until at about three o'clock in the afternoon they were taken on board a ship lying in the Bengkulu roads. '[H]ad this dreadful accident occurred a day later', Sophia wrote to Mary Anne Flint,

> or had the smallest of the many favourable circumstances a merciful God combined for our preservation been wanting[,] we should have perished the most dreadful of deaths – the shock has been a great one – the loss a ruinous one – but we must be thankful & still cling to that faith & hope which has enabled us to bear so much.[76]

They landed at Bengkulu practically destitute, with only the clothes they stood in. 'I had not even a pr of Stockings on –', Sophia wrote, '& in this place … there is nothing to be had – we have [no] covering – clothes I cannot call them –'.[77] Sophia lost not only her wardrobe but also her valuable collection of jewellery given to her by her parents and her husband. Raffles lost a diamond ring which Princess Charlotte had given him before he left England. Altogether, their losses amounted to between £20,000 and £30,000.[78]

On 8 April they embarked on the *Mariner* (John Herbert) with the same party as before but this time with the addition of Captain Charles Young and the crew of the ill-fated *Fame*. Off the Cape of Good Hope the ship experienced the worst gales that Captain Herbert had ever experienced and Sophia had to be boarded up in her couch with ropes. After a passage of 11 weeks the *Mariner* reached St. Helena, where they received a hospitable welcome from the Governor, Brigadier-General Alexander Walker (1764–1831), and his wife.

Shortly after their arrival, Raffles received the distressing news of the death of his mother four months earlier. She had outlived her husband Captain Raffles by 13 years, and after residing for a time with her youngest daughter Ann at St. Anne's Cottage, Hampstead, she had moved to Margate in Kent to live with her sister Elizabeth,[79] before finally being cared for by Raffles's friend, the wool merchant J.T. Simes, and his family at Stoke Newington in London.[80] Her coffin was taken for burial in the graveyard of the nearby St. Mary's Old Church, her headstone bearing the inscription, 'Beneath are deposited the remains of Mrs. Anne [*sic*] Raffles Relict of Captn. Raffles and mother of

Surviving gravestone of Sir Stamford Raffles's mother
*Photograph courtesy of Isaiah Levy*

Sir T. Stamford Raffles Lieutenant Governor of Bencoolen. She departed this life the 8th of February 1824 aged 69 years'.[81]

The news of his mother's death so shortly before his expected arrival in England was a particularly hard blow for Raffles, who wrote to his sister Mary Anne Flint in Singapore on 1 July 1824: 'My health and Spirits will not admit of my dwelling on it – Heaven rest her Soul!'[82] Lady Raffles wrote to her on the following day, on the eve of their departure from St. Helena: 'Tom is certainly much better (that is) the nervous excitement & consequent agony of pain has subsided & he only suffers from debility & occasional bilious attacks'.[83] The *Mariner* crossed the Line on 12 July and arrived off Plymouth on 20 August. Raffles and Sophia landed two days later.

# CHAPTER SEVEN

## Lady Raffles after the Death of her Husband

Bowood House, Wiltshire, the seat of the Marquess of Lansdowne
*The Revd. Francis O. Morris,* County Seats *(London, 1880)*

SOPHIA COULD NOT CONTAIN her excitement at the prospect of being reunited with her daughter Ella, who was being cared for by her parents, and she and Raffles immediately left Plymouth for Cheltenham, where they arrived on 24 August. They rented 'a snug house', No. 2 Wellington Place, where they remained until mid-November, Sophia having accompanied her husband to London in September for a few days so that he could make his report to the Directors of the East India Company. They stayed at Thomas's Hotel in Berkeley Square,[1] and because of illness she spent much of her time in bed, but her health improved after they returned to Cheltenham. She wrote to Mary Anne Flint on 10 October 1824 informing her that they had been able to collect together a few comforts and were 'endeavouring to gain a little health & strength for our winter campaign'.[2] At the end of October, Raffles spent a few days at 'Bowood' in Wiltshire, the seat of Henry, Marquis of Lansdowne, where he met again his old friend Thomas Moore, who recorded in his Journal that Raffles had shown him there 'maps of his new settlement at Singapore'.[3]

On 16 November Sophia and her husband left Cheltenham for London, where Raffles took a short lease on No. 104 Piccadilly, opposite Green Park.[4] The house proved unsatisfactory, and in February 1825 they moved to No. 23 Lower Grosvenor Street, after Raffles purchased the lease from Sir Humphry Davy (1778–1829).[5] In April, preparatory to making a tour along the south coast in 'remarkably fine' weather, they stayed at the Marine Hotel in Brighton, where the Russian Ambassador, Prince Lieven (1774–1839), and his wife, Princess Lieven (1784–1857), were also staying.[6] In June they attended Mrs. Bennett's Ball, at which the Marquis and Marchioness Lansdowne and Thomas Moore were also present.[7] In the following month, in accordance with Sophia's wish to

Henry Petty-Fitzmaurice (1780–1863), 3rd Marquess of Lansdowne

'High Wood', Middlesex

live principally in the country, 'tho' not further than from 20 to 40 miles from London', they moved to 'High Wood', a small estate of some 120 acres near Hendon in Middlesex.[8] Raffles laid out £18,000 for the house and the lands before learning in February 1826 that his bankers in Java had failed, leaving him with a loss of £16,000.[9] Two months later, in a letter dated 12 April 1826, he received an additional demand from the East India Company for the repayment of £22,272, which included his salary when he was in England in 1816–17 and moneys expended during his missions to Singapore and Aceh in 1819.[10]

This totally unexpected demand, together with other growing financial pressures, undoubtedly contributed to his death on 5 July 1826, a day before his 45th birthday. Sophia found his body at the bottom of the spiral staircase at 'High Wood' in the morning, and in the afternoon the celebrated surgeon Sir Everard Home (1756–1832) carried out an autopsy which disclosed, after removing the cranium, that the anterior part of the right frontal bone was twice as thick as the left, that the outer covering of the brain was in a highly inflamed state, and that in the right lateral ventricle there was 'a coagulum of blood' larger than a pigeon's egg, all pointing to arterio-venous malformation, with resulting haemorrhaging.[11] Sophia arranged for his burial at the nearby 13th-century parish Church of St. Mary in Hendon. A month later she wrote to the Revd. Dr. Thomas Raffles:

> [A]las Time softens but does not cure my sorrow – & I feel the spark of life so faint within me – I see the hand of God drawing me nearer & nearer to the World of Spirits & this makes me anxious to put my House in order & fulfil the few duties left me to perform – [lest] I should be summoned from this scene of trial to my place of everlasting peace … my thoughts are so wild & sad – my heart is broken – .[12]

She, in fact, lived for another 32 years though it has to be said that her thoughts were constantly on death and her spiritual reunion with her husband and children. Religion came to play a central role in her life, which was also sustained by the need to care for her daughter Ella ('Ella Bella'), and her nephew, William Charles Raffles Flint.

One of the earliest reported events in Sophia's life after the death of her husband was a tour she made on 18 May 1827 with a party of friends to inspect the underground excavation of the Thames Tunnel, then being carried out by a private company under the direction of (Sir) Marc Isambard Brunel (1769–1849) as principal engineer, and his son, Isambard Kingdom Brunel (1806–1859), as resident engineer. The deputy on the project was the Irish civil engineer Richard Beamish (1798–1873), who was apparently a friend of Sophia's, having declined a post at Fort Marlborough offered to him by Raffles in 1818. On the morning of Sophia's tour, the men excavating the Tunnel noticed a disturbance of the ground at Nos. 6 and 7 frames and were reluctant to return to work.

Ella Raffles (1821–1840), daughter of Sir Stamford Raffles
*Marble bust, Rome, 1833*

Diving Bell used in the construction of the Thames Tunnel
*W. Thornbury and E. Walford,* Old and New London *(London, 1879–85)*

The same phenomenon occurred on the flood-tide in the afternoon, and by the time of the visit of Sophia and her friends at five o'clock both Beamish and the Brunels were extremely apprehensive, Marc Brunel recording in his Journal of 18 May:

> Visited by Lady Raffles and a numerous party. Having had an intimation by Mr. Beamish of their intended visit, I waited to receive and to accompany them, not only from the interest I felt at being acquainted with Lady Raffles, but also from motives of solicitude, knowing that she intended to visit the frames. Indeed, my apprehensions were increasing daily ... I attended Lady Raffles and party to the frames, most uneasy all the while, as if I had a presentiment, not so much of the approaching catastrophe to the extent it has occurred, but of what might result from the misbehaviour of some of the men, as was the case when the Irish labourers ran away from the pumps and the stage. I left the works at half-past five, leaving everything comparatively well: Mr. Beamish continued on duty.[13]

At seven o'clock in the evening, as the spring-tide swept up the Thames, the roof of the Tunnel was breached, endangering the men at work, but by their exertions, and extreme good fortune, a tragedy was averted and no lives were lost. Sophia, on the reading of the incident in the newspapers, must have felt a sense of relief, and her experience probably explains why in March of the following year, after a number of workers perished in a similar accident, she contributed £3.0s.0d to a fund in aid of 'the sorrowing widows of those men who unhappily perished in the Thames Tunnel'.[14]

In June 1828 Sophia was listed among the 'distinguished Fashionables' who visited an Exhibition of portraits of illustrious people in English history at the booksellers Joseph Harding and John Lepard at No. 4 Pall Mall,[15] and in August she was reported in the newspapers to have been a victim of a burglary at 'High Wood', where two men, William Ryan, 'a man about 27 years of age', and John George, 'a diminutive man, about 22 years of age', stole a toy-box, two pairs of scissors, two thimbles, two pocket handkerchiefs, a work-box, and a missionary subscription-box containing 10 shillings.[16] They had entered the house through the school-room window at between three and four o'clock in the morning, but were heard by the butler, John Crosswell, who was sleeping in his pantry, and they ran away. They were later apprehended by the Bow Street horse patrol and were charged there 'with burglariously entering the dwelling-house of Lady Raffles, the widow of the late Sir Stamford Raffles, at Mill Hill, Hendon'.[17] The men left their hats behind and the magistrates directed that they should be placed on their heads, when they 'appeared to fit exceedingly well'. Crosswell testified that the two prisoners resembled 'in size and person' the two thieves he saw running away, and he said 'her ladyship had informed him that she was awoke as early as one o'clock by some noise in the house, and she pulled the bell, but could not hear the bell ring, which, it appears, was buffed by the thieves'.[18] The prisoners were remanded to a later hearing, but were eventually discharged. Less fortunate was an 18-year-old Irish workman named Daniel Kelly, who stole a shovel worth 2s.6d. from Lady Raffles's London house in Lower Grosvenor Street when she was living there in July 1829, and largely on the evidence of the butler John Crosswell he was sentenced to transportation to Van Diemen's Land (Tasmania) for seven years.[19]

# MEMOIR

OF THE

## LIFE AND PUBLIC SERVICES

OF

# SIR THOMAS STAMFORD RAFFLES, F.R.S. &c.

PARTICULARLY IN THE GOVERNMENT OF JAVA, 1811—1816,

AND OF

BENCOOLEN AND ITS DEPENDENCIES, 1817—1824;

WITH DETAILS OF THE

COMMERCE AND RESOURCES OF THE EASTERN ARCHIPELAGO,

AND

*SELECTIONS FROM HIS CORRESPONDENCE.*

## BY HIS WIDOW.

LONDON:

JOHN MURRAY, ALBEMARLE STREET.

MDCCCXXX.

Title-page of Lady Raffles's Memoir of her husband, 1830

Despite these distractions, Sophia continued to work on her monumental account of her husband's life and career in Asia. Initially, she had hoped that the Revd. Dr. Thomas Raffles would write the book, but when he declined she undertook the task herself, even though she believed that she was ill-equipped to do so. She succeeded so well that her large quarto volume soon became the acknowledged primary source of information on Raffles's life.[20] She contracted with John Murray to publish the book in 1830, together with a second edition of Raffles's *History of Java*, but she had to meet the printing costs, which amounted to the large sum of £1,700.[21] She also paid substantial fees to Sir Francis Leggat Chantrey (1781–1841) to have a statue of Raffles erected in Westminster Abbey, despite the fact that her financial resources were under severe strain.[22] She repaid £10,000 to the East India Company in settlement of Raffles's debt, and continued to meet the heavy burden of retaining both her London and country houses. In April 1829 she decided to place 'High Wood' on the market, but it failed to sell,[23] and in the same month she invited Mary Anne Flint and her daughter Sophia to stay with her when they arrived from Singapore,[24] following the death of Captain Flint from dysentery in the previous year.[25] Mary Anne had been left virtually destitute and she moved with her daughter to Blois in France, where living costs were much lower than in England.

Faced with her own financial problems, Sophia decided to adopt a similar solution and live abroad. By good fortune, she was able to rent 'High Wood' in April 1830 on a three-year lease, and she immediately set off for the Continent with Ella, William Charles Raffles Flint, her brother Captain William Hollamby Hull, and his wife Jane Charlotte, travelling from Dover to Calais in HM packet *Crusader*. In Bonn she spent two days in the company of the Sanskrit scholar, August Wilhelm von Schlegel (1767–1845),[26] and then proceeded to Basel, where she stayed in the room she had shared with Raffles 13 years previously, resulting, as she wrote, in 'many painful thoughts'.[27] From Basel, she proceeded by way of Biel, Neuchatel and Lausanne to Geneva. During the summer, she travelled to Bern, Zurich and Interlaken, and in the spring of 1831, having left Charles with a tutor at Geneva, she travelled with Ella to Milan and Genoa, and then on to Pisa and Florence. She returned to Geneva in June and remained there during the winter, her name and sorrows, as she wrote, having won for her 'the kindness & interest' of the inhabitants.[28] She

Madame de Staël's bedroom at Coppet, near Geneva

had also by this time formed a close relationship with Adélaide (Adele) de Staël (née Vernet), the widow of Auguste, elder son of the French woman of letters, Madame de Staël (1766–1817), their only son surviving long enough to give her, by the laws of Geneva, the inheritance of Coppet, where Sophia often stayed in the room of the late Madame de Staël.[29]

In 1832 she travelled to Rome with Charles and Ella, who had her portrait painted by Antoine Chatelain (1794–1859), her likeness to her father, with her chestnut-coloured hair, by now becoming very pronounced. On 16 January 1833 Sophia was one of some 500 guests, including 120 English residents at Rome, who attended the first ball of the season given at the Palace by the Austrian Ambassador and his wife, Count and Countess Lutzen, when the 'Fashionables', including a host of Princes, Princesses, Dukes and Duchesses, presented 'a blaze of beauty and rank, such as have oftener graced the houses of Lady Jersey and Lady Londonderry, in the west-end' of London. It was almost certainly

Baron Christian Charles Josias Bunsen
(1791–1860)
*Engraving by H. Adlard after a portrait by Tosting*
*from Frances Baroness Bunsen,* A Memoir of Baron
Bunsen *(London, 1868)*

Frances Baroness Bunsen (1791–1876)
*Engraving after a portrait by C.H. Jeens from A.J.C.*
*Hare,* The Life and Letters of Francis Baroness
Bunsen *(London, 1879)*

on this occasion that Sophia met Frances, Baroness Bunsen (née Waddington) (1791–1876), wife of Baron Christian Charles Josias Bunsen (1791–1860), Minister Plenipotentiary of Prussia in Rome,[30] with whom she formed one of her most intimate and lasting friendships. Baroness Bunsen recorded her initial impressions of Sophia in a letter to her mother in March 1833:

> Lady Raffles is the widow of the Governor of Java, and is one of our new acquaintance[s] of the winter who will not be blended in the mass of those seen for a moment and thought of no more: the combined impression produced by her manner, countenance, and conversation, prepares one to believe, or even guess before-hand, all that is great and good attributed to her. She brought us a letter from Madame de Staël, whom she had known long and well at Geneva. She has an only child, a girl of twelve years old, the wreck of a large family which fell a sacrifice to the climate of Java [sic].[31]

After spending a 'delightful' winter with her brother William Hollamby Hull and his wife in Rome,[32] she returned to Geneva, unable to return to England because she could find no purchasers for 'High Wood' or her London house, and also because she lost in that year what she described as 'a considerable sum of money'.[33] She planned to send William Charles Raffles Flint to Cambridge to begin his theological studies, but as he was not yet 15 she calculated that she still had a couple of years before she needed to return to England. During October 1833 she stayed with Adele de Staël at Coppet, their bond as widows enhanced by deep religious feelings, and she spent the winter of 1833–4 at Geneva at the Maison Grande. In the summer she was again at Coppet, before setting out in August for Paris, where she stayed for a couple of months. Then, because of her mother's failing health, she went to live with her at No. 12 Oriel Place, Cheltenham, her return to England being also decided by problems connected with William Charles Raffles Flint's education and by concerns about 'High Wood'. In December she tried again to sell the property, but despite advertising it weekly in a number of country newspapers little or no interest was shown. In April 1835 she confessed that she was 'quite at a loss what steps to take – the impossibility of my residing there being quite decided –'.[34]

She occupied herself as best she could by preparing a second revised edition of the *Memoir* of her husband, and went to stay for three weeks at the house in Bedford Square, London, of the Tory politician, Sir Robert Harry Inglis, who had assisted her with the first edition of the book.[35] The new edition was printed by William Clowes & Sons of London, and published in May 1835 in two volumes octavo by James Duncan of No. 37 Paternoster-Row. It was dedicated to Baron Bunsen, who had also given her advice on the book, including the suggestion that she should include more information about her own life with Raffles. This she found impossible to do, without 'drawing aside too far the veil from that domestic altar which, to all who have been admitted to its highest and holiest duties, is very sacred'.[36]

Her next visit was to No. 19 St. James's Square, the London residence of her friend, the Right Revd. Charles Richard Sumner (1790–1874), Bishop of Winchester,[37] whom she had met at Geneva when he ministered to the English congregation. After visiting other friends in Buckinghamshire, she planned to go to Brighton, but, on a whim, she returned to 'High Wood', where she found the house in such poor condition that she felt something had to be done. She moved in immediately and, after getting things in order, she confided to the Revd. Dr. Thomas Raffles that 'the pain of the first bitter recollections' were now over, and that she was 'able to enjoy the peace & quiet of this sweet spot'.[38] She wrote to him again later: 'I am beginning to enter into all the enjoyment this beautiful Place is so capable to affording, & I trust it will be the good pleasure of God to permit me to remain in it – I really by his Providence was brought here contrary to my intentions, & I therefore hope for a blessing upon the step'.[39]

Although her financial position was far from secure, she arranged for Mary Anne Flint and her daughter Sophia to return from Blois, and she undertook to provide for the education of both Sophia and William Charles Raffles Flint. This necessitated giving up her horses and carriage for a time, and refusing an invitation in February 1836 to visit Dr. Raffles in Liverpool because of the expense involved.[40] A month later, on 10 March, she was distressed by the death of her 73-year-old mother at Cheltenham,[41] her father having died at a similar age at Farquhar House, Highgate, on 5 April 1831.[42] She lost another member of her family with the death at Cheltenham on 29 September 1837 of her sister-in-law, Mary Anne Flint, and two days later of her sister, Emily

Dorothy Hull, who died at Prestbury.[43] She arranged for both of them to be buried in the same vault as her mother, and she set about trying to recover for Mary Anne Flint's children her 'little property' in Singapore by engaging the services of the Singapore merchants, Alexander Laurie Johnston (d. 1850), and Alexander Guthrie (1796–1865)[44].

Because of her financial position she spent the summer of 1838 with Ella and Sophia Flint at 'High Wood', but she obtained tickets to attend the Coronation of Queen Victoria in Westminster Abbey on 28 June.[45] Towards the end of August she and Ella visited friends in the country, and they stayed for some time with her sister Alice Mudge at 'Beechwood', near Plymouth. She grew increasingly concerned about the health of Sophia Flint and decided to take her back to 'High Wood' to obtain medical advice before placing her with a clergyman's family at Blackheath.[46]

In March 1839 Sophia was appointed a member of the Committee of 'The Ladies' West-end Association' to promote the objects of the Colonial Church Society aimed at maintaining clergymen, catechists, and schoolmasters in the British colonies, and to aid in the erection of churches and the procurement of missionaries.[47] In late May and early June she had as her guests at 'High Wood' her old friends Baron and Baroness Bunsen, who described the view from her house:

> She looks down from a height, over green slopes and fine groups of trees, upon a broad and fertile expanse of wood and cultivated ground, bounded by the heights upon which Harrow is situated and which are crowned by its church spire. We had the most delightful weather, and those days, in her society, were perfectly ideal. She ever deepens the first impression she made, and the more opportunity one has of contemplating her on all sides, the more perfect is the effect produced of completeness of grace, dignity, and proportion. Ella is good and pleasing and her head very handsome.[48]

Sophia herself had written of Baron Bunsen two years earlier as being 'the only person I have ever met possessing the same combination of talent, & charm of mind so peculiar in Sir Stamford',[49] and he in turn described her at

'High Wood' as 'the former Queen of the East amidst her relics, and surrounded by the remains of her station'.[50]

During the summer of 1839 she was unwell, but after recovering she and Ella spent 10 days in late November and early December with the Right Revd. Charles Richard Sumner at Winchester. He was the younger brother of the Archbishop of Canterbury, John Bird Sumner (1780–1862), and two of his four sons had shared the same tutor as William Charles Raffles Flint. The eldest of the sons, John Sumner, who later became Rector of Buriton, was ordained into the ministry during their visit, making it, as Sophia felt, 'a moment of deep interest to Ella & myself'. Ella's engagement to John Sumner was announced shortly afterwards, with the marriage planned for the following summer, but in February, after their return to 'High Wood', she broke a blood vessel, and the eminent physician Dr. William Frederick Chambers (1786–1855) was called in, and he was joined shortly afterwards by a Dr. Phillips. On 8 April Sophia wrote from Winchester House to the Bunsens describing Ella's state of health:

> We have the assurance of the Physicians that the unfavourable symptoms are gradually diminishing, but the cough is still unsubdued – and on this hangs life or death – She is reduced to a Skeleton, & has not a trace of her former blooming self – I have felt more than ever during this heavy chastisement that God is Love & I know he will spare me if it is possible – .[51]

Chambers advised Sophia to take Ella to the seaside at Hastings, and on Good Friday they moved to No. 59, The Marina, St. Leonards-on-Sea, on the Sussex coast. The change of air and a different medication led to a brief rally, but in early May the spasms returned, and there was a rapid decline in her condition. She died at 5.30 on the morning of 5 May in the presence of a nurse named Ann Clifford. She was 19 years of age. Her last words were, 'Mother, Mother, where is she?'[52]

The coffin was placed in the room where she died, and in the following days Sophia sat weeping beside it, which William Charles Raffles Flint found 'heart-rending and agonizing in the extreme'.[53] She was buried on 12 May in the presence of Bishop Sumner, his son John, who bore his loss with 'the most becoming fortitude and resignation', members of Sophia's family, and her old friend, the Revd. Samuel Wilberforce (1805–1873), Canon of Winchester, whose family had lived next to her at 'High Wood'.[54] He described in a letter to his wife the harrowing scenes before the burial:

> It was an awful time: I trust that I prayed: I am sure many did and the deep sobbing of poor Lady Raffles and John [Sumner] was most affecting. Then Lady Raffles had to be removed: and it was almost too much. She clung to the coffin and kissed its repulsive blackness: saying in a sort of thrilling whisper of agony "My child, my child, my babe. Must I leave thee. Cannot I keep even this. My child, my babe". The Bishop took her hand: and bid her for love to her who was gone bear this one more struggle: and she rose and left the room with her brother.[55]

The death of Ella, terrible in itself, was made worse for Sophia as she had represented the last living link with her beloved husband, whom she had so closely resembled. She wrote to the Bunsens from St. Leonards-on-Sea on 2 June 1840:

> I am left to wander alone in the World in which I no longer feel any interest, whilst there was one Being to whose Happiness I could contribute Life had some value – but now all the energies of my mind are thrown back upon myself as useless & valueless, for all [were] centered in my beautiful child and God so loved her he took her to himself and it is blessed to be the Mother of Saints and angels … I grieve that I have lost my child – I long to have her back again – … I see nothing but her earthly form – hear nothing but her constant gentle call of Mother – Mother – … I am so exhausted in body – & so low in Spirit – that I have not been able to remove from this place – or to bear the journey even to London – .[56]

For three weeks after the funeral, John Sumner stayed with her at St. Leonards, but when he left she went to visit her sister Alice Mudge at 'Beechwood'. She then moved to London, but at the end of the year she was drawn back to St. Leonards-on-Sea and stayed at No. 60, The Marina, next to the house where Ella died. She later joined her friend Sir Robert Harry Inglis in London early in the New Year, and after William Charles Raffles Flint's graduation she set out with him and her maid for Berne and Geneva. In July 1841 Baroness Bunsen met her at Lucerne: 'Lady Raffles is an astonishing person – I wonder and admire the more I see her, and I have the comfort of feeling that it is soothing to her to be here'.[57]

She returned to 'High Wood' in September or early October 1842, by which time Bunsen had been appointed Minister Plenipotentiary and Envoy Extraordinary to Frederick William IV of Prussia at the Court of St. James and she was often in his and his wife's company at the Prussian Embassy in Carlton Terrace, London, at their house, Herstmonceux Place, in East Sussex, or, from early 1844, at Oak Hill, near Barnet, only four miles from 'High Wood'.[58] Sophia met Mendelssohn through the Bunsens, and on 15 November 1847 she was present at a dinner at the Embassy when her friends, the Duc de Broglie and Sir Robert Inglis, were present.[59]

Five days later, on 20 November 1847, Bunsen arranged a grand reception at the Embassy for Sophia to meet James Brooke (1803–68), Rajah of Sarawak.[60] Brooke was the centre of great interest in London at the time, and after dinner 'a small circle assembled'[61] to hear him discuss his exploits in Borneo. Brooke claimed to have been inspired by Raffles, and Bunsen noted this fact when two days after the reception he commented on Lord Ellesmere's review of Keppel's *Journal of H.M.S. Dido* in the *Quarterly Review*:[62]

> Both by the original work and by the review a great interest has been excited about Mr. Brooke, which we have warmly shared; but it cannot be said that after having seen him the feeling has been kept up at the same pitch. However willing one may be to make every allowance for his desire to shrink from being made a show of, yet still, every allowance made, he proved "dry as a remainder-biscuit after a voyage". The favourable appearances are

to be characterised by negatives; he is unassuming, unpretending, unobtrusive: but the degree of curiosity that remains is only as to whether he *can* warm or kindle, *be* warmed or *be* kindled.[63]

Whether or not Brooke made a similar impression on Sophia is unknown, but he wrote to her from Cheltenham on 14 January 1848 expressing the hope that he would have 'the pleasure of bidding you adieu before my departure and I trust with all the confidence of an old friend you will let me know whether I can be of any service in the East, or whether there is any thing in its jungle or its waters that you covet'.[64]

The Bunsens were among the most regular of Sophia's guests at 'High Wood', and their second son, Ernest von Bunsen, and his wife, Elizabeth Gurney, daughter of the philanthropist and banker, Samuel Gurney (1786–1856), spent a few days of their honeymoon there in August 1845.[65] With the prospect of their retirement in 1854, the Bunsens wrote to Sophia proposing that they should move to 'High Wood' and share the living costs with her,[66] but she declined:

> I appreciate the feeling that suggested the thought of my poor unworthy self, but if I had the means which I have not, my sufferings & weakness which God alone knows[,] render me quite unable to undertake the position & the latter encreases daily, & it is my feeling & conviction that before the year closes my broken heart will be at rest – I will not enter into particulars[,] my Income is so limited & the claims upon me so many, I have great difficulty in keeping out of debt – .[67]

The Bunsens left England for Heidelberg, and four years later they moved to the Mediterranean to escape the German winter. They were at Nice when they learned from their daughter-in-law of Lady Raffles's death at 'High Wood' on 12 December 1858: 'Your letter with the moving intelligence of dear Lady Raffles's release has just reached us. We all join you in thanking God for the termination of such a living death as she had existed through for years'.[68]

Sir James Brooke (1803–1868), Rajah of Sarawak
*Engraving by W. Holl after a portrait by Sir Francis Grant, 1848*

During the last years of her life, Sophia had lost two of her soldier brothers, Captain John Watson Hull of the 10th and 14th Regiments of Bengal Native Infantry, who died at Dromore, County Down, on 10 November 1842,[69] and Major Lawrence Nilson Hull of the 16th Native Infantry Grenadiers, who died from wounds sustained on 23 December 1845 when leading his regiment at Ferozepore during the first Sikh War.[70] She was survived by four members of the family, her brother Captain William Hollamby Hull, who died at St. Leonards-on-Sea on 30 January 1862,[71] and her sisters, Alice Watson Mudge, who died in 1862,[72] Elizabeth Mary Ann Page, who died at Rugby, Warwickshire, on 21 October 1887,[73] and Mary Jane Auber, who died at St. Helier's, Jersey, on 5 December 1873.[74] It was the latter who nursed her during her final illness at 'High Wood', and she was present when she died there, afterwards arranging for her burial at St. Paul's Church, Mill Hill, in Middlesex. The exact circumstances of her death were not recorded, but she died in the confident belief that after her long tormented life she would at last be happily reunited with her beloved husband and children. 'I have the strangest feeling', she wrote in July 1840,

> that my bright & beloved Husband, is surrounded by all his Children, that they are rejoicing & in delightful communion enjoying their & my happy Home, whilst I am a lonely Wanderer who cannot be permitted to rejoin this blessed circle & I feel that they are longing to have me with them – & then I am really to rest in the blessed assurance that the night is far spent, the day is at hand – & I too shall soon be one of the waiting Spirits in the Paradise of God – .[75]

Many letters of condolence were received by her nephew, the Revd. William Charles Raffles Flint,[76] including one from her old friend, Dr. Thomas Horsfield, the American naturalist and Keeper of the East India Company Museum, who had accompanied her on the memorable journey to the Minangkabau highlands of central Sumatra 40 years earlier, when, as he now wrote, 'I witnessed her remarkable character and qualifications'.[77] By her Will dated 6 September 1855 and proved in the Principal Registry of the Court of Probate on 6 January 1859, she left the bulk of her estate, including 'High Wood', to her niece, Jenny Rosdew Flint, wife of the Revd. William Charles Raffles Flint, and daughter of her sister Alice and Lieutenant-Colonel Richard Mudge.[78] To her youngest surviving sister, Elizabeth Mary Ann Page, widow of the Revd. Thomas Page, she left the proceeds from a bond of £2,000 settled on her by her father at the time of her marriage, and to her butler, Edward Goddard, her cook, Louise Steward, and her maid, Ann Harding, one year's wages as 'a token of regard for their long and faithful Services'. To Mary Grimes, her life-long friend, the nurse who had accompanied her to west Sumatra in 1818, and taken Ella to England in 1822, she left an annuity of £30.

It is impossible to say what her wealth was at the time of her death as no sums are specified in the Will, but stocks in English and Foreign funds are recorded. Three years earlier, when Peter Auber and William Brown Ramsay were replaced as Trustees by her brother, Captain William Hollamby Hull, the sums of £8,734.5s.9d. in consols, and £2,199.6s.3d. in three per cents, are mentioned.[79] The returns from these investments, and from rents from the farms had to meet the costs of 'High Wood', including the wages of seven servants (at the time of the 1851 Census). The house and the estate, consisting of nearly 100 acres, were put up for sale by auction in London by Jenny Rosdew Flint on 27 May 1859, but the sum realised is unknown.[80] The estate was only 20 acres smaller in size than when Raffles purchased it in 1825, so it would seem that she retained most of the land during her tenure of 'High Wood'.[81]

# Epilogue

THE DEATH OF LADY RAFFLES, preceded by that of her daughter Ella in 1840, and Raffles's sister Leonora in 1855,[1] ended the direct family line of Sir Stamford Raffles. Thereafter the Raffles family continued essentially through three branches:

1. The family of the Revd. William Charles Raffles Flint, son of Sir Stamford Raffles's sister, Mary Anne Flint,[2] and Captain William Flint R.N.;[3]

2. The family of the children from the previous marriage of Mary Anne to Quintin Dick Thompson;[4] and

3. The family of the Revd. Dr. Thomas Raffles, son of William Raffles,[5] half-brother of Captain Benjamin Raffles.

Of this last family, it should be noted that the Revd. Dr. Thomas Raffles, son of William and Rachel Raffles (née Dunsby),[6] was born on 17 May 1788 and died on 18 August 1863. On 18 April 1815 he married Mary Catherine Hargreaves, the only daughter of James Hargreaves (b. 7 August 1745, d. 22 September 1812), a brewer of Highfield and Smithfield Streets, Liverpool, and Mary (née Winter) (d. 24 September 1824), and by her had five children:

Mary Rachel Raffles, b. 6 May 1817, d. 10 January 1887
Thomas Stamford Raffles, b. 18 September 1818, d. 23 January 1891[7]
James Hargreaves Raffles, b. 2 February 1826, d. at Bass, Victoria, 14 January 1872
William Winter Raffles, b. 20 July 1830, d. 9 February 1895
Reginald Dugdale Raffles, b. 2 July 1833, buried 7 November 1833, aged four months.

# Notes

**ABBREVIATIONS**

***BKI*** *Bijdragen tot de Taal-, Land- en Volkenkunde* (KITLV, Leiden)

**BL** British Library (London)

**HEIC** Honourable East India Company

***JMBRAS*** *Journal Malaysian (Malayan) Branch Royal Asiatic Society* (Singapore, Kuala Lumpur)

***JSBRAS*** *Journal Straits Branch Royal Asiatic Society* (Singapore)

***J. Soc. Biblphy nat. Hist.*** *Journal of the Society for the Bibliography of Natural History* (London)

**MSS. Eur.** European Manuscripts (Asia, Pacific & Africa Collections, British Library (London)

**NLS** National Library of Scotland (Edinburgh)

**NLWC** National Library of Wales Collection (Aberystwyth)

**Trans. Linn. Soc.** *Transactions of the Linnean Society* (London)

***VKI*** *Verhandelingen van het Koninklijk Instituut voor Taal-, Land- en Volkenkunde* (Leiden)

# PREFACE

————◆————

[1] Victoria Glendinning, *Raffles and the Golden Opportunity 1781–1826* (London, 2012), pp. 3–4, 14–15, wrongly asserts that the ship *Martin* (George Hooper), in which Benjamin Raffles served as an apprentice, was engaged in the slave trade with Antigua. Captain Raffles is described as 'a slave-trader' who 'abandoned his family' in the online site, 'Raffles and the Golden Opportunity'.

[2] Maurice Collis, *Raffles* (London, 1966), p. 22 also assumes that Raffles's father was engaged in the slave trade with the West Indies.

# CHAPTER ONE
## *Sir Stamford Raffles's Father and Grandfather*
————◆————

[1] George Oliver, *The History and Antiquities of the Town and Minster of Beverley, in the County of York* (Beverley, 1829), p. 293.

[2] John Bastin, *Letters and Books of Sir Stamford Raffles and Lady Raffles: The Tang Holdings Collection of Autograph Letters and Books of Sir Stamford Raffles and Lady Raffles* (Singapore, 2009), pp. 18, 192–3; D.C. Boulger, *The Life of Sir Stamford Raffles* (London, 1897), pp. 3–4.

[3] Lady Raffles, *Memoir of the Life and Public Services of Sir Thomas Stamford Raffles, F.R.S. &c.* (London, 1830), p. 2.

[4] The names Raffles, Raffels, Raffeles, Raffelles and Raffules appear in the 17th-century records of Berwick-upon-Tweed, including Thomas, son of Thomas Raffels in 1619; Elizabeth, daughter of Thomas Raffels in 1622; William, son of Thomas Raffles in 1627, the latter being described as 'the waite'; Beniamin, son of Thomas Raffelles in 1630; John, son of Thomas Raffelles in 1633; Rachell, daughter of Thomas Raffeles in 1635; Benjamine Raffels, married to Marie Mortine on 1 May 1655; Thomas, son of Beniamine Raffelles in 1656; Barbara, daughter of Thomas Raffles in 1694, and so on. There are references to a Margaret Raffles, who was baptised in the Church of the Holy Trinity on 29 January 1690, and to a Thomas Raffles who died on 3 May 1717, but the name begins to fade from Berwick-upon-Tweed records thereafter, and, apart from a George Raffles, no one of that name is listed during the 19th century.

[5] Lady Raffles, *Memoir*, p. 2.

[6] Strutton Ground, a corruption of Stourton Ground, named after the mansion of the Lords Dacre. It was described at the time as 'a good, handsome, long, well built and inhabited Street, which runs up to Tethill-fields, almost against the new Work-House

for employing poor People'. Today it forms the continuation of Horseferry Road into Victoria Street.

[7] We have found no evidence of this Thomas Raffles having been abroad.

[8] Thomas Raffles was still alive in June 1743 but we cannot be certain if he was the Thomas Raffles of Duck Lane in the parish of St. John the Evangelist Westminster who is recorded in September 1767 under the designation of 'Taylor', as the entry may have been carried over, as occurred in other records, and we have found no further entries of the name of Thomas Raffles in Duck Lane in the Westminster Rate Books after 1742. His wife Elizabeth Raffles was buried at St. Margaret's Church Westminster on 28 May 1744.

[9] The burial is recorded of a certain Thomas Raffle at St. Margaret's Church Westminster on 17 June 1715, without a final 's' to the surname.

[10] Anne Raffles married William Cassell or Caffol or Cafell in St. Margaret's Church Westminster on 1 January 1735.

[11] Mary, or possibly Margaret Raffles, who married James Winter in St. Mary's Church Whitechapel on 29 September 1731. A certain Mary Raffles was buried at St. Margaret's Church Westminster in 1719.

[12] Susannah Raffles's name varies in the records, sometimes with the omission of the final 'h', so that the correct spelling of her name and that of her daughter is uncertain.

[13] Elizabeth Raffles married James Gaddrer on 15 August 1758 in St. Martin-in-the-Fields, Westminster, with her father Thomas Raffles as witness.

[14] The date of her death is uncertain but she appears to have been the Mary Raffles who was buried on 15 February 1780 in the graveyard of St. Faith under St. Paul's, London, and who had been a witness three years earlier to the marriage of her brother Captain Benjamin Raffles and Ann Lyde on 21 November 1776 (Chapter Two). There was, however, another Mary Raffles (Captain Benjamin Raffles's aunt), born on 4 August 1718 and baptised on 15 August 1718, who could have been the witness to the marriage, but not the third known Mary Raffles, wife of Henry Raffles, as she was illiterate and would have been unable to sign the marriage register.

[15] Susannah Julia Raffles married Ambrose Carter, a neighbour of Nathaniel Phillips's Pleasant Hill plantation in Jamaica, about 1770, and by him had four sons and three daughters: Dr. Ambrose Carter, who was born around 1772 and died in Jamaica in 1796; Elizabeth Carter, who was born about 1774; William Carter, who was born in 1776 and died in Jamaica in 1812; Ann Carter, who was born in Jamaica in 1778; Thomas Carter, who was born on 20 December 1780, baptised in St. Mary's Church Islington, London, and died in Jamaica about 1782; Leonora Sophia Carter, who was

born in Jamaica about 1783; and Benjamin Carter (named after Captain Benjamin Raffles), who was born at Barking Lodge, St. Thomas in the East, Jamaica, one week before his mother was buried on 19 August 1784, aged 38. Susannah's father, Thomas Raffles, received news of his daughter's death in London and on 1 November 1784 he added a Codicil to his Will directing that her share of his moneys should go to her six living children, to be applied by the father, Ambrose Carter, for their use and benefit. Thomas Raffles died shortly afterwards, and was buried on 28 November 1784 at St. Mary's Church Islington.

[16] St. Margaret's Church Westminster stands between Westminster Abbey and the Houses of Parliament and so became known as 'the parish church of the House of Commons'. Sir Walter Raleigh ('Rawleige') and John Milton are buried there.

[17] Autobiographical fragment of Thomas Raffles, Dr. Williams's Library, University of London. He states in this document that his father was left with eight children on the death of his first wife, but the statement was recorded many years later and he was possibly confused by the additional children born to his father after his second marriage in 1750. The records of Christ's Hospital state that at the time of the enrolment of Thomas Raffles Jr. in April 1748 his father was a housekeeper with six children, and not seven, as stated by his son, Thomas Raffles.

[18] The birth of John Raffles occurred less than three months after Thomas Raffles's marriage to Jane Gibson, which may explain why they were married at Alexander Keith's New Little Chapel and not St. George's Chapel, Mayfair. John Raffles subsequently married Jane Tute on 15 December 1773, his sister Margaret Raffles being one of the witnesses to the marriage. It was short-lived, as he remarried, as a widower, on 21 November 1776 a spinster named Elizabeth Hare. His only daughter, Caroline-Matilda, first married William Mills of Frocester House, near Stroud, their union producing two sons, William and John, both of whom became clergymen. By her second marriage to James Harmer of Bewdly she had a son and a daughter. Sir Stamford Raffles, after his return from Java in 1816, visited his Uncle John at Hayley, near Birmingham, and also his cousin, Caroline-Matilda, at Bewdly, as he informed his cousin, the Revd. Dr. Thomas Raffles, in a letter dated 3 September 1816: 'As you might have expected, we were received with the greatest hospitality & affection by my Uncle John and family – He is exactly what he was with the advantage of being a better Christian and as for my Aunt [Elizabeth] I think she is if possible a more extraordinary Character than ever – ... It was impossible to leave Bewdly at the time I had fixed & therefore I spent two days with Caroline instead of one – I like Harmer very much and think Caroline much improved –' (Bastin, *Letters and Books of Sir Stamford Raffles*, pp. 92–3, 236, note 19). John Raffles died at his house at Stourport and was buried at Lower Mitton, Worcestershire, on 11 March 1819, his Will being proved in August of that year. His widow Elizabeth subsequently married Richard Jones, an architect and surveyor of Foregate Street, Worcester, and she died there on 18 March 1824, aged 65.

[19] William Raffles was admitted as a Scholar to St. Paul's School in January 1762 at the age of 10. In 1767 he obtained articles of Clerkship as a solicitor or attorney to Michael Barbour of Fetter Lane, London, and he later formed a legal practice, Parnell & Raffles, in London. He married Rachel Dunsby (born 9 December 1752, daughter of Mary and Richard Dunsby, a Staymaker of Wells, Norfolk) at St. Leonard's Shoreditch, London, on 20 May 1778. They lived at No. 14 Princes (Princelet) Street, Spitalfields, where the young Thomas Stamford Raffles often visited, and where, as his cousin the Revd. Dr. Thomas Raffles recalled in his 'Reminiscences', he made a visit after he returned from Java in 1816: 'One of his first visits was to his Aunt, for they were very fond of each other … & walking the length of Princes S$^t$. knocked at old Number 14, & on the opening of the door went at once into the sort of Parlour Kitchen where my Mother was, busied as usual about her household affairs – "I knew well", he said, "where at this time of the day I should find you", & taking his accustomed seat in an old armed chair by the fire side where he had often sat – made her at once by his affectionate & playful manner, quite unconscious of the elevation to which he had attained since he had last sat there. "Aunt", he said, "you know I used to tell you when a boy that I should be a Duke before I die". "Ah", she replied, "& I used to say that it would be Duke of *Puddle Dock*" – which was a proverb in London at that day, referring to a wretched locality at Wapping: & with which aspiring lads, who had great notions of the greatness they should hereafter attain, were twitted.' (Bastin, *Letters and Books of Sir Stamford Raffles*, p. 228). There are four extant letters of Raffles to his uncle William Raffles (ibid., pp. 190–5), who served for many years as joint vestry clerk of Christ Church Spitalfields, and who was buried there on 14 November 1825, five days after his death. His wife Rachel was also buried in the graveyard after she died on 15 July 1832 in the parish of St. Mary's, Islington. William and Rachel Raffles had three children: Elizabeth Margaret Raffles, who was born on 5 July and baptised on 1 August 1779; Mary Jane Raffles, who was born on 17 January 1787; and the Revd. Dr. Thomas Raffles, who was born on 17 May 1788. (On the Revd. Dr. Thomas Raffles's family, see Epilogue.) Mary Jane Raffles married her brother's school-friend James Baldwin Brown (1785–1843), Barrister-at-Law of the Inner Temple, on 17 September 1817 in London. He practised on the northern circuit and at the Lancashire quarter sessions, and was the author of a number of books, including *Memoirs of the Public and Private Life of John Howard, the Philanthropist* (London, 1818). After her husband's death on 23 November 1843, Mary Jane went to live with her brother in Liverpool, where she died on 8 February 1858. Her eldest son, James Baldwin Brown (1820–1884), was one of the first graduates of London University, and he became almost as well-known as a Congregational Minister as his uncle, but he declined an invitation to succeed him at the Great George Street Chapel in Liverpool.

[20] The date of Margaret Raffles's death is unrecorded, but she is mentioned in her father's Will of 1784 so she must have been alive at that time.

[21] As stated in the Autobiographical fragment of his son, Thomas Raffles, Dr. Williams's Library, University of London.

[22] Doctors' Commons, or the College of Advocates and Doctors of Common Law, consisted of a court or common hall, with a library and dining room attached. There were also houses round two squares in which the chambers of the Judges and Advocates were located, the larger of the squares leading to Knightrider Street.

[23] *The Gentleman's Magazine*, vol. 54, pt. 2 (1784), p. 956.

[24] Autobiographical fragment of Thomas Raffles, Dr. Williams's Library, University of London. It is interesting that later, when established as a merchant in Jamaica, Thomas himself took on a pupil from Christ's Hospital as an apprentice (Peter Wilson Coldham, *The Complete Book of Emigrants 1751–1776*, Genealogical Publishing Company, Baltimore, 1987, p. 90): '28 November [1770], John Smith apprenticed from Christ's Hospital to his friend Mr. James Gibbs, watchmaker of Fetter Lane, and Mr. Thomas Raffles of Doctors Commons to serve his son Mr. Thomas Raffles of Port Morant, Jamaica, merchant'. On 1 February 1780 Thomas Raffles married Ann Raven, a widow of St. Bride, Fleet Street, London. The following year he was a school master and, according to an insurance record of that year, he lived at No. 101 Dorset Street, Salisbury Court, London. He had a step-daughter named Ann Raven, who was buried in Bunhill Fields burial grounds Islington, London, on 10 July 1783. His wife Ann was also interred in Bunhill Fields burial grounds on 24 January 1796, aged 55, and he was buried there on 8 February 1798, aged 60.

[25] Benjamin, in turn, was followed at Christ's Hospital in April 1751 by his brother Henry, who remained at school until 11 June 1757. He was apprenticed on 3 July 1757 for eight years to a London tinplate worker named John Clayton, 'to learn his Art'. On 28 February 1775 he married in St. Clement Danes Church Westminster an illiterate woman named Mary Ward, who signed the marriage register with two crosses. He died sometime before the date of his father's Will in 1784 in which his widow was left £5.

[26] One of the privileges of the Royal Mathematical School was that the boys were presented annually at Court during the first Drawing Room of the year, previously on the first day of the year but latterly on the Queen's Birthday (*Annals of Christ's Hospital from its Foundation to the Present Time and of the Original Conventual Church of the Grey Friars, By an Old Blue* (London, 1867), p. 36).

[27] Mss. 399, American and Canadian Ciphering Books. It is interesting that Captain Raffles's leather-bound ciphering book contains Sir Stamford Raffles's 'ownership form', so the book obviously came into his possession after the death of his father in 1811 (Nerida F. Ellerton and McKenzie A. Clements, *Summary of Ciphering Books in Phillips Library, Salem, Massachusetts*, no. 14).

[28] Nerida F. Ellerton and M.A. Clements, *Rewriting the History of School Mathematics in North America 1607–1861: The Central Role of Cyphering Books* (Dordrecht, 2012), p. 28.

# CHAPTER TWO
## Captain Benjamin Raffles and the West India Trade

[1] According to another description of the ship she was of 250 tons burthen with a crew of 30 and armed with 12 carriage guns.

[2] One of the owners of the *Martin* was Richard Oliver, who owned slaves and sugar farms in Antigua. The other owners of the ship were Thomas Stanton, James Welford, Richard Hazard, John Shakespeare and Bouchier Cleeve, who lived and had his business next door to Lawrence Cole, who became a partner of Thomas Bingley Sr. (Chapter Two, note 4).

[3] *London Chronicle or Universal Evening Post*, London, 23–26 February 1765.

[4] The relationship between Captain Raffles and Thomas Bingley Sr. must have been close as Captain Raffles named his son after him: Thomas Stamford Bingley Raffles. The name was dropped, however, when Raffles was re-baptised in England by the Revd. John Lindeman in 1784 (Chapter Two, note 28). Thomas Bingley Sr. married Ann Doncaster on 29 July 1759 at St. Michael's Church Cornhill, and he was buried there on 19 August 1797, aged 66. In his Will he left rings to his friends, Captain Benjamin Raffles, and his wife, Ann. His son, Thomas Bingley Jr., also an insurance broker of 21 Birchin Lane, London, was born on 20 August 1761 and later married Margaret Jackson. He held £1,000 in East India Company stock and he and Charles Hamond signed the Bond for £500 required by Thomas Stamford Raffles when he was appointed a junior clerk on the Company's permanent establishment in 1800. Thomas Bingley Jr. subsequently fell on hard times, and he proceeded to Java, where he arrived in September 1812 as a passenger on the *Diana* (J. Bowman) from Portsmouth. He stayed with Raffles at Batavia and also at Government House, Buitenzorg, where he died on 20 August 1813, and was buried in the Botanical Garden (Kebun Raya). Raffles appointed him to a number of government posts, including Superintendent of Tonnage and Cargoes in October 1812, and in May 1813 Vice-President of the Orphan Chamber. The *Java Government Gazette* of 28 August 1813, in reporting his death, also described him as a 'Free Merchant'.

[5] Betty Wood (ed.) et al., 'The Letters of Simon Taylor of Jamaica to Chaloner Arcedekne, 1765–1775', *Travel, Trade and Power in the Atlantic 1765–1884*, Camden Miscellany, vol. XXXV, Fifth Series, vol. 19 (Cambridge, 2002), pp. 7, 11.

[6] *Lloyd's Evening Post*, London, 16–18 September 1765.

[7] *General Evening Post*, London, 17–19 July 1766.

[8] *London Evening Post*, 9–11 April 1767.

[9] Simon Taylor wrote to Benjamin Cowell (Arcedekne's brother-in-law) from Kingston on 24 March 1768: 'By the Account Current you will see that there are four hdds. of Sugar remaining to be accounted for. They were sent alongside of Capt. Raffles's ship last year and by the negligence of the Sailors they did not check the Hdds, so on taking out one the others ran to Leeward and oversatt the boat by which they were excessively damaged. The Capt. was with me two days ago and we are to settle the matter on my going to Windward as it is well known there & he himself is convinced that he must pay for them.' (Wood, *Travel, Trade and Power*, p. 56).

[10] Ibid., p. 41.

[11] *The London Evening Post*, 11 July 1767, reported the arrival of the *Morant* off the Downs: 'A letter from Capt. Raffles, arrived in the Downs from Jamaica, says, "On our passage we spoke with Capt. Brown, from the Bay of Honduras for Rotterdam, who says, as he passed thro' the Gulph he saw a large ship, with three decks, on shore upon the Florida coast, but there being little wind when he past her, could not go near her to see who she was: it was about the 3d or 4th of June when he passed her."'

[12] *St. James's Chronicle or the British Evening Post*, London, 17–19 August 1769.

[13] *Bingley Weekly Journal or the Universal Gazette*, London, 15 September 1770; *Gazetteer and New Daily Advertiser*, London, 26 September 1770.

[14] *Public Advertiser*, London, 25 September 1770.

[15] Nathaniel Phillips was born in England in 1733 and arrived at Kingston in 1759. He subsequently became the owner of the Pleasant Hill plantation of 985 acres outside Port Morant in the sugar district of St. Thomas in the East. In the 1760s, when Captain Raffles first met him, the estate had a cattle mill and watermill and a population of 120 slaves. He later acquired three other properties in St. Thomas in the East, two sugar plantations known as Phillipsfield and Suffolk Park, and a livestock pen called Boxford Lodge, in which Ambrose Carter, Captain Raffles's brother-in-law, was involved (Chapter One, note 15). Phillips's plantation neighbours at St. Thomas in the East were Thomas and Leonora Sophia Stamford, after whom Thomas Stamford Raffles and his sister Leonora were named (Chapter Three, notes 2, 4). Thomas Stamford was the Overseer of the Harbourhead Estate in Jamaica from 1766 to 1777, when it was owned by William Beckford (1709–1770) and his heirs, and he was probably the owner of the house and racing stables at Newmarket in England, since his estate in Jamaica was similarly named and his slaves branded 'TS'. He is listed as a subscriber in *A Short Dissertation on the Jamaica Bath Waters*, which was printed in Kingston in 1784. On his death in that or the following year, his widow Leonora Stamford inherited the Newmarket plantation and married there on 1 June 1786 Ambrose Carter, whose first wife, Susannah Julia Raffles, sister of Captain Raffles, was buried at his sugar plantation, Barking Lodge, St. Thomas in the East, Jamaica,

on 19 August 1784 (Chapter One, note 15). Ambrose Carter died on 25 November 1793 of 'a putrid fever', probably yellow fever, which raged in Jamaica at the time, and was buried at Barking Lodge. His widow Leonora Carter died on 17 June 1838 at 5 Skinner Place, Holloway Road, London, aged 104, having received three years earlier, as an absentee Jamaica land-owner, compensation from the British Government of £426.6s.11d. for 22 slaves on the Newmarket estate of her former husband, Thomas Stamford. Nathaniel Phillips returned to live permanently in London in 1789, his Jamaica properties then being worth £160,000 (Jamaica currency), together with 706 slaves valued at £50,000. His business offices were in Mincing Lane, London, and in 1793 he purchased an estate of 600 acres at Slebech, near Haverfordwest in Pembrokeshire, Wales, in which he invested part of his fortune. He died at Slebech Hall on 30 December 1813 and was buried on 7 January 1814. He was an intimate friend of Captain Raffles and was possibly responsible for securing him the position of ship's master with the London shipping firm of Hibbert, Purrier & Horton with which he had close business connections. Phillips had six illegitimate children by a free mulatto woman named Charlotte Wynter, two of whom, Elizabeth Wynter, known as 'Betsy', who was born on 15 July 1779, and Richard Wynter, who was born on 27 November 1782 (and baptised on 7 March 1783 as Richard Phillips), were taken to England in March 1789 aboard Captain Raffles's ship *West Indian* with Phillips's servant, Mary Vine, with instructions that the children were to be under Captain Raffles's care until he received further orders from Phillips (NLWC: Slebech Papers, Accounts, item 5387, image 92). The two children lived with the Raffles family, Richard, aged seven, being placed in the Mansion House Boarding School in Hammersmith, the same school as was also attended by Thomas Stamford Raffles (Chapter Three, note 8), and Elizabeth, aged 10, in a girl's school in Islington. On 27 November 1802 Elizabeth married at St. Mary's Newington in Surrey an old friend of the Raffles family, John Thomas Simes, a wool broker of No. 58 Coleman Street, London, and the High Street, Stoke Newington. Thomas Stamford Raffles and his mother were both witnesses to the marriage, and after he became Lieutenant-Governor of Fort Marlborough in 1818 Raffles took with him to west Sumatra the Simes's 14-year-old son, John, and appointed him to the new British post at Kalumbangan Bay in southern Sumatra, where he died in December 1818. Richard Wynter, after returning to Jamaica in 1798 to learn about sugar production at his father's plantation, Pleasant Hill, also joined Raffles in west Sumatra, where he established a sugar plantation and mill in the village of Bentiring, five miles east of Fort Marlborough. Raffles invested money in the plantation but he and Winter (as he was now known) lost heavily in the venture after Fort Marlborough and the British out-settlements were ceded to the Netherlands by the Treaty of London in 1824. Winter cohabited at Bengkulu with a local woman named Raleayah, by whom he had three children, including two boys, William Richard Winter and Charles Winter, who were baptised at Fort Marlborough on 16 October 1824. Some time afterwards, he moved his family to Singapore, where he was appointed as an Assistant in the Accountant's and Pay Office, a post probably secured for him by Raffles. Winter was by now suffering from poor health and he died at Singapore on 12 September 1827, shortly after learning of Raffles's death in

England in July of the previous year. In his Will, sworn at Singapore on 13 August 1827, a month before his death, and proved on 19 July 1832, Winter states that he had been obliged to leave west Sumatra after the transference of the British settlements to the Netherlands because it was 'no longer possible to obtain a livelihood but under the most precarious circumstances', and that as a result he had sacrificed property 'to a considerable amount'. At the time of his death, his two sons were at school in Penang and his daughter was with her mother in Singapore. Richard Winter was a childhood companion of Raffles, and with his unrivalled knowledge of slavery in the West Indies he must have been an important influence in shaping Raffles's hatred of slavery and related forms of forced labour. (Information on Nathaniel Phillips in the first part of this note follows: Kenneth Morgan (2004), Jamaican material in the Slebech Papers; an introduction, http://www.britishonlinearchives.co.uk/9781851171811.php. © 2006–2015 Microform Academic Publishers.)

[16] Nathaniel Phillips to Hibbert, Purrier & Horton, 9 August 1770, NLWC: Slebech Papers, Letter Book, item 11485, image 197 (quotation courtesy of Microform Academic Publishers and National Library of Wales). Hibbert, Purrier & Horton of London, are also recorded as Hibbert, Purrier & Co., London, and Hibbert & Co., London, in *Lloyd's Register*.

[17] Autobiographical fragment of Thomas Raffles, Dr. Williams's Library, University of London.

[18] Nathaniel Phillips to Thomas Hibbert Jr., London, 16 April 1772, NLWC: Slebech Papers, Letter Book, item 11485, image 218 (quotation courtesy of Microform Academic Publishers and the National Library of Wales).

[19] Nathaniel Phillips to William Thomson, 1 July 1772, NLWC: Slebech Papers, Letter Book, item 11485, image 221 (quotation courtesy of Microform Academic Publishers and the National Library of Wales).

[20] Nathaniel Phillips to William Thomson, 10 October 1773, Slebech Papers, Letter Book, item 11485, image 233 (quotation courtesy of Microform Academic Publishers and the National Library of Wales).

[21] Nathaniel Phillips Accounts, Business Records Accounts for 24 February 1773, NLWC: Slebech Papers, item 11703, image 44; Business Records Accounts for 1 August 1774; Slebech Papers, item 11725, image 97 (courtesy of Microform Academic Publishers and the National Library of Wales).

[22] *Morning Chronicle and London Advertiser*, 3 August 1775.

[23] Autobiographical fragment of Thomas Raffles, Dr. Williams's Library, University of London. The date of the arrival of the *Charlotte* (Green) on 1 August 1775 is confirmed in the Shipping News of the same date: 'At Dover, the … Charlotte, Green,

from New Providence'. Thomas Raffles subsequently became a teacher (Chapter One, note 24) and is described as a Master of St. Brides School, London, in his Will dated 5 January 1798, and proved 9 February 1798, in which he bequeathed to his brother, Captain Benjamin Raffles, 'forty Pounds if dead before me to his children provided that whatever sum he may be indebted to me at the time of my decease may be [?] deducted from the said forty Pounds'.

[24] Wood, *Travel, Trade and Power*, pp. 151–2.

[25] It seems that Captain Raffles contracted at this time for a 1/12th share in the *Ann*, which he later realised in the sum of £167.9.9 in April 1783 after taking command of the ship *West Indian*.

[26] Nathaniel Phillips to Hibbert, Purrier & Horton, 19 May 1776, NLWC: Slebech Papers, Letter Book, item 11485, image 248 (quotation courtesy of Microform Academic Publishers and the National Library of Wales).

[27] Ann Lyde was born in 1755 and was probably baptised at St. Mary's Church Teddington in Middlesex. Her parents (Sir Stamford Raffles's maternal grandparents) were Edward Lyde of the parish of St. Martin-in-the-Fields, Westminster, 'an eminent Oilman', whose business was situated at No. 459 The Strand, and Ann Salter of Cleveland-court, St. James, who is described in a newspaper report of their marriage in St. James's Chapel on 12 December 1743 as 'an agreeable Lady, and [of] a good fortune'. She was his second wife and was born on 9 December 1716, the daughter of Edward Slater and Ann Peach, following their marriage on 6 May 1712. He was Door or Chamber Keeper to the Privy Council and Clerk of His Majesty's Spicery, and he died at his official lodging in St. James's on 20 October 1732, his wife being interred with him in St. Mary's Church Wimbledon on 18 October 1749. Ann Lyde's father, Edward Lyde, was born in 1706 and was first married to Anne Bell at St. Martin-in-the-Fields on 30 April 1725. He was buried on 5 June 1768 in the graveyard of St. Mary's Church Teddington, his second wife Ann being interred with him on 16 April 1770. He left considerable freehold and leasehold property in Kent, Middlesex, and London, and in his Will he named his five children as beneficiaries, including Ann, and her two sisters, Harriot, who was born on 24 June 1750, and baptised on 6 July at St. Martin-in-the-Fields, Middlesex, and Elizabeth, who was born on 7 August 1752 and baptised there seven days later. Elizabeth married Charles Hamond, a London tea merchant, in St. Lawrence's Church Old Jewry on 13 May 1773, her first daughter Esther being born at his property of Sackett's Hill House, Thanet, Kent. Her son, Elton Hamond, was born on 4 November 1774 and baptised in St. Lawrence's Church Old Jewry on 24 November, but he died soon afterwards, and was succeeded by another son named Elton Hamond, who was born on 28 May 1786 and baptised on 28 June in St. Lawrence's Church Old Jewry. Elizabeth Hamond subsequently separated from her husband, as stated in his Will of 1807, his death occurring on 14 October of that year. She died on 2 February 1843 at her residence at Upper Marine Terrace, Margate,

where her sister, Ann Lyde (Sir Stamford Raffles's mother) often stayed during the latter years of her life. (A letter of condolence from Elizabeth Hamond to Lady Raffles on the death of Raffles dated Margate 10 July 1826 is in BL:MSS.Eur.D.742/9.) Ann Lyde – Ann Raffles – died in February 1824 and was buried on the 14th of that month at the Old Church St. Mary's Stoke Newington, London, a few months before her son arrived in England from west Sumatra. Raffles's cousin, Elton Hamond, to whom he assigned responsibility for bringing out a second edition of his *History of Java*, committed suicide in 1819 (Bastin, *Letters and Books of Sir Stamford Raffles*, p. 75, note 66).

[28] The Revd. John Lindeman was the son of Susanna Lindeman (née Leigh) and William Lindeman of the parish of St. Martin-in-the-Fields, an oilman and some-time partner of Edward Lyde of No. 459 The Strand, London. William and Susanna were married at St. Martin-in-the-Fields on 15 February 1746 and after her death in December 1754 he married Elizabeth Champ on 25 May 1766 at Shoreditch in London, one of the witnesses to the marriage being Thomas Raffles Sr. William Lindeman was buried on 30 October 1791 at St. Mary Mounthaw in London, his son, the Revd. John Lindeman, being an executor of his Will. The Revd. John Lindeman was born on 26 July 1748 and baptised at St. Dunstan's Church West, London, on 21 August 1748. In October 1758, at the age of 10, he was admitted to St. Paul's School, London, and on 7 December 1763 he was indentured for seven years to Samuel Butler as a haberdasher. He subsequently matriculated in Easter 1767 as a Scholar of Corpus Christi, Cambridge, and graduated B.A. in 1771 and M.A. in 1775. He was ordained deacon on 26 May 1771 and priest on 21 September 1772. He was Rector of St. Mary Somerset (with St. Mary Mounthaw), London, from 1773 until August 1777, when he became Rector of the parish Church of St. Michael and All Angels at Eaton Bishop in Herefordshire. He was collated to the Vicarage of Sithney, near Helston, in Cornwall in March 1799, and he died there on 24 September 1819 from apoplexy. He married Harriot Lyde, sister of Ann Lyde, on 5 November 1771 in the Church of St. Clement Danes Westminster, and by her had seven children, including three daughters: Mary Ann, who was born at Eaton Bishop on 26 October 1779, married Richard Wise M.D. (1784–1869) at Sithney on 17 July 1812, and died at the Ladock Rectory in Cornwall in April 1862; Susan, who married John Covey, a widower, on 4 October 1832 at Fawley in Hampshire; and Lucy, who was baptised on 16 September 1785 at Eaton Bishop in Herefordshire, married a teacher named Timothy Kelly on 12 January 1808 in St. James's Church Westminster, and was buried at St. Peter's Church Bromyard in Herefordshire on 21 December 1814. Her mother, Harriot Lindeman, died on 8 June 1795 at Eaton Bishop in Herefordshire. The Revd. John Lindeman re-baptised the three-year-old Thomas Stamford Raffles at the parish Church of St. Michael and All Angels on 4 July 1784, when his mother was staying with her sister at Eaton Bishop, apparently omitting during the ceremony the name of 'Bingley' (Chapter Two, note 4). Lindeman and his daughter Mary Ann visited the ship *Lady Raffles* at Falmouth in November 1817 before her voyage to west Sumatra, and Raffles and Lady Raffles returned the visit to Sithney a couple of days later (Bastin, *J. Soc. Biblphy nat. Hist.*, vol. 6, pt. 5 (1973), p. 362, note 215). They were accompanied on the visit by the British

naval surgeon Dr. Joseph Arnold (1782–1818), who wrote an unflattering account of Lindeman in a letter to the banker Dawson Turner dated 7 November 1817 (ibid., pp. 324, 362, note 215).

[29] Mary Raffles, sister of Benjamin Raffles's father, Thomas Raffles, was born in 1718 and died in 1796. She was admitted to St. Thomas's Hospital, Southwark, on 25 August 1796 and was 'taken' three days later.

[30] In the Shipping News of 21 June 1779 the *San Juan Baptula* is recorded as having sailed for Carthagena with a Captain Raffles in command, and later, on 25 October 1785, the same name appears as the commander of the *Quebec*, bound from Honduras to Bristol. These are either printing mistakes, which are common, or we are dealing with the unlikely prospect of a different Captain Raffles. There is similar confusion in the account given by Wurtzburg (*Raffles of the Eastern Isles*, p. 19) of the death of a Captain Raffles of the *Sebastiana* on a voyage to Falmouth in 1797. This account was said to have been based on a report in *The Columbian Magazine: or Monthly Miscellany* of June 1797, but the death reported is not that of Captain Raffles but of the ship's carpenter, Andrew Monteath, whose death is also reported in the *True Briton* of 1 September 1797: 'Died. – Mr. Andrew Monteath, carpenter, after an illness of two days'. When a death was reported on board ship, it was customary to name the captain of the ship, and this clearly led to Wurtzburg's error. The identity of the Captain Raffles who is named as commander of the *Sebastiana* is impossible to establish, but the name is not repeated in any subsequent source. The misspelling of names in the shipping reports was not uncommon and, indeed, we have an instance in a report of 19 November 1791 where a Captain Raffles or Ruffles is stated to have put his ship aground four days earlier off Ipswich.

[31] Chapter Two, note 15. In the family papers of the Revd. William Charles Raffles Flint, Stamford is identified as a Doctor in Jamaica (Bastin, *Letters and Books of Sir Stamford Raffles*, p. 17), but this is clearly a mistake.

[32] Nathaniel Phillips accounts with Hibbert, Purrier & Co., Business Records Accounts, NLWC: Slebech Papers, item 11788, image 226 (quotation courtesy of Microform Academic Publishers and the National Library of Wales).

[33] *The Royal Gazette*, Volume IV, no. 168 (29 June – 6 July 1782). David Hannay, citing Colquhoun's *Treatise on the Commerce and Police of the River Thames*, states that in 1792 there were 346 London vessels of 101,484 tons (including repeated voyages or calculating each voyage as a ship) in the West India trade, compared with 53 ships of 41,456 tons engaged in the trade with Asia (*Letters written by Sir Samuel Hood (Viscount Hood) in 1781-2-3*, Navy Records Society (London, 1895), vol. III, p. xxii).

[34] *General Evening Post*, London, 16–18 January 1783.

[35] *General Evening Post*, London, 1–4 March 1783; *Felix Farley's Bristol Journal*, Bristol, 8 March 1783; *Leeds Intelligencer*, 11 March 1783.

[36] *Public Advertiser*, London, 19 June 1787; *Caledonian Mercury*, 23 June 1787.

[37] Captain Raffles commanded three ships owned by Hibbert, Purrier & Horton before 1776 and the *Ann* between 1776 and 1782. He was master of the *West Indian* between 1782 and 1789 owned by Hibbert, Purrier & Co., and from 1790 until 1796 he commanded the new *West Indian* and the *Lord Rodney* owned by Hibbert Fuhr & Hibbert. Hibbert & Co. of 9 Mincing Lane, London, also owned cotton mills and exported cloth to Europe and South Africa, where it was traded for slaves for Jamaica after Thomas Hibbert (1710–1780) arrived at Kingston in 1734. As well as the ships above, Hibbert & Co. owned the *Mary Ann*, *Ann*, *Hibbert*, and *George Hibbert*, all of them engaged in the direct trade between London and Jamaica. In 1771 Horatio Nelson (1758–1805) worked as a 'youngster' on the merchant ship *Mary Anne* (John Rathbone) belonging to the house of Hibbert, Purrier & Horton on a voyage to the West Indies.

[38] *Public Advertiser*, London, 15 November 1790; *Diary or Woodfall's Register*, London, 20 November 1790.

[39] *Lloyd's Evening Post*, London, 16–18 March 1791.

[40] *Evening Mail*, London, 3–6 June 1791; *Lloyd's List*, London, 3 June 1791.

[41] *James's Chronicle or the British Evening Post*, London, 22–25 October 1791.

[42] *Lloyd's List*, London, 5 June 1792.

[43] *Public Advertiser*, London, 11 June 1792.

[44] *Lloyd's Evening Post*, London, 29–31 October 1792.

[45] *Lloyd's Evening Post*, London, 31 October – 2 November 1792; *London Chronicle*, 1–3 November 1792; *Public Advertiser*, London, 3 November 1792.

[46] On 5 February 1793 HMS *Providence* arrived off Jamaica and, after calling first at Port Royal, sailed on to Port Morant, where some of the trees were unloaded and planted in the Botanic Garden and in other places in the island, where they flourished.

[47] Thomas Barritt to Nathaniel Phillips, 18 January 1794, NLWC: Slebech Papers, Letters, item 8426, image 399 (quotation courtesy of Microform Academic Publishers and the National Library of Wales).

[48] *Lloyd's Evening Post*, London, 13–16 December 1793.

[49] *London Chronicle*, 24–26 July 1794.

[50] Thomas Barritt noted in a letter to Nathaniel Phillips dated 14 May 1794, with regard to this voyage, that 'Captain Raffles gets a Barrel of good Sugar for M$^{rs}$. Raffles as usual', NLWC: Slebech Papers, Letters, item 8428, image 413 (quotation courtesy of Microform Academic Publishers and the National Library of Wales).

[51] *Lloyd's List*, London, 14 November 1794.

[52] *Oracle and Public Advertiser*, London, 20 August 1795; *Lloyd's List*, London, 21 August 1795.

[53] The ravages of yellow fever became so severe that the shortage of seamen in the West India trade led to sums as high as 30 or 40 guineas being paid to them (*Reading Mercury*, 6 October 1784). Ambrose Carter (Chapter Two, note 15) may have died from the disease.

[54] Thomas Barritt to Nathaniel Phillips, 15 April 1796, NLWC: Slebech Papers, Letters, item 11570, image 13 (quotation courtesy of Microform Academic Publishers and the National Library of Wales).

[55] Captain Raffles to Nathaniel Phillips, 6 May 1796, NLWC: Slebech Papers, Letters, item 9171, images 136–8 (quotation courtesy of Microform Academic Publishers and the National Library of Wales).

[56] Rear-Admiral Sir Hugh Cloberry Christian (1747–1798) served in the West Indies between 1779 and 1782. He was knighted in 1796 and appointed Commander-in-Chief in the West Indies in the same year.

[57] Thomas Barritt to Nathaniel Phillips, 15 July 1796, NLWC: Slebech Papers, Letters, item 11576, image 44–5 (quotation courtesy of Microform Academic Publishers and the National Library of Wales).

[58] *Oracle and Public Advertiser*, London, 6 September 1796.

[59] *Daily Advertiser*, London, issue 21176, 14 October 1796; *Oracle and Public Advertiser*, London, 18 October 1796.

[60] George Hibbert to Nathaniel Phillips, 8 October 1796, NLWC: Slebech Papers, Letters, item 9197, image 215 (quotation courtesy of Microform Academic Publishers and the National Library of Wales).

[61] The *Catherine*, lying at Bell Wharf on the Thames, was advertised for sale by James Margetson, a Broker of No. 4, Fenchurch-building, London, in September 1791. The ship 'not long ago had entire Copper-works, and underwent a complete and substantial Repair'.

[62] Thomas Barritt to Nathaniel Phillips, 26 March 1798, NLWC: Slebech Papers, Letters, item 11592, image 151 (quotation courtesy of Microform Academic Publishers and the National Library of Wales).

[63] Thomas Barritt to Nathaniel Phillips, 12 June 1798, NLWC: Slebech Papers, Letters, item 11594, image 161 (quotation courtesy of Microform Academic Publishers and the National Library of Wales).

[64] Thomas Barritt to Nathaniel Phillips, 10 August 1798, NLWC: Slebech Papers, Letters, item 11595, image 171 (quotation courtesy of Microform Academic Publishers and the National Library of Wales).

[65] Thomas Barritt to Nathaniel Phillips, 26 October 1798, NLWC: Slebech Papers, Letters, item 11597, image 183 (quotation courtesy of Microform Academic Publishers and the National Library of Wales).

[66] Thomas Barritt to Nathaniel Phillips, 22 November 1798, NLWC: Slebech Papers, Letters, item 11599, image 187 (quotation courtesy of Microform Academic Publishers and the National Library of Wales).

[67] In September 1794, a ship named *Uxbridge* of 350 tons with 10 mounted carriage guns, sailing from Liverpool for Philadelphia, advertised accommodation for passengers and 'Measurement Goods at 35s. per Ton'. Applications were to be made to a certain 'Peter Kennion' of Liverpool, a name not dissimilar to J. Kenyon, who is listed in *Lloyds Register* of 1799 as owner of the *Uxbridge* (*Manchester Mercury*, 9 September 1794).

[68] Thomas Barritt to Nathaniel Phillips, 10 April 1799, NLWC: Slebech Papers, Letters, 11600, images 208, 209 (quotation courtesy of Microform Academic Publishers and the National Library of Wales).

[69] Thomas Barritt to Nathaniel Phillips, 10 April 1799, NLWC: Slebech Papers, Letters, item 11600, image 209 (quotation courtesy of Microform Academic Publishers and the National Library of Wales).

[70] Thomas Barritt to Nathaniel Phillips, 15 May 1799, NLWC: Slebech Papers, Letters, item 11602, image 223 (quotation courtesy of Microform Academic Publishers and the National Library of Wales).

[71] Thomas Barritt to Nathaniel Phillips, 5 June 1799, NLWC: Slebech Papers, Letters, item 11603, image 226 (quotation courtesy of Microform Academic Publishers and the National Library of Wales).

[72] Thomas Barritt to Nathaniel Phillips, 11 July 1799, NLWC: Slebech Papers, Letters, item 11604, image 234 (quotation courtesy of Microform Academic Publishers and the National Library of Wales).

[73] Thomas Barritt to Nathaniel Phillips, 2 August 1799, NLWC: Slebech Papers, Letters, item 11604, image 242 (quotation courtesy of Microform Academic Publishers and the National Library of Wales).

[74] Leonora Sophia Stamford married Captain Raffles's brother-in-law Ambrose Carter in 1786 (Chapter Two, note 15).

[75] Thomas Barritt to Nathaniel Phillips, 16 November 1800, NLWC: Slebech Papers, Letters, item 11615, image 319 (quotation courtesy of Microform Academic Publishers and the National Library of Wales).

[76] Louise Sanger, Information Centre Deputy Manager, Group Communications, Lloyd's Register, email dated 15 April 2014.

## CHAPTER THREE
### Captain Benjamin Raffles and his Family

[1] Three other children of Captain Benjamin and Ann Raffles had died earlier: Ann Raffles, who was born on 27 August 1779, baptised on 26 September 1779 at St. Dunstan in the East, London, and buried on 14 January 1780 in the south vault under the school of St. Dunstan's; Elizabeth Raffles, who was born on 4 March 1787, baptised on 14 March 1787 at St. Benet Fink Church, Threadneedle Street, London, died at Walcott Place, Lambeth, on 3 March 1791 and buried at St. Mary's Church Lambeth on 9 March 1791; and Benjamin Raffles, who was born on 12 April 1788 and died three days later. It also seems likely that Captain Raffles and his wife Ann had another daughter named Elizabeth, who was buried on 8 February 1778 at St. Botolph, Aldgate, being the first child of that name in the family.

[2] Thomas Stamford Bingley Raffles was born on board his father's ship *Ann* in the harbour of Port Morant, Jamaica, on 6 July 1781, or 5 July by sea-reckoning. He was named after his father's friends, Thomas Stamford, an overseer of the William Beckford estate in Jamaica (Chapter Two, note 15) and Thomas Bingley Sr., an insurance broker of Exchange Alley, Cornhill, later of 21 Birchen Lane, Cornhill, London (Chapter Two, note 4).

[3] Harriot Raffles, the eldest sister of Thomas Stamford Raffles, was born on 27 November 1783 and was baptised at the Church of St. Michael and All Angels at Eaton Bishop in Herefordshire on 4 July 1784 by the Revd. John Lindeman, when her brother was also re-baptised, following his initial baptism aboard his father's ship *Ann* in the harbour of Port Morant, Jamaica. She was named after her mother's sister Harriot, wife of the Revd. Lindeman (Chapter Two, note 28), and in 1810 she accompanied her sister Leonora to Penang and subsequently to Melaka, where Raffles was engaged as Agent to the Governor-General Lord Minto, who described

them favourably in letters to his family. Harriot, Leonora, and their sister Mary Anne Flint, all sailed in the British invasion fleet to Java in 1811, but Harriot, unlike her sisters, was unsuccessful in finding a husband. In October 1813 she accompanied her sister Mary Anne and her husband Captain William Flint R.N. to London aboard the *Lord Eldon* (Jacob Cowles), and eventually, on 17 October 1816, she married Tobias Browne of Kentish Town, an official at Somerset House. Raffles was a witness to the marriage, and he wrote to his cousin the Revd. Dr. Thomas Raffles soon afterwards: 'My Sister Harriet you will perhaps have perceived by the Papers is married to *her* M$^r$. Brown – he seems a very steady good kind of Man and likely to make her happy – he is a Widower with one Child and has an office in Somerset House' (Bastin, *Letters and Books of Sir Stamford Raffles*, p. 99; p. 70, note 22). Raffles's reference to '*her* M$^r$ Brown' is to the marriage of his sister Leonora to Thomas Campbell Brown, and to that of the Revd. Dr. Thomas Raffles's sister, Mary Jane, to James Baldwin Brown, a Barrister-at-Law. Harriot died on 28 February 1818, aged 34, while staying with her mother at St. Ann's Cottage, Hampstead, and was buried on 7 March 1818 at the nearby St. John's Church. She had given birth to a son, Stamford Raffles Brown, on 5 August 1817, but he died and was also buried at Hampstead on 3 January 1818. Tobias Browne subsequently married Ann Edgar, also of Kentish Town, on 24 August 1820.

[4] Leonora Raffles was born on 8 July and baptised on 5 August 1785 at St. Mary's Church Islington, Middlesex. She was named after her godmother, Leonora Sophia Stamford, wife of Thomas Stamford, the plantation Overseer in Jamaica after whom Raffles was named (Chapter Two, note 15). On 22 November 1810, shortly after her arrival at Penang with her sister Harriot, Leonora was married at a ceremony conducted by William Edward Phillips to a 38-year-old widower named Billington Loftie, Acting Surgeon at Prince of Wales Island. He was born on 10 June 1772 at Wingham in Kent, the son of the Revd. John Loftie (d. 1800) and Charlotte (née Billington) (d. 1834), and was appointed Assistant Surgeon on the Madras medical establishment in 1798 on the nomination of the Deputy Chairman of the East India Company, Stephen Lushington. He served as Garrison Surgeon at Melaka, where he married his first wife, Johanna, and by her had a daughter named Charlotte, who returned to England in 1812 and subsequently married Captain J.M.A. Lucas of the Bengal military establishment on 9 October 1828. Johanna died on 30 January 1810 at Penang, after her husband's appointment as Acting Surgeon, so that Loftie's marriage to Leonora was only 10 months after the death of his first wife. Following the British conquest of Java, and Raffles's appointment as Lieutenant-Governor of the island, Leonora settled at Surabaya with her husband, who was placed in charge of the General Hospital. On 10 December 1811, he was appointed by Raffles as Superintending Surgeon of the Eastern Districts on a monthly salary of Sp.$300 but he died at Semarang three months later, on 12 March 1812. Thereafter Leonora stayed at Semarang with her sister Mary Anne Flint and her husband Captain Flint, and subsequently with Raffles at Buitenzorg, where on 20 April 1813 she married Thomas Campbell Brown, an Assistant Surgeon on the Bengal medical establishment, who from 28 November 1812 had been performing 'the civil duties at the station of Buitenzorg'. In June 1813 he was

appointed Superintendent of the Press, and in November to the more lucrative post of Timber Storekeeper at Semarang in place of his brother-in-law Captain William Flint, after he left Java with his wife for England. Later, as Superintendent General of the Forests, Brown had to make way for Flint when he returned to Java in July 1815, and this caused family friction, which led to Brown and Leonora falling out with the Flints and also with Raffles. After the restitution of Dutch rule in Java, Brown returned to his old post of Assistant Surgeon at Cuttack in India, and in November 1818 he attempted a reconciliation with Raffles when the latter was in Calcutta, the subject forming part of a letter Raffles wrote to his sister Mary Anne Flint shortly afterwards (BL:MSS.Eur.D.742/17). In 1826 Brown was appointed Superintending Surgeon in the Kurnool division, and he died of inflammation of the chest at Judhpur on 22 October 1839. His father, George Brown, was a Surgeon of Derry in Ireland, and this was probably the reason why Leonora settled at Shipquay Street, Templemore, Derry, after her return from India. She was visited there in July 1850 by her cousin, the Revd. Dr. Thomas Raffles, and she died there on 5 July 1855, aged 70, the last member of Captain Benjamin Raffles's immediate family.

[5] Mary Anne Raffles was born on 21 May and baptised on 26 June 1789 at St. Mary's Church Lambeth. At the age of 16 she accompanied Raffles and Olivia to Penang, where she was married to Quintin Dick Thompson, Sub-Warehousekeeper and Deputy-Paymaster of the new Presidency government, on 28 December 1805 by the Chaplain, the Revd. Atwill Lake, the witnesses to the marriage being Raffles and William Dick, Surgeon on the Prince of Wales Island establishment. Mary Anne had three children by Quintin Dick Thompson: Acheson Quintin Dick Thompson, who was born on 22 October 1806, Charlotte Raffles Drury Thompson, who was born on 2 May 1808, and William O'Bryen Drury Thompson, who was born on 29 May 1809 and died shortly afterwards (Chapter Five, note 31). An interesting account of Mary Anne and Quintin Dick's young family at Penang is contained in *The Marquesan Journal of Edward Robarts 1797–1824*, (ed.) G. Dening (Canberra, 1974), pp. 12, 200–5. After Thomson's death on 29 June 1809, at the age of 26, Mary Anne married at Melaka on 2 May 1811 William Lawrence Flint, son of a Scottish landowner of Clackmannan, and a Post Captain in the Royal Navy commanding the ship *Teignmouth*. She was described at this time by the Governor-General Lord Minto as 'a very pretty woman' and as a 'beauty'. Following the British conquest of Java she and her husband lived at Semarang, but because of disputes about his position as Prize Agent of the East India Company, and his requirement as a Post Captain to report to the Admiralty, she left Java with him in October 1813 for England, together with their first child, Stamford Raffles Charles Flint (born at Semarang on 16 September 1812), and her sister Harriot, aboard the *Lord Eldon* (Jacob Cowles). Flint returned to Java on the *Isabella* in 1815, but Mary Anne remained with her mother at Hampstead, where her son Stamford died on 7 April 1816. After the arrival of Raffles from Java in July 1816, she went to live with him at No. 3 The Crescent, Cheltenham, and later at No. 23 Berners Street, London. She accompanied him and Lady Raffles on a tour of the Continent during June and July 1817 but she was still without her husband when

she went to Portsmouth to see them off for west Sumatra on the ship *Lady Raffles* (H. Auber). On her return to London she stayed at No. 16 Kensington Square, London, with the family of Major John Torriano (1751–1825) of the Bombay Artillery, whose eldest daughter, Eliza Ella Torriano, had been her companion on the tour of the Continent. (In 1818 Eliza married Gerard De Visme of Bryanston Street, Portman Square, London, who was appointed an executor of Raffles's Will, and in 1826 her sister Jane Charlotte Torriano married Lady Raffles's brother William Hollamby Hull (Chapter Six, note 11).) Later, Mary Anne was invited to visit the Duke and Duchess of Somerset. When her husband Captain Flint returned to England in 1818, they dined with Raffles's friend Captain David Macdonald of the Indian Navy (Chapter Five, note 36) and met another of Raffles's friends, the Irish poet Thomas Moore, who found the evening 'very dull' (W.S. Dowden (ed.), *The Journal of Thomas Moore* (Newark, 1983), vol. I, p. 77). The Flints left England for India on 25 July 1819 with their son William Charles Raffles Flint (who had been born at Cheltenham on 31 March 1819) aboard the private ship *Rochester* (D. Sutton) and arrived at Calcutta on 21 December, where they were met by Raffles and taken by him to Bengkulu aboard the *Indiana* (James Pearl). Flint went on to Java to settle matters relating to the Serondol estate, but Mary Anne remained at Bengkulu until September 1820, when she left to join her husband at Singapore after he had arrived there on 23 April 1820 to take up the post of Master Attendant. They lived in Singapore during the next eight years, until in September 1828, in an attempt to recover his health, Flint sailed in the East Indiaman *William Fairlie* (Thomas Blair) for China. He died on board ship on 3 October from dysentery, leaving his wife practically destitute. Lady Raffles reported Mary Anne's return to England in a letter to the Revd. Dr. Thomas Raffles dated 6 June 1829: 'Poor Marianne has been confined to her room ever since her arrival, her situation is pitiable – & her prospects as to this World very sad – Captain Flint has died without leaving Will – paper or Me$^m$. of any kind so you may imagine the difficulty of realising the property he has left [in Singapore] at such a distance from this country – ' (Bastin, *Letters and Books of Sir Stamford Raffles*, pp. 328, 402–3). The returns on this property were meagre and she was obliged to live at Blois in France with her daughter Sophia, who had been born at Singapore in March 1823. In 1836 she returned to Cheltenham, where she was visited in May of that year by Raffles's former aide-de-camp, Captain Thomas Otho Travers, and they passed some hours together 'recalling to our minds old times and old friends amongst whom time had brought about many and sad changes' (MS. Journal, May 1836). She died at Cheltenham of 'natural decay' on 29 September 1837, and was buried on 7 October in the same vault as Lady Raffles's mother, Sophia Hull, and sister Emily Dorothy Hull, who had died at Prestbury on 1 October 1837. Lady Raffles described Mary Anne accurately as 'one of those gentle spirits that bends to all circumstances'.

[6] Ann Raffles, the second to be named after her mother in Captain Raffles's family, following the death of the first in 1780, was born on 9 April and baptised on 12 May 1793 at St. Mary's Church Lambeth. She was a difficult child and lived with her mother until the latter's death on 8 February 1824 when she went to stay at Edinburgh

with her cousin Mary Anne Wise, daughter of the Revd. John Lindeman, and wife of the surgeon Richard Wise (Chapter Two, note 28). Raffles wrote to his sister Mary Anne Flint in Singapore on 21 December 1824: 'Ann is well and in Scotland with her cousin M[rs]. Wyse – I have given her an allowance of £150 p[er] annum which I hope will enable her to have every comfort' (BL:MSS.Eur.D. 742/17). He wrote to her again on 25 May 1825: 'I am sorry to inform you of the death of our poor Sister Anne – She died at Edinburgh on the 23[d] – where she was remaining with her cousins M[r]. & M[rs]. Wise – She had rapidly declined for the last month or two and died of a confirmed consumption – Thank god, she had the best advice, and was surrounded by friends, so that the last moments were rendered as easy as circumstances admitted' (BL:MSS.Eur.D.741/17). Lady Raffles wrote to Mary Anne Flint on 25 June 1825: 'Anne's death you will have heard of from M[rs]. Simes & Tom – poor thing[,] it seems to have been a mercy to herself & all those connected with her, for her weaknesses & waywardness encreased every day till at last they were by all accounts beyond endurance – Simes' were her best friends throughout' (BL:MSS.Eur.D.742/15). Ann Raffles left £440.8s.11d. in her Will, which was the subject of dispute as she left £400 to her cousin Susan Covey (née Lindeman), sister of Mary Anne Wise, the expected beneficiary (Chapter Two, note 28). A letter of Mary Anne Wise to Lady Raffles dated 10 December 1830 is in BL:MSS.Eur.D.742/18, together with two letters to her from Richard Wise in BL:MSS.Eur.D.742/9 and BL:MSS.Eur.D.742/18.

[7] Nathaniel Phillips Diaries, Slebech Papers, Diaries, item 9404, image 162 (courtesy of Microform Academic Publishers and the National Library of Wales). Captain Raffles under the designation of 'Mariner' is recorded earlier, on 14 November 1767, as living in St. Ann's, Blackfriars, London, probably at his father's house, but at the time of his marriage on 21 November 1776 he was a resident in the parish of St. Botolph, Aldgate, London.

[8] Mansion House Boarding School was situated at the west end of King Street, Hammersmith, and when Raffles became a pupil at the school around 1793 it was under the charge of the Headmaster, Dr. James Anderson. (See Thomas Faulkner, *The History and Antiquities of the Parish of Hammersmith, Interspersed with Biographical Notices of Illustrious and Eminent Persons, who have been born, or who have resided in the Parish, during the Three Preceding Centuries* (London, 1839), pp. 261–2.) His contemporary at the school was Richard Wynter (Chapter Two, note 15) and a copy of his school fees, paid by his father Nathaniel Phillips, is in NLWC: Slebech Papers, Accounts, item 5377, image 59 (courtesy of Microform Academic Publishers and the National Library of Wales). These fees would have been similar to those paid by Captain Raffles for his son before he was withdrawn from the school.

[9] The London *Daily Advertiser* of 15 November 1796 printed a notice of sale of a freehold property in Mitcham 'in the Possession of Mr. Raffles', consisting of 'Garden-Ground, with a Mefluage, Barn, Stable, Cart Lodge, Farm-Yard, Still-House, and several large Pieces of rich land, in the Mitcham Common Fields, in the Whole about

18 Acres'. This 'Mr. Raffles' seems to have had no connection with Benjamin Raffles's family.

[10] Raffles to the Revd. Dr. Thomas Raffles, 14 October 1819, Private collection.

[11] Ibid. The difficulties facing Ann Raffles in 1811 were increased by her being involved in a series of Chancery Court cases in that and succeeding years arising from her administration of the Will of her half-sister, Mary Cole of Chelsea, Middlesex, which was proved on 17 October 1799. See 1811 Biging v Lyde; 1812 Biging v Raffles, and 1816 Raffles v Lyde (National Archives, Kew: C 13/2103/11; C 13/2108/21 and C 13/2502/57). In Biging v Raffles *The London Gazette* on 1 July 1815 reported that Ann Raffles had lost the case.

[12] Lamb to Sothey, 27 December 1798, E.V. Lucas (ed.), *The Letters of Charles Lamb* (London, 1935), vol. I, p. 144.

[13] Bastin, *Letters and Books of Sir Stamford Raffles*, pp. 25–6.

[14] Ibid., p. 23.

[15] Land Tax Records, Surrey History Centre, Woking, Surrey.

[16] Boulger, *Life of Sir Stamford Raffles*, p. 11.

[17] *The Picture of London, for 1802; being a Correct Guide to All the Curiosities, Amusements, Exhibitions, Public Establishments, and remarkable Objects, in and near London; With a Collection of Appropriate Tables. For the Use of Strangers, Foreigners, and all Persons who are not Intimately Acquainted with the British Metropolis* (London, 1802), pp. 118–9.

[18] Handwritten words in Captain Raffles's Petition are underlined. It is interesting that in his Petition he refers to the *Lord Rodney* as the last ship he commanded when, in fact, he was later master of the *Catherine* and the *Uxbridge*. But the *Lord Rodney* was clearly a special ship, built at Wells's yard on the Thames on a new construction with all her 34 guns on one deck and the figure of Lord Rodney carved at her head and the words 'Jamaica preserved' and 'Valour rewarded' inscribed on her sides.

[19] Chapter Four, note 40.

[20] Bastin, *Letters and Books of Sir Stamford Raffles*, pp. 38, 71, note 24.

[21] In a letter to his uncle William Raffles, written from Java on 29 October 1812, Raffles expressed his thanks for the assistance he had given his mother on the occasion: 'My Mother informs me that she is much indebted to you for your kind attention to her in the hour of trouble and at the time of my poor father's death, and I should not

do justice to my feelings did I not avail myself of the earliest opportunity to express my acknowledgements' (Bastin, *Letters and Books of Sir Stamford Raffles*, p. 194).

## CHAPTER FOUR
### *Sir Stamford Raffles's First Wife: Olivia Mariamne Devenish*

[1] Robert J. Devenish and Charles H. McLaughlin, *Historical and Genealogical Records of the Devenish Families of England and Ireland* (Chicago, 1948), pp. 286–9; Wurtzburg, *Raffles of the Eastern Isles*, Appendix I, 'Olivia Mariamne Raffles', pp. 744–6.

[2] Castle Dana is usually given as her place of birth but this must be in error for Casheltauna, Four Mile House, Roscommon Town, County of Roscommon.

[3] Olivia Raffles to John Leyden, 3 August 1808, NLS:MSS 971, fol. 55r.

[4] V.C.P. Hodson, *List of the Officers of the Bengal Army 1758–1834* (London, 1928), vol. II, p. 52.

[5] Charlotte Louisa Hawkins Dempster to Maud Raffles, 1909, Private collection.

[6] The *Rose* was a three-deck East Indiaman of 801 or 810 tons built at the Wells shipyard at Rotherhithe on the Thames in 1786. She sailed from the Downs on 21 February 1787 and arrived at Madras on 2 June 1787. Charlotte Louisa Hawkins Dempster in her letter to Maud Raffles in 1909 states that Olivia joined the ship at Youghal in southern Ireland, but this detail is certainly incorrect.

[7] John Hamilton Dempster was the son of John Dempster of Dunnichen, who died on 2 November 1754, and his second wife [Margaret] Stewart (née Hamilton), whom he married on 13 November 1740 and who died at Dundee on 27 January 1780. For details of his life, see John Evans, *The Gentleman Usher: The Life and Times of George Dempster (1732–1818) Member of Parliament and Laird of Dunnichen and Skibo* (Barnsley, 2005).

[8] Evans, *The Gentleman Usher*, passim.

[9] Ibid., pp. 153–4.

[10] Charlotte Louisa Hawkins Dempster to Maud Raffles, 1909, Private collection. Harriet was known before her marriage as Harriet Milton, the last name being formed from the last six letters of her father's middle name, Hamilton. Charlotte Louisa Hawkins Dempster in her posthumously published autobiography, *The Manners of My Time* (London, 1920), affirms that Harriet Soper Dempster's mother was 'Olivia Marianne [*sic*] Devenish of Castle Dana, Co. Roscommon, a young lady whose

extraction was partly Irish and partly Circassian, and whose beauty finally secured for her, in 1803 [*sic*], a union with Mr Stamford Raffles'. This statement, and a similar one in her letter to Maud Raffles in 1909, establishes Charlotte Louisa Hawkins Dempster as the sole source of the story that Harriet was the illegitimate child of John Hamilton Dempster and Olivia Mariamne Devenish. She was also the sole source of the connected story, contained in her letter of 1909, that the child was the result of Olivia's relationship with Dempster on board the *Rose* during the voyage of the ship to India. Evans in his book *The Gentleman Usher* accepts the fact that Olivia and Dempster were Harriet's parents (pp. 152–3) but proposes an alternative theory that their intimacy occurred early in 1785 when Dempster's ship *Ganges* was in Cork harbour undergoing temporary repairs and when, one may add, Olivia was only 14 years old. Apart from some highly speculative remarks about how the news of this liaison and the birth of Harriet was viewed by Dempster's own family, and the family of his erstwhile bride, Jean Fergusson ('the Fergusson and Dempster families found this a difficult period and were at pains to avoid scandal and to arrange matters with as much discretion as could be mustered', p. 153), there is no contemporary evidence to support his account of an illicit connection between Dempster and Olivia occurring in Ireland at this time. It seems that Evans has been drawn to his theory because of a calculation of Harriet's age and date of birth based on a former tablet erected in her memory at Ashburton Church, Cornwall, which, he says, 'recorded that she was 25 when she died in October 1810 – hence the 1785 date of birth' (p. 356, note 69). Harriet Dempster died at Ashburton on 16 October 1810 (not 17 October, as stated by Evans) 'of a lingering illness, which she bore with all the calmness of pious resignation'. She died on a visit with her husband to his town of Ashburton, and was buried seven days after her death, so that in all likelihood he was the one responsible for erecting the memorial tablet and recording her incorrect age, as occurred on a similar occasion when Anne Brontë died away from home at Scarborough in Yorkshire in 1849 and five errors were made in the inscription on her gravestone (Juliet Barker, *The Brontës*, London, 1995, p. 699). In any case, the Ashburton tablet was weathered, and the date of Harriet's age of 23 could easily have been misread as 25, which, on the basis of Evan's argument, would point to Harriet being conceived on board the *Rose* in 1787 and born at Madras later that year. There is, however, an overriding argument in favour of the liaison having occurred between Olivia and Dempster on board the *Rose* and that is the degree of authority of Charlotte Louisa Hawkins Dempster's testimony. She was, after all, Harriet's granddaughter, and her testimony rests, as she declared in her letter to Maud Raffles in 1909, on the 'report … among her Dempster grandchildren & their servants' at Skibo, where she herself was among those growing up there during the 1830s and 1840s. If one accepts the first part of her account that Olivia and Dempster were the parents of Harriet, then the second part of her account, that their affair occurred on board ship, has to be accepted since there is no other contemporary evidence, or authoritative source, to contradict it.

[11] Charlotte Louisa Hawkins Dempster to Maud Raffles, 1909, Private collection.

[12] For details of the loss of the *Earl Talbot*, see *Bombay Courier*, 3 January 1801; Evans, *The Gentleman Usher*, pp. 264–6.

[13] Register of Weddings in Bombay between 1 January and 22 March, inclusive: January 17, 1806, Chaplain A. Burrows.

[14] *London Gazette*, 28 July 1803. Harriet returned from India with her husband on board the 818-ton East Indiaman *Earl St. Vincent* (John Brook Sampson). The ship arrived in London on 1 June 1803 so Soper's application for a Royal Licence to change his name was made shortly after his arrival.

[15] F.E.P., Reprinted from *The Genealogist*, vols. xix-xxiii (n.s.): *Marriages at Fort St. George Madras* (Exeter, 1907), p. 46: 1793: 'May 26. Jacob Cassivelaun Fancourt, Esq., & Miss Olivia Devonish' [*sic*].

[16] The *Pitt* was built in 1780 on the Thames for George Mackenzie Macaulay, an alderman of the City of London, and was the first regular East Indiaman engaged to carry convicts to Australia. After embarking some 344 male and 58 female convicts in England, the ship arrived at Sydney in February 1792 and then sailed for India, where she was taken up by the East India Company to carry freight to England, sailing from Diamond Harbour in March 1793 and arriving off the Downs on 7 August. She was back in the direct India trade in the 1794–5 season with Edward Manning continuing as commander, but he was replaced by John Gerrard for the season of 1796–8. See Charles Bateson, *The Convict Ships 1787–1868* (Glasgow, 1969), pp. 139–45.

[17] Robert Hobart, Baron Hobart, 4th Earl of Buckinghamshire (1760–1816), Governor of Madras (1794–1798), was recalled because of differences with the Governor-General, Sir John Shore, 1st Baron Teignmouth (1751–1834). He was Secretary for War and the Colonies between 1801 and 1804, and President of the India Board of Control during 1812–16 when Raffles was Lieutenant-Governor of Java.

[18] It is interesting, in perhaps giving a picture of Anglo-Indian military life at this time, that the young Charles Edward Clayton (1788–1808) returned to Calcutta as an Ensign on 10 December 1805 and was subsequently posted as Lieutenant to the 17th Bengal Native Infantry on 19 February 1806. He was drowned on 8 September 1808 while attempting to cross the Jumna River. His sister, Emma Maria, who was born on 20 May 1791, also returned to India, and was married at Dinapore in August 1810 to Lieutenant (later Captain) George Barker (1786–1819), of the 12th Bengal Native Infantry, who died at Muttra on 13 July 1819. She died in 1820–21.

[19] *The London Gazette*, 1 October 1796.

[20] Old Bailey Proceedings online (www.oldbaileyonline.org, version 7.0, 15 January 2015), December 1798, trial of MARY GORING (t17981205-4).

[21] Peter H. Marshall, *William Godwin* (Yale University Press, New Haven, 1984).

[22] Ibid., pp. 189–90.

[23] *The Diary of William Godwin*, (eds) Victoria Myers, David O'Shaughnessy and Mark Philp (Oxford: Oxford Digital Library, 2010), http://godwindiary.bodleian.ox.ac.uk: 1 December 1798: 'Dine at Chandler's: Tea w. him, at O Fancourt's'; 4 December 1798: 'Sup at O Fancourt's w. Chandler'; 9 December 1798: 'tea O Fancourt's, w. Chandler'; 21 December 1798: 'tea O Fancourt's, read'; 26 December 1798: 'Dine at O Fancourt's, w. Chandler & C Bence'; 27 December 1798: 'tea O Fancourt's, adv. [ise?] Chandler; 18 January 1799: 'Call on Chandler[n] [not at home?] & O Fancourt'; 19 January 1799: 'Smith, Northcote, Chandler & O Fancourt dine'; 31 January 1799: 'M[rs]. F. affirms, that the subjects of the Mahometan princes in India are all Moors, & the subjects of the Hindoo princes all Hindoos'; 1 February 1799: 'dine at Fancourt's, with Mrs Vardon, C Bence, Hodson & Chandler'; 22 June 1799: 'Chandler dines: tea O Fancourt's, w. him & Mrs Delany: meet Macquin: Circus, the Seasons, w. C[handler] & O F[ancourt]'; 10 September 1799: 'Chandler calls; dine with him at O Fancourt's'; 14 September 1799: 'dine at West End, w. Chandler & O Fancourt'; 11 December 1799: 'call on Chandler[n] [not at home?], O Fancourt'; 24 December 1799: 'call on O Fanc[t] na' [not at home?]; 26 December 1799: 'dine at O Fancourt's, w. Chandler'; 1 January 1800: 'Dine at O Fancourt's, w. Northcote, M[c] Quin, Chandler, Litchfied, & Hutchinson & Mrs Gurney'; 6 January 1800: 'dine at Fancourt's, w. Northcote, Macquin & Chandler'; 11 May 1802: 'Call on O Fancourt'.

[24] Abbé Ange Denis MacQuin was born at Meaux, where he was subsequently Professor of Belles-Lettres. He arrived in England in 1792 and in the following year was appointed heraldic draughtsman to the College of Arms. He published various miscellaneous works, including a number on heraldry, on which subject he was well informed. Godwin records in his Diary that he had already met MacQuin before the meeting at Olivia's on 22 June 1799.

[25] James Northcote was born at Plymouth on 2 October 1746 and was assisted in becoming a painter by the Devonshire family of the divine Dr. Zachariah Mudge (1694–1769), who had connections with the family of Sir Joshua Reynolds (1723–1792). In 1771 Northcote gained entry to Reynold's studio in London, where he served for five years, exhibiting at the Royal Academy and becoming a R.A. in 1787. He was residing at No. 39 Argyle Street, London, when he became acquainted with Olivia Fancourt in 1799. Shortly afterwards, in 1802, he met the essayist and art critic, William Hazlitt (1778–1830), who published his *Conversations of James Northcote, R.A.* in book form in 1830. Sir Joshua Reynolds and Dr. Zachariah Mudge were frequently mentioned in these conversations, and Olivia possibly heard from Northcote of the Devonshire family of the Mudges with whom Raffles's second wife Sophia Hull later became connected through the marriage of her younger sister Alice Watson Hull (1787–1862) with Lieutenant-Colonel Richard Zachariah Mudge (1790–1854) (Chapter Six, note 4).

[26] Chandler to Godwin, 18 January [1800], Bodleian Library, Oxford: Abinger Collection Shelfmark MS. Abinger c.5, fols. 64–5.

[27] Chandler to Godwin, 20 January 1800, Bodleian Library, Oxford: Abinger Collection Shelfmark MS Abinger C 5, fol. 68. The reference to Aspasia in this connection is particularly flattering to Olivia as Aspasia was celebrated in Athens for her genius and beauty, and was so noted for her eloquence and knowledge of politics that Socrates took lessons from her. On Henry Fuseli, see Franziska Lentzsch, et al., *Füssli: The Wild Swiss* (Zürich, 2005).

[28] In 1800 Chandler's *Sir Hubert, An Heroic Ballad* was published in octavo format in London at 7s.6d.; printed by J. Bonsor, Salisbury Square; and sold by Messrs. J. and E. Kerby, Bond Street; Vernor and Hood, Poultry; and Lackington, Allen, and Co., Finsbury Square. In November 1805 the *Staffordshire Advertiser* also published 'A New Song' by Chandler, to be sung to the tune of *Rule Britannia*, the words, it must be said, hardly improving on the original: 'When lawless pow'r the sceptre won, / To scourge for Heav'n a guilty land, / The Tyrant trembled on his Throne, / While Britons sung Great Jove's command. / Rule Britannia! rule the Sea / For Britons still are great and free.'

[29] The hill fort at Rayakottai was of great strategic importance during the Mysore Wars. It had been ceded to the British in 1792 and General Harris's army encamped under its walls in 1799 during its march on Seringapatam. The subject is represented in an oil painting on canvas by Thomas Daniell, 'View of Ryacotta Fort, South India', and also as Plate 12 in Series Three of Thomas and William Daniell's *Oriental Scenery* (London, 1795–1808).

[30] Marshall, *Godwin*, pp. 249–50.

[31] Godwin seems to have met Moore on 8 January 1802 and dined with him on the following day.

[32] W.S. Dowden (ed.), *The Letters of Thomas Moore* (Oxford, 1964), vol. I, p. 30.

[33] Ibid., vol. 1, p. 35.

[34] *The Morning Post*, 3 June 1802.

[35] Boulger, *Life of Sir Stamford Raffles*, p. 14.

[36] A.H. Hill (ed.), 'The Hikayat of Munshi Abdullah', *JMBRAS*, vol. XXVIII, pt. 3 (1955), pp. 72–3.

[37] Raffles to the Revd. Dr. Thomas Raffles, 'At Sea 14th October 1819', Private collection; Boulger, *Life of Sir Stamford Raffles*, p. 22.

[38] Olivia Raffles to John Leyden, 3 August 1808, NLS:MS 971, fol. 55v.

[39] On Charles Hamond, see Chapter Two, note 27.

[40] Raffles to William Raffles, 24 February 1809 (Bastin, *Letters and Books of Sir Stamford Raffles*, p. 192; see also p. 34, note 56). Richard Stephens Taylor was an attorney at Field Court, Gray's Inn, in the County of Middlesex. He appeared as an attorney in an Old Bailey case in 1803, and he was obviously used to handling money matters as he advertised as possessing funds for mortgage investments. He married Sophia Shepcutt, also at St. George's Church, Bloomsbury, on 4 July 1807. He died in 1822 aged 52.

[41] Boulger, *Life of Sir Stamford Raffles*, p. 16; Wurtzburg, *Raffles of the Eastern Isles*, p. 746; Bastin, *Letters and Books of Sir Stamford Raffles*, p. 29.

[42] Andrew Plimer resided first at No. 3 Golden Square and at No. 8 from 1797 until 1806, in which year he went to live in the country, his household furniture and other effects, including 'a small collection of Paintings and Drawings', being sold at his house in Golden Square.

[43] George Williamson, *Andrew & Nathaniel Plimer* (London, 1903), App. VII, p. 133: 'Two Ladies and a Gentleman, members of the family of Dempster of Skibo and Dunnichen, but names unknown'. See Evans, *The Gentleman Usher*, p. 381, note 8. If Harriet had travelled to London from Scotland in March or April 1805 to see Olivia before she left England she would have been four months pregnant and might possibly have been accompanied by her one-year-old son, George Soper Dempster, who had been born on 26 February 1804. This would have been a burdensome journey for her and it might therefore be the case that her miniature portrait and that of her mother were painted by Andrew Plimer when she arrived in England from India aboard the *Earl St. Vincent* in June 1803.

[44] Ibid.; Evans, *The Gentleman Usher*, p. 281.

[45] The latest attribution to Andrew Plimer is given in Christie's Catalogue describing the miniature portrait of Harriet sold on 2 June 2009 as part of the Dr. William Lindsay Gordon Collection. The Catalogue gives the provenance of the miniature as Mrs. D. Salt, Christie's, London, 27 February 1968, lot 84, and the Alvin J. Huss Collection, Sotheby's, London, 4 December 1985, lot 113, with references to D. Foskett, *Collecting Miniatures* (Woodbridge, 1979), illustrated p. 382, pl. 1120C; and D. Foskett, *Miniatures: Dictionary and Guide* (Woodbridge, 1987), illustrated p. 382, pl. 110C. Further confirmation of the miniature being by Andrew Plimer is the number *83* below the image, conforming to his system of numbering his miniatures.

[46] Graham Reynolds, *English Portrait Miniatures* (London, 1952), p. 178.

[47] C. Northcote Parkinson, *War in the Eastern Seas 1793–1815* (London, 1954), pp. 221–35.

[48] Ibid., pp. 269–71; C. Northcote Parkinson, *Edward Pellew: Viscount Exmouth Admiral of the Red* (London, 1934), pp. 338–9.

[49] Troubridge wrote to Lord Sidmouth three days after the action: 'Blenheim at Sea, Aug 10th 1805': 'I fancy he thought we were all Indiamen, for the moment he made the *Blenheim* out through the Haze, he bore away, and without separating from my valuable charges it was impossible to pursue him …' He added, in the British naval spirit of the age: 'I trust I shall yet have the good fortune to fall in with him when unencumber'd with Convoy, and the Contest I think will be short, to see him and not be able to bring him to close Action has fretted me much, for if I had one wish more particular than another, it was to fight Mr. Linois …' (Parkinson, *Edward Pellew*, p. 339).

[50] Raffles subsequently claimed reimbursement for the costs due to the diversion of the *Ganges* to Calcutta (Marcus Langdon, *Penang: The Fourth Presidency of India 1805–1830* (Penang, 2013), p. 238, note 133).

[51] Ibid., p. 238.

# CHAPTER FIVE
## *Olivia Mariamne Raffles in Penang, Melaka and Java*

[1] Leyden to Ballantyne, 24 October 1805, Sir Walter Scott, 'Biographical Memoir of John Leyden, M.D.', *The Edinburgh Annual Register, for 1811*, vol. IV, pt. 2 (1813), p. lx.

[2] Raffles to William Erskine, 10 September 1815, NLS:MS 971, fols. 146–153v; John Bastin, *John Leyden and Thomas Stamford Raffles* (Eastbourne, 2006), p. 70.

[3] Bastin, *John Leyden and Thomas Stamford Raffles*, p. 18.

[4] T.S. Raffles, 'On the Maláyu Nation, with a translation of its Maritime Institutions', *Asiatick Researches*, vol. XII (1812), pp. 102–58.

[5] Lord Minto to Lady Minto, 25 February 1811, The Countess of Minto, *Lord Minto in India: Life and Letters of Gilbert Elliot, First Earl of Minto from 1807 to 1814 while Governor-General of India* (London, 1880), p. 254.

[6] Scott, *Edinburgh Annual Register, for 1811*, vol. IV, pt. 2 (1813), p. xlix.

[7] Olivia Raffles to Leyden, 3 August 1808, NLS:MS 971, fol. 55r.

[8] Leyden to Olivia Raffles, 7 January 1806, Boulger, *Life of Sir Stamford Raffles*, pp. 19–21.

[9] Leyden to Olivia Raffles, 6 March 1806, NLS:MS 971, fol. 42v.

[10] Raffles to Leyden, 24 May 1806, BL:MSS.Eur.D.29, fol. 121; Bastin, *John Leyden and Thomas Stamford Raffles*, p. 41.

[11] Boulger, *Life of Sir Stamford Raffles*, p. 76.

[12] Olivia Raffles to Leyden, 3 August 1808, NLS:MS 971, fols. 55r–56v.

[13] John Dickens was appointed judge and advocate at Prince of Wales Island in April 1801 and assumed his judicial duties in August of that year. See Bastin, *John Leyden and Thomas Stamford Raffles*, p. 101, note 96; Wurtzburg, *Raffles of the Eastern Isles*, pp. 63–4.

[14] Sir Edmond Stanley, first Recorder of Prince of Wales Island, where he arrived on 2 April 1808. See Wurtzburg, *Raffles of the Eastern Isles*, p. 63.

[15] Charlotte Raffles Drury Thompson was born three months earlier, on 2 May 1808. See Chapter Three, note 5; Chapter Five, note 31.

[16] Leyden to Olivia Raffles, September/October 1808, NLS:MS 971, fol. 87.

[17] Leyden to Olivia Raffles, December 1805, NLS:MS 971, fols. 111r–111v. A variant version is printed in the Revd. James Morton, *The Poetical Remains of the Late Dr. John Leyden, with Memoirs of His Life* (London, 1819), pp. 168–9.

[18] Lord Minto to Lady Minto, 31 May 1811, Countess of Minto, *Lord Minto in India*, p. 265.

[19] Anon., *United Services Journal* (January 1836), cited Wurtzburg, *Raffles of the Eastern Isles*, p. 65.

[20] The book is in a Private collection.

[21] Raffles to the Revd. Dr. Thomas Raffles, 16 January 1817, Bastin, *Letters and Books of Sir Stamford Raffles*, p. 106.

[22] W.S. Dowden (ed.), *The Journal of Thomas Moore* (Newark, 1983), vol. I, p. 146.

[23] Ibid., vol. II, p. 772.

[24] Olivia Raffles to Leyden, 3 August 1808, NLS:MS 971, fol. 56v; Wurtzburg, *Raffles of the Eastern Isles*, p. 66.

[25] Bastin, *John Leyden and Thomas Stamford Raffles*, p. 106, note 126.

[26] Wurtzburg, *Raffles of the Eastern Isles*, p. 85.

[27] Ibid., pp. 85–6.

[28] John and Christopher Bastin, 'Some Old Penang Tombstones', *JMBRAS*, vol. XXXVII, pt. 1 (1954), p. 161; Alan Harfield, *Christian Cemeteries of Penang & Perak* (London, 1987), pp. 129–30, 163.

[29] Raffles to Baron McClelland, 1 March 1810, BL:MSS.Eur.D.742/21.

[30] Raffles to Quintin Dick, 19 August 1809, 25 August 1809, Sotheby's London Bibliotheca Phillippica sale, 29 June 1965, lot 233. The second letter was subsequently re-sold as lot 13 in Sotheby's sale of English Literature on 17 December 2009.

[31] Acheson Quintin Dick Thompson, who was born on 22 October 1806, married on 21 September 1837 Isabella Madden, eldest daughter of the Revd. Michael Dodgson Madden, Chancellor of St. Canice, County Kilkenny, and by her had three sons and one daughter. He inherited Annaverna on the death of Baron McClelland in 1831 and he died at Kaukapakapa, Auckland, New Zealand, on 14 January 1883, his wife having died in London on 9 July 1875, aged 71. Charlotte Raffles Drury Thompson was born on 2 May 1808 and married on 24 March 1835 the Hon. Charles Andrew Knox Stuart, second son of 2nd Earl Castle Stewart. He was born on 23 April 1810 and succeeded his brother Edward to become 4th Earl Castle Stewart on 20 February 1857, his only son, Henry James, succeeding as the 5th Earl Castle Stewart on his death on 12 September 1874. Charlotte Raffles Drury Thompson died at Torquay on 1 February 1906, the last family member to have known Raffles alive. Raffles and Lady Raffles met Baron McClelland and his wife in London in 1824 and Raffles reported on the two children to their mother, Mary Anne Flint in Singapore, in a letter dated 6 October 1824: 'Acheson is one of the finest handsomest & elegant young men I every met with – tall & in the face the image of his father & Mother – of the former more particular[ly] – he has a beautiful complexion – fine Teeth and his hair of a fine shade – he has now been two years at College and it soon will be determined whether he is to be a Lawyer or a Parson – … Charlotte is every thing you could wish but by no means so handsome as Acheson – She is more like what Leonora was … that is to say she has more of the Raffles face than any other – but she is nevertheless very good l[oo] king – very well bred – most affectionate & in short quite captivating – Even the Baron talks of the probability of her marrying in a year or two.' (BL:MSS.Eur.D.742/17). In a letter of condolence to Lady Raffles on the death of Raffles dated Anaverna 22 July 1826, Charlotte Thompson wrote: 'In the late sad event I feel the loss of one who if I had required his protection would not have withheld it' (BL:MSS.Eur.D.742/9).

[32] Boulger, *Life of Sir Stamford Raffles*, pp. 88–9.

[33] As well as Raffles, there also regularly gathered at Leyden's house in Calcutta in 1810 John Adam, Secretary of the Military Department of the Supreme Government, and the Chinese scholar Thomas Manning (1772–1840), where philological and theological subjects were discussed (*Asiatic Journal*, vol. XXXIII, n.s. (1840), p. 183; J.C. Marshman, *Life and Times of Carey, Marshman, and Ward embracing the History of the Serampore Mission* (London, 1859), vol. I, pp. 437–8). Manning and Raffles became close friends in Calcutta in 1810, Leyden referring in a contemporary undated letter to Manning to 'your Chum T. Raffles' (NLS:MS 1809, f.45). Manning is remembered because of his friendship with the English essayist, Charles Lamb, who was a clerk in the Accountant's Office in the India House when Raffles was employed in the Secretary's Office. There is no evidence that Raffles was in any way associated with Lamb, but he would certainly have known about him and it may have been this tenuous link that formed the initial basis of his friendship with Manning in Calcutta.

[34] Leyden to Olivia Raffles, 22 August 1810, NLS:MS 971, fol. 73r.

[35] Leyden to Olivia Raffles, 22 October, 1810, NLS:MS 971, fol. 76r.

[36] D. Macdonald, *A Narrative of the Early Life and Services of Capt.ⁿ D. Macdonald, I.N.* (Weymouth, n.d.), pp. 65–6. On Macdonald, see Bastin, *John Leyden and Thomas Stamford Raffles*, p. 104, note 118, and p. 122.

[37] Bastin, *Letters and Books of Sir Stamford Raffles*, p. 73, note 47.

[38] Hill, *JMBRAS*, vol. XXVIII, pt. 3 (1955), pp. 77–8.

[39] Raffles to Leyden, 15 December 1810, BL:MSS.Eur.F.148/3, fol. 182r.

[40] On Captain William Lawrence Flint, see Chapter Three, note 5; C.A. Gibson-Hill, 'The Master Attendants at Singapore, 1819–67', *JMBRAS*, vol. XXXIII, pt. 1 (1960), pp. 16–32.

[41] Bastin, *John Leyden and Thomas Stamford Raffles*, pp. 109–10, note 142.

[42] On Captain Thomas Taylor, see ibid., p. 112, note 151.

[43] On Archibald Seton, see Langdon, *Penang: The Fourth Presidency of India*, pp. 274–7; Bastin, *John Leyden and Thomas Stamford Raffles*, pp. 104–5, note 120.

[44] Bastin, *John Leyden and Thomas Stamford Raffles*, p. 54.

[45] Lord Minto to Lady Minto, 31 May 1811, Countess of Minto, *Lord Minto in India*, pp. 264–5.

[46] Lord Minto to Miss Casamaijor, 24 May 1811, Private collection.

[47] Chapter Three, note 4.

[48] Chapter Three, note 3.

[49] William Thorn, *Memoir of the Conquest of Java; with the subsequent Operations of the British Forces in the Oriental Archipelago* (London, 1815), pp. 6–11.

[50] C.E. Wurtzburg, 'Who Planned the Sea Route of the Java Expedition in 1811?', *The Mariner's Mirror*, vol. 37, no. 2 (April 1951), pp. 104–8.

[51] Thorn, *Memoir of the Conquest of Java*, pp. 41–79.

[52] Bastin, *John Leyden and Thomas Stamford Raffles*, pp. 61–3.

[53] Bastin, *Olivia Mariamne Raffles*, pp. 86–9.

[54] BL:MSS.Eur.F.148/30, fols. 69r–70v. Lord Minto replied to this letter briefly in April 1812, declaring, somewhat ungraciously, that the Madurese musical instrument she had sent him had arrived in a damaged state. These were the only letters that passed between them, and, indeed, her letter to him is one of only two extant letters of hers, the other one being her letter to Leyden dated 3 August 1808 (NLS:MS 971, fols. 55r–56v).

[55] Archer and Bastin, *The Raffles Drawings*, pp. 70–1.

[56] Raffles to William Brown Ramsay, 21 October 1812, BL:MSS.Eur.D.742/20.

[57] Bastin, *Olivia Mariamne Raffles*, p. 97.

[58] *Java Government Gazette*, 18 April 1812.

[59] Bastin, *Olivia Mariamne Raffles*, pp. 101, 104.

[60] *Java Government Gazette*, 12 September 1812.

[61] Ibid., 2 January 1813.

[62] Ibid., 23 January 1813.

[63] Ibid., 20 February 1813.

[64] Chapter Three, note 4.

[65] *Java Government Gazette*, 12 June 1813.

66 Raffles to William Brown Ramsay, 30 June 1813, BL:MSS.Eur.D.742/20.

67 Same to same, 15 September 1813, ibid.

68 Same to same, 10 October 1813, ibid.

69 On Major-General Sir Miles Nightingall, see John Bastin, 'The Java Journal of Dr Joseph Arnold', *JMBRAS*, vol. XLVI, pt. 1 (1973), pp. 41–2, note 220; Bastin, *The Letters and Books of Sir Stamford Raffles*, p. 215, note 208.

70 *Java Government Gazette*, 11 December 1813.

71 Bastin, *Olivia Marianne Raffles*, pp. 111–127; *Java Government Gazette*, 18 December 1813, 25 December 1813.

72 *Java Government Gazette*, 19 February 1814.

73 Ibid.

74 On Florentia Elizabeth Nightingall, see Bastin, *JMBRAS*, vol. XLVI, pt. 1 (1973), p. 43, note 230. In a letter of condolence to Lady Raffles on the death of Raffles dated 18 September 1826, Lady Nightingall wrote: 'the loss of a being I so sincerely loved, & respected, there were very few for whom I had so great a regard & I have truly wept his loss' (BL:MSS.Eur.D.742/9).

75 Travers, *Journal*, p. 44.

76 *Java Government Gazette*, 26 March 1814; Travers, *Journal*, p. 47; Bastin, *JMBRAS*, vol. XLVI, pt. 1 (1973), p. 12, note 70.

77 *Java Government Gazette*, 2 April 1814.

78 Ibid., 11 June 1814.

79 Ibid. On the Java Auxiliary Bible Society, see Bastin, *Letters and Books of Sir Stamford Raffles*, p. 199, note 33.

80 *Java Government Gazette*, 11 June 1814.

81 *Java Government Gazette*, 16 July 1814.

82 Ibid., 30 July 1814.

83 Ibid.

84 Ibid., 20 August 1814.

85 Ibid., 27 August 1814.

86 Ibid.

87 *Java Government Gazette*, 1 October 1814.

88 Ibid., 15 October 1814.

89 Ibid., 22 October 1814.

90 Raffles to William Brown Ramsay, 6 March 1814, BL:MSS.Eur.D.742/20.

91 Apart from a brief statement in the *Java Government Gazette*, 3 December 1814.

92 Caroline Marie Currie, 23–28 November 1814, Private collection.

93 Raffles to William Erskine, 10 September 1815, NLS:MS 971, fol. 151.

94 Boulger, *Life of Sir Stamford Raffles*, p. 18.

## CHAPTER SIX
### *Sir Stamford Raffles's Second Wife: Sophia Hull*

1 Sophia Hull was born in Millman Street, London, on 5 May 1786, and baptised at St. Andrew's Church, Holborn.

2 James Watson Hull Sr. was born on 11 July 1758, the eldest son of Anthony Hull of Lisburn, County Antrim (d. 25 August 1795) by his first wife Alice Watson (d. 22 February 1767), daughter of James Watson of Brooke Hill, County Antrim, and sister of the celebrated Commodore John Watson, Superintendent of the Bombay Marine, who was killed during the siege of the Mahratta fort on the island of Salsette in 1774. James Watson Hull Sr. had 15 children by his wife Sophia (née Hollamby), who was born on 5 September 1762, the youngest of 21 children, one of whom was William Hollamby, Quartermaster on HMS *Discovery* during Captain James Cook's third voyage to the Pacific. She died at No. 12 Oriel Place, Cheltenham, on 10 March 1836. James Watson Hull Sr. died at Farquhar House, Hornsey Lane, Highgate, after a long illness on 5 April 1831 and was buried at St. George's Church Bloomsbury, where Raffles and his first wife, Olivia Mariamne Devenish, were married in 1805. James Watson Hull Sr.'s daughter Margaret Redman Hull, who died at Highgate on 4 June 1827, was also buried in the same church. Eleven of his 15 children are listed in the notes. His other four children were: (i) James Watson Hull, who was born at Bombay on 23 May 1785 and appointed Ensign in HM 43rd Regiment on 24 July 1800. He was promoted Lieutenant on 24 July 1802 and Captain on 11 June 1807. He distinguished himself in the Peninsular War at Vimiero in 1808 and was severely

wounded at the Battle of Coa (Corunna) on 24 July 1810. He retired from the army in May 1812, and after an unfortunate marriage, which led to his falling out with his father, he left for America, where he died in November 1824. (ii) Trevor Hull, who was born on 6 July 1793 at York and died on 14 February 1803 at Great Baddow, Essex. (iii) Mary Hollamby Hull, who was born on 1 July 1788 at Belvidere, County Down, and died at the same place on 1 December1789, and (iv) Maria Ann Hull, who was born on 18 September 1801 at Great Baddow, Essex, and died there four days later, on 22 September 1801.

[3] Mary Jane Hull was born 14 August 1795 at Petergate, York, and married Peter Auber, Assistant Secretary of the East India Company, on 4 December 1815 at Great Baddow, Essex. She died on 5 December 1873 at St. Helier's, Jersey.

[4] Alice Watson Hull was born on 22 June 1787 at Belvidere, County Down, and married Captain (later Lieutenant-Colonel) Richard Zachariah Mudge (b. 1790) of the Royal Engineers on 1 September 1817. She had two daughters by him, Sophia Elizabeth Mudge, who married the Revd. John R. Bogue, and Jenny Rosdew Mudge, who married the Revd. William Charles Raffles Flint, son of Mary Anne Flint (née Raffles), and who was the principal beneficiary of Lady Raffles's Will, inheriting 'High Wood' on her death in 1858. Lieutenant-Colonel Mudge died in September 1854 and his wife Alice Watson Hull in 1862. See Bastin, *Letters and Books of Sir Stamford Raffles*, p. 234, note 6; p. 410, note 117; p. 411, note 152.

[5] Margaret Redman Hull, who was born on 24 August 1794 at Petergate, York, and died unmarried on 4 June 1827 at her father's house in Highgate. Emily Dorothy Hull, who was born on 4 March 1800 at Great Baddow, Essex, and died unmarried on 1 October 1837 at St. Herbert's Cottage, Prestbury. She was buried in the same vault at Cheltenham as her mother, Sophia Hull.

[6] Elizabeth Mary Ann Hull was born on 17 August 1802 at Great Baddow, Essex, and married the Revd. Thomas Page, M.A. (Oxford), of St. Paul's Church Cheltenham, on 3 November 1834. He was later Minister of Christ Church, Virginia Water, where in 1843 he was the subject of an assassination attempt by an unknown assailant firing a shot through the parsonage window. He died as the incumbent of St. Matthew's Church Rugby, Warwickshire, on 5 November 1852. She died on 21 October 1887. For William Hollamby Hull, see Chapter Six, note 11; Edward Anthony Hull, Chapter Six, note 39; Robert Redmond Hull, Chapter Six, note 51; Lawrence Nilson Hull, Chapter Six, note 54; and John Watson Hull, Chapter Seven, note 69

[7] Raffles to the Revd. Thomas Raffles, 23 February 1817, Bastin, *Letters and Books of Sir Stamford Raffles*, p. 108.

[8] Travers, MS. Journal, February 1817, Private collection.

[9] Arnold to Dawson Turner, 9 July 1818, Bastin, *J. Soc. Biblphy nat. History*, vol. 6, pt. 5 (1973), p. 328.

[10] Revd. Thomas Raffles, *Letters, during a Tour through some parts of France, Savoy, Switzerland, Germany, and The Netherlands in the Summer of 1817* (Liverpool, 1818).

[11] William Hollamby Hull was born on 1 September 1790 at Belvidere, County Down, and entered the Royal Naval College on 23 May 1804. Three years later, on 3 June 1807, he was appointed Midshipman on HMS *Niobe* (John Wentworth Loring) and he saw action in this and other ships in the Mediterranean and Channel stations during the Napoleonic Wars. He was promoted Lieutenant on 1 June 1811 and was retired on half pay in May 1814. He toured the Continent with Raffles and his sister, Lady Raffles, in 1817, and accompanied them to west Sumatra aboard the *Lady Raffles* (H. Auber) later that year. He was appointed by Raffles, with W.H. Johnston R.N., to survey Teluk Kalumbajan in southern Sumatra (*Memoir*, facing p. 311), and he sailed with Raffles and Lady Raffles aboard the brig *Udney* in September 1818 for Calcutta, where he joined a ship for England. He married on 2 May 1826 his second cousin, Jane Charlotte Torriano (eldest daughter of Major John Samuel Torriano (1751–1825) of the Bombay Artillery and Kensington Volunteer Corps), and he and his wife visited Rome with Lady Raffles in the winter of 1832–3. He was an executor of Raffles's Will, in which he was bequeathed £500, and he sat on the Council of the Zoological Society of London as Lady Raffles's representative. He died without issue at St. Leonards-on-Sea on 30 January 1862 and was buried at Battle, near Hastings, his effects being declared at under £3,000. His widow died at No. 13 Cambridge Road, Hove, Sussex, on 26 September 1878, her personal estate being sworn under £35,000.

[12] Chapter Three, note 5; Bastin, *Letters and Books of Sir Stamford Raffles*, p. 71, note 25; p. 74, note 59.

[13] Bastin, *Letters and Books of Sir Stamford Raffles*, pp. 79–81, *passim*.

[14] Chapter Three, note 5.

[15] Falck was in charge of the Department of Foreign Affairs during the period of French rule in the Netherlands and subsequently Secretary-General of the Colonies. After the restoration of the House of Orange, he was appointed Secretary of State and Minister of Education, National Industry, and Colonies. In 1823 he was nominated Emissary Extraordinary to resume negotiations in London on colonial matters, which led in August of the following year to the Treaty of London and recognition of Singapore as a British possession. A letter from Falck to Raffles dated 7 October 1824 is in BL:MSS. Eur.D.742/3.

[16] Travers, MS. Journal, July 1817, Private collection.

[17] Chapter One, note 18.

[18] Bastin, *Letters and Books of Sir Stamford Raffles*, p. 118.

[19] Ibid., pp. 118, 170, 204, notes 89, 93.

[20] Ibid, p. 119.

[21] Ibid.

[22] Ibid., p. 209, note 138.

[23] Bastin, *John Leyden and Thomas Stamford Raffles*, pp. 108–9, note 138.

[24] Bastin, *Letters and Books of Sir Stamford Raffles*, pp. 204, note 94, 119.

[25] Ibid., p. 204, note 94; p. 406, note 48.

[26] Lady Raffles to the Duchess of Somerset, 21 October 1817, BL:MSS.Eur.D.742/26.

[27] Bastin, *Letters and Books of Sir Stamford Raffles*, p. 75, note 63.

[28] Ibid., p. 208, note 130.

[29] Ibid., pp. 76, note 73; 404, note 20.

[30] By Lady Raffles's Will, dated 6 September 1855, Nurse Grimes was left an annuity of £30.

[31] Arnold to Dawson Turner, 24 October 1817, *J. Soc. Biblphy nat. History*, vol. 6, pt. 5 (1973), p. 322.

[32] Raffles to the Duchess of Somerset, 8 April 1818: 'She has been christen'd *Charlotte Sophia Toonjong Segára*, the latter designation at the suggestion of the Raden in compliment to my Javan friends and with reference to her having been born at Sea – in English it would be *"Lotus of the Sea"*' (BL:MSS.Eur.D.742/24). Raffles had his daughter christened shortly after his arrival at Bengkulu by the Chaplain, the Revd. Christopher Winter, at the small St. George's Chapel in the presence of Malay and Bugis officers: Charlotte Sophia Somerset Tunjung Segara. Although the child was named after Charlotte, Duchess of Somerset, the name obviously had an additional significance for him. In a letter from Singapore dated 10 June 1819 to Colonel John Peter Addenbrooke (1753–1821), former equerry to Princess Charlotte, he stated that by giving his children the names of Charlotte and Leopold they would be 'commemorated in my domestic circle, as names every dear and ever respected; and that of my daughter will be associated with the emblem of purity, handed down in remembrance of one whose virtues and interests will never be forgotten' (*JSBRAS*, no. 2 (1878), p. 180).

[33] Lady Raffles to the Revd. Dr. Thomas Raffles, 14 April 1818, Bastin, *Letters and Books of Sir Stamford Raffles*, p. 289. On Raden Rana Dipura, ibid., p. 404, note 12.

[34] Raffles to the Duchess of Somerset, 8 April 1818, BL:MSS.Eur.D.742/24.

[35] John Bastin, *The Founding of Singapore 1819* (Singapore, 2012), p. 172, note 171.

[36] William Robert Jennings was 'provisional chief authority' at Fort Marlborough acting in place of the Resident George John Siddons, who was on sick leave. Jennings's wife Mary Anne, daughter of Edward Malone of Hampton, Middlesex, had married Jennings at St. John's Church, Calcutta, four years earlier, on 10 February 1814, but she could hardly have been the most welcoming of hostesses to Raffles and his exhausted family as she was suffering from an 'affliction of the most distressing nature', made worse by the effects of the earthquakes. From this time, 'the symptoms of her approaching dissolution were particularly apparent', and she died a month later on 22 April 1818 (*Asiatic Journal*, vol. VII, no. 37, January 1819, p. 117). The burial service was attended by Raffles, Lady Raffles, and 'the ladies and gentlemen of the settlement, together with several Native Chiefs'.

[37] Raffles to Marsden, 7 April 1818, Lady Raffles, *Memoir*, p. 293.

[38] Lady Raffles to the Duchess of Somerset, 9 April 1818, BL:MSS.Eur.D.742/26.

[39] Edward Anthony Hull was born on 14 March 1801 at Great Baddow, Essex, and was appointed a Cadet in the Bengal Army in 1816 and Ensign in the 2/10th Regiment of Bengal Native Infantry. He was interred in the same tomb in South Street Burial Ground in Calcutta as his relative, Lieutenant-Colonel John Popham Watson of HM 75th Regiment of Foot, who died on 8 June 1804. Hull is described on the tombstone as 'a youth of the sweetest disposition and fairest promise' (*The Bengal Obituary* (Calcutta, 1851), p. 165).

[40] Arnold to Dawson Turner, 9 July 1818, Bastin, *J. Soc. Biblphy nat. History*, vol. 6, pt. 5 (1973), p. 328.

[41] Lady Raffles, *Memoir*, pp. 315–38; Bastin, *Founding of Singapore*, p. 14.

[42] R. Brown, 'An Account of a New Genus of Plants, named RAFFLESIA', *Trans. Linn. Soc.*, vol. XIII, pt. 1 (1821), pp. 201–34.

[43] Lady Raffles, *Memoir*, pp. 340–66.

[44] John Bastin, *Essays on Indonesian and Malayan History* (Singapore, 1961), pp. 170–1.

[45] Lady Raffles to the Revd. Dr. Thomas Raffles, 8 April 1820, Private collection. For British newspaper accounts of the journey to Minangkabau, see Bastin, *Letters and Books of Sir Stamford Raffles*, p. 212, note 180.

[46] Lady Raffles, *Memoir*, pp. 367–72.

[47] Bastin, *Founding of Singapore*, pp. 1–32.

[48] Bastin, *Letters and Books of Sir Stamford Raffles*, p. 237, notes 30, 32; Bastin, *J. Soc. Biblphy nat. History*, vol. 6, pt. 5 (1973), pp. 360–1, notes 199, 201.

[49] Bastin, *Founding of Singapore*, pp. 98–105.

[50] Travers, *Journal*, p. 139.

[51] Robert Redman Hull was born on 12 September 1789 at Belvidere, County Down, and was appointed a Cadet in the Bengal Army in 1804 and Ensign shortly after his arrival in India on 6 April 1806. He was posted Ensign to the 10th Regiment of Bengal Native Infantry and promoted Lieutenant on 16 July 1807. He served in Baghelkhand in 1813 and in the Third Mahratta War (1817–18), and was promoted Brevet Captain on 1 January 1819. The issue of a sick certificate enabled him to join Raffles on board the *Indiana* (James Pearl) early in 1820 and travel with him to Bengkulu, where he died unmarried on 21 October 1820. The monument erected to him at Bengkulu is illustrated in A. Harfield, *Bencoolen: A History of the Honourable East India Company's Garrison on the West Coast of Sumatra (1685–1825)* (Barton-on-Sea, 1995), p. 483.

[52] Bastin, *Letters and Books of Sir Stamford Raffles*, p. 74, note 54.

[53] Lady Raffles, *Memoir*, p. 481.

[54] Lawrence Nilson Hull, who was named after his father's friend, Brigadier-General Lawrence Nilson, Commander-in-Chief at Bombay in 1785–86, was born on 7 January 1799 at Great Baddow, Essex. He was appointed a Cadet in the Bengal Army in 1814, Ensign on (16 December 1814) 21 August 1815 in the 2/10th Bengal Native Infantry, Lieutenant on 21 July 1818, Captain on 7 March 1826, and Major on 28 November 1839 in the 16th Bengal Native Infantry Grenadiers. He served in the Nepal War in 1816, the Third Mahratta War in 1817–18, the First Afghan War in 1838–9, and the First Sikh War, and died on 23 December 1845 from wounds received the previous day while leading his regiment at Ferozepore. He was described by a fellow officer in the action as being 'the admiration of every man who saw him leading and cheering on the 16th Grenadiers'. He served earlier at Bengkulu under Raffles and he accompanied him and his sister Lady Raffles to Singapore in 1822, and to England in the *Mariner* (John Herbert) in 1824. He was unmarried. See Bastin, *Letters and Books of Sir Stamford Raffles*, p. 211, note 164.

[55] Lady Raffles, *Memoir*, p. 452.

[56] Chapter Six, note 11.

[57] Raffles to Peter Auber, 7 July 1820: 'Leopold is by far the finest child of the three; he is handsome, bold, and intelligent, and struts about the house with an air of the most complete independence' (Lady Raffles, *Memoir*, p. 454). Reporting Leopold's death to his god-father, Thomas Murdoch, on 12 April 1822, Raffles described him as 'the pride and hope of my life' (BL:MSS.Eur.D.742/22), and to Mary Anne Flint on 28 June 1821, the day after his death, he wrote: 'My whole Soul was wrapped up in him' (BL:MSS.Eur.D.742/17). He was obviously an exceptional child, Dr. William Jack stating in a letter to Nathaniel Wallich on 18 July 1821 that he was 'one of the finest and loveliest children I ever saw' (*JSBRAS*, no. 73 (1916), p. 234).

[58] Lady Raffles, *Memoir*, p. 500.

[59] Bastin, *Letters and Books of Sir Stamford Raffles*, p. 75, note 63.

[60] Ibid., p. 76, note 72. Raffles informed his sister Mary Anne Flint of his death on 4 January 1822: 'A new and most unexpected affliction overwhelms us – Last night robbed us of our last and only remaining Boy – Cooksey – He had long been ailing with his teeth, but had seemingly got the better of it till two days ago when he was seized with a violent Bowl Complaint – even this was checked and we retired to rest last night leaving him in apparently a tranquil and reviving Sleep – We were soon called up, and in less than half an hour he was a Corpse – poor fellow he now lies in his Coffin – Charlotte too does not recover as we could wish, she is miserably altered, a perfect Skeleton without life and Spirits & scarcely knows any one –' (BL:MSS. Eur.D.742/17).

[61] Raffles to Thomas Murdoch, 12 April 1822, Lady Raffles, *Memoir*, p. 512; BL:MSS. Eur.D.742/22. On Thomas Murdoch, see Mildred Archer and John Bastin, *The Raffles Drawings in the India Office Library London* (Oxford University Press, Kuala Lumpur, 1978), p. 94, note 7. Raffles's letters to Murdoch and Murdoch's letters to Raffles are in BL:MSS.Eur.D.742/22 and BL:MSS.Eur.D.742/3 respectively. Murdoch's letter of condolence to Lady Raffles on the death of Raffles dated 26 July 1826 is in BL:MSS. Eur.D.742/9.

[62] Raffles to Peter Auber, 26 February 1822, Lady Raffles, *Memoir*, p. 507.

[63] Bastin, *Letters and Books of Sir Stamford Raffles*, pp. 210–11, note 162.

[64] Raffles wrote to Charlotte, Duchess of Somerset on 30 November 1822: 'I am at present engaged in establishing a Constitution for Singapore the principles of which will I hope ensure its prosperity – the utmost possible freedom of Trade and equal rights to all with protection of property & person[,] all the objects to be attained and I shall spare no pains to establish such Laws and Regulations as may be most conducive to them –' (BL:MSS.Eur.D.742/24).

[65] Ibid.

[66] Gibson-Hill, *JMBRAS*, vol. XXXIII, pt. 1 (1960), pp. 16–32.

[67] Archer and Bastin, *The Raffles Drawings*, pp. 20–1.

[68] John Bastin, *William Farquhar: First Resident and Commandant of Singapore* (Eastbourne, 2005).

[69] Raffles to the Revd. Dr. Thomas Raffles, 1 October 1822, Bastin, *Letters and Books of Sir Stamford Raffles*, pp. 150–3.

[70] Archer and Bastin, *The Raffles Drawings*, pp. 28–31; Bastin, *Letters and Books of Sir Stamford Raffles*, p. 210, note 158.

[71] Bastin, *Letters and Books of Sir Stamford Raffles*, p. 210, note 155.

[72] Raffles to Auber, 20 December 1823, Lady Raffles, *Memoir*, p. 564.

[73] Lady Raffles, *Memoir*, p. 563; Bastin, *Founding of Singapore*, p. 155, note 42. Documents relating to the sale and disposal of Salmond's lands at Bengkulu during 1823–4 are in BL:MSS.Eur.D.742/5.

[74] Raffles to Macquoid, 7 February 1824, formerly in the possession of the late Mrs. Dorothy Nixon, Secretary of the Kuala Lumpur Book Club.

[75] Lady Raffles, *Memoir*, pp. 566–9.

[76] Lady Raffles to Mary Anne Flint, 22 March 1824, BL:MSS.Eur.D.742/15.

[77] Ibid.

[78] Raffles to the Court of Directors, 8 February 1824, Lady Raffles, *Memoir*, pp. 569–74. A similar statement of the same date by Raffles and a certificate confirming the loss of his property on the *Fame* are in BL:MSS.Eur.D.742/4.

[79] Chapter Two, note 27.

[80] Bastin, *Letters and Books of Sir Stamford Raffles*, pp. 71–2, note 26.

[81] Hackney Archives, London: BW/E 16 (plan of graveyard), 929.5 (LH/05) Index to plan (Eileen Mortimer, 1983). Ann Raffles's grave is no. 10 on the plan (and T10 in the index).

[82] Raffles to Mary Anne Flint, 1 July 1824, BL:MSS.Eur.D.742/17.

[83] Lady Raffles to Mary Anne Flint, 2 July 1824, BL:MSS.Eur.D.742/15.

## CHAPTER SEVEN
### *Lady Raffles after the Death of her Husband*
———◆◆———

[1] *The Morning Post*, 23 September 1824.

[2] Lady Raffles to Mary Anne Flint, 10 October 1824, BL:MSS.Eur.D.742/15.

[3] Dowden, *Journal of Thomas Moore*, vol. 2, p. 772.

[4] Bastin, *Letters and Books of Sir Stamford Raffles*, p. 213, note 192; pp. 165, 167; p. 241, note 49.

[5] Ibid., p.. 213, note 192; pp. 165, 167; p. 241, note 49.

[6] *The Morning Post*, 14 April 1825. The *Sussex Advertiser* of 4 April 1825 included the names of Raffles and Lady Raffles in the subscription book 'of the well established and managed Reading Saloon' at Brighton.

[7] *The Morning Post*, 9 June 1825.

[8] Bastin, *Letters and Books of Sir Stamford Raffles*, pp. 170, 174 and *passim*.

[9] Ibid., pp. 217, 218, notes 238, 240.

[10] Boulger, *Life of Sir Stamford Raffles*, pp. 368–80.

[11] J.C.M. Khoo, C.G. Kwa, L.Y. Khoo, 'The Death of Sir Thomas Stamford Raffles (1781–1826)', *Singapore Medical Journal*, vol. 39, pt. 12 (1998), pp. 564–5. For the post-mortem report by Sir Everard Home, see BL:MSS.Eur.D.742/9; *The Gentleman's Magazine*, vol. XCVI, pt. 2 (1826), p. 275. Home was surgeon to St. George's Hospital, London, from 1793 to 1827, and the first President of the Royal College of Surgeons. He and Raffles became friendly in 1817, and Raffles and his aide-de-camp, Captain Thomas Otho Travers, accompanied Home's two daughters to the Queen's Drawing Room in February of that year. Home was one of Raffles's supporters on his election as a Fellow of the Royal Society in March 1817 and Raffles corresponded with him from Bengkulu and Singapore. See Bastin, *Letters and Books of Sir Stamford Raffles*, p. 241, note 50.

[12] Lady Raffles to the Revd. Dr. Thomas Raffles, 6 August 1826, ibid., pp. 304–5.

[13] Journal of Marc Brunel, 18 May 1827, cited Isambard Brunel, *The Life of Isambard Kingdom Brunel Civil Engineer* (London, 1870), pp. 28–9.

[14] *London Standard*, 9 March 1828.

[15] *The Morning Post*, 16 June 1828.

[16] *London Standard*, 27 August 1828.

[17] Ibid.

[18] Ibid.

[19] The Middlesex Sessions report on the trial of Daniel Kelly states: 'JOHN CROSSWELL. I am butler to Mrs. [*sic*] Sophia Raffles – she is a widow, and lives in Grosvenor-square. I know this shovel to be hers – it was safe on the 26th of July about the middle of the day; the beadle afterwards brought it. JOHN LACEY. I am an officer. I took the shovel from the prisoner on the 27th of July, between nine and ten o'clock in the morning; I took him to the watch-house; I had been watching him in several areas – I saw him bring something out of the prosecutrix's area, and then go down Davies-street, where he offered the shovel to a man who was making a sewer. *Prisoner's Defence.* I went down to take the dust, and left my shovel in the area – I went back for it and found this; my own was gone; I put it into my sack, and thought at first it was my own. JOHN CROSSWELL. He had been there for dust, but he was not the regular dustman.' The unfortunate Kelly was found guilty and ordered to be transported to Van Diemen's Land for seven years. He sailed in the *Royal George* on 12 June 1830 and arrived at Hobart on 18 October 1830. Two years later, he was given 12 lashes for not doing his allotted work, with his tea and sugar also stopped, and he subsequently received additional lashes and hard labour for absconding. Happily, *The Hobart Town Gazette* of 30 June 1837 reported that in that year he was issued with a Ticket-of-Leave.

[20] John Bastin, *Lady Raffles's Memoir of the Life and Public Services of Sir Thomas Stamford Raffles* (Eastbourne, 2004).

[21] John Bastin, *Sir Stamford Raffles's The History of Java: A Bibliographical Essay* (Eastbourne, 2004), pp. 53–6.

[22] John Bastin, 'Raffles in Marble & Bronze', *The Straits Times Annual for 1972* (Singapore, 1971), pp. 58–63; 'The Bust of Sir Stamford Raffles', Archer and Bastin, *The Raffles Drawings in the India Office Library London*, pp. 10–14; Bastin, *Letters and Books of Sir Stamford Raffles*, p. 407, note 62.

[23] *The Times* of London printed the following advertisement on 9 April 1829: 'MR. GEORGE ROBINS has the pleasure to announce, that he is directed to SELL by AUCTION, on Thursday, May 7, at 12, a distinguished FREEHOLD PROPERTY, which partakes of the state of a village residence of a superior character, on Highwood-hill, has for many years been proverbial, no less for its external appearance, than the very great conveniences which will be found to preside throughout the interior of

this favoured retreat; it is judiciously seated on a lofty and commanding spot, giving very great facility to views which can hardly be surpassed in any part of England. The terrace walk is of considerable extent, and adorned by a multitudinous collection of all that is rare and estimable in plants and flowering shrubs. The kitchen gardens are extensive, and the fruit trees prolific, and of the best kind. The pleasure grounds and shrubbery walks extend nearly one mile, and are well sheltered from the north and easterly winds, and it would almost appear, from the extraordinary tact that is manifest every where, that the genius of Repton must have been enlisted into the service; it was from this interesting spot that Lady Russell dated her memorable letters. Sir Stamford Raffles, whose good taste has always been admitted, expended many thousand pounds in rendering complete this seductive and most desirable property. The estate comprehends, in ground, ONE HUNDRED AND TWENTY-TWO ACRES of excellent land, which completely environ the mansion. There is also (and to be sold in separate lots) 7 cottages, and a residence, with public-house, &c.; also a farm-house and suitable buildings. The estate may be viewed 21 days prior to the sale: particulars had at Highwood-Hill House; also the Three Cranes, Edgware; Abercorn Arms, Stanmore; Essex Arms, Watford; Bell, Hendon; of Messrs Amory and Coles, solicitors, Throgmorton-street; at the Mart; and in Covent-garden.' The date of the auction was subsequently changed to 11 June 1829, but the property did not sell. For the later sale of 'High Wood' in 1859, see Chapter Seven, note 80.

[24] Sophia Flint was born in Singapore in March 1823 (Chapter Three, note 5).

[25] Chapter Three, note 5; Bastin, *Letters and Books of Sir Stamford Raffles*, p. 74, note 59.

[26] Bastin, *Letters and Books of Sir Stamford Raffles*, p. 354; pp. 408–9, note 91. Letters and other material relating to Lady Raffles's visit to the Continent in 1831–33 is in BL:MSS.Eur.D.742/11.

[27] Lady Raffles to the Revd. Dr. Thomas Raffles, 29 May 1830, ibid., p. 354.

[28] Lady Raffles to the Revd. Dr. Thomas Raffles, 24 February 1832, ibid., p. 358.

[29] Ibid., p. 409, note 99. A letter of condolence from Adélaide de Staël dated 12 July [1858] on the death of Lady Raffles is in BL:MSS.Eur.D.742/19.

[30] A.J.C. Hare, *The Life and Letters of Frances Baroness Bunsen* (London, 1879); Frances Bunsen, *A Memoir of Baron Bunsen Late Minister Plenipotentiary and Envoy Extraordinary of His Majesty Frederic William IV, at the Court of St. James* (London, 1868); Bastin, *Letters and Books of Sir Stamford Raffles*, p. 410, note 130; p. 411, note 131.

[31] Hare, *Life and Letters of Frances Baroness Bunsen*, vol. I, p. 397; Baroness Bunsen, *Memoir of Baron Bunsen*, vol. I, p. 380.

[32] Lady Raffles to the Revd. Dr. Thomas Raffles, 24 October 1833, Bastin, *Letters and Books of Sir Stamford Raffles*, p. 360.

[33] Ibid.

[34] Lady Raffles to the Revd. Dr. Thomas Raffles, [16 April 1835], Bastin, *Letters and Books of Sir Stamford Raffles*, p. 372. A letter regarding the valuation of the house and lands of 'High Wood' dated 19 November 1834 is in BL:MSS.Eur.D.742/13a.

[35] Lady Raffles to the Revd. Dr. Thomas Raffles, [16 April 1835], Bastin, *Letters and Books of Sir Stamford Raffles*, pp. 372, 406, note 48. Sir Robert Harry Inglis and his wife Mary Inglis were among Lady Raffles's most intimate friends. Later, when she was residing at Bedford Square at the time of the 1841 Census, her name is recorded at their address along with those of William Charles Raffles Flint and servants in the house. Sir Robert Inglis wrote a letter of condolence dated 11 July 1826 to Lady Raffles on Raffles's death (BL:MSS.Eur.D.742/9) and also a letter dated 23 February 1830 acknowledging her gift of a copy of her *Memoir* (BL:MSS.Eur.D.742/10). Lady Mary Inglis wrote a letter of condolence to Mary Jane Auber from Bedford Square on the death of Lady Raffles in 1858 (BL:MSS.Eur.D.742/19).

[36] Lady Raffles, *Memoir* (1835), vol. I, p. [iii], Dedication 'To His Excellency The Chevalier Bunsen', 16 June 1835.

[37] Rev. George Henry Sumner, *Life of Charles Richard Sumner, D.D., Bishop of Winchester, and Prelate of the Most Noble Order of the Garter, During a Forty Years Episcopate* (London, 1876).

[38] Lady Raffles to the Revd. Dr. Thomas Raffles, 3 August 1835, Bastin, *Letters and Books of Sir Stamford Raffles*, p. 374.

[39] Lady Raffles to the Revd. Dr. Thomas Raffles, [High Wood 1835], ibid., p. 376.

[40] Lady Raffles to the Revd. Dr. Thomas Raffles, 10 February 1836, Bastin, *Letters and Books of Sir Stamford Raffles*, p. 378. Lady Raffles certainly replaced her carriage and horses sometime afterwards, as her carriage was involved in an accident in London in May 1850 when a cab-driver named William Scott was summoned for 'wilful negligence' by crashing into it. 'James Harvey, coachman to Lady Raffles, had pulled up the carriage before a shop in Regent-quadrant ... and while the footman was in the act of letting out her ladyship, there was a sudden crash at the back of the carriage. The coachman looked over the top of the carriage, and saw that a cab had driven in the back panel. ... Thomas Turner, the footman, said when the carriage stopped he did not see that any cab was behind it. The coachmaker's bill was produced. The damage was estimated at 4£.10s. Defendant said he was called to take up. As he was in the act of doing so, the coachman backed and caused the accident. This, however, was denied.

Mr. Bingham decided that the defendant was liable for the amount; he would inflict the nominal fine of 6d., and order him to pay the amount of the coachmaker's bill. Defendant said he was a very poor man with a large family, and totally unable to pay the amount. Mr. Bingham had no objection to give time; no doubt her ladyship would be disposed to give the defendant every indulgence. The solicitor for her ladyship said she was an excellent person, and would listen to his claim of indulgence; but the coachman said her ladyship had already declared that she would listen to no appeal, but would leave it to the magistrate. Mr. Bingham said, that being the case, he should order him to pay the damage in two months, by four instalments' (*London Daily News*, 27 May 1850).

[41] Lady Raffles to the Revd. Dr. Thomas Raffles, 16 May [1836], Bastin, *Letters and Books of Sir Stamford Raffles*, p. 380.

[42] As already noted, he was buried at the parish church of St. George, Bloomsbury. By his Will he left his children various sums of money, including for his daughters, Sophia Raffles, Alice Watson Mudge, and Mary Jane Auber, the release of £2,000 each from the bonds under their marriage settlements.

[43] Lady Raffles to the Rev. Dr. Thomas Raffles, 10 October [1837], Bastin, *Letters and Books of Sir Stamford Raffles*, p. 386.

[44] Ibid., Appendix, pp. 402–3.

[45] Lady Raffles to the Revd. Dr. Thomas Raffles, 26 June [1838], ibid., p. 392.

[46] Lady Raffles to the Revd. Dr. Thomas Raffles, 21 January 1839, ibid., p. 396.

[47] *The Morning Chronicle*, 22 March 1839.

[48] Hare, *Life and Letters of Frances Baroness Bunsen*, vol. I, p. 512.

[49] Lady Raffles to the Revd. Dr. Thomas Raffles, 24 April 1837, Bastin, *Letters and Books of Sir Stamford Raffles*, p. 384.

[50] Baroness Bunsen, *Memoir of Baron Bunsen*, vol. I, p. 512.

[51] Lady Raffles to Baron and Baroness Bunsen, 8 April 1840, Geheimes Staatsarchiv Preussischer Kulturbesitz: Familienarchiv von Bunsen, B nr. 108, Bd. 1–2.

[52] William Charles Raffles Flint to Baron Bunsen, 11 May 1840, ibid.

[53] Ibid.

[54] Bastin, *Letters and Books of Sir Stamford Raffles*, pp. 239–40, note 47. There are nine letters of Samuel Wilberforce to Lady Raffles dated from 2 March 1841 to 16 February 1857 in BL:MSS.Eur.D.742/7.

[55] David Newsome, *The Parting of Friends: The Wilberforces and Henry Manning* (Grand Rapids, Michigan, 1966), p. 239.

[56] Lady Raffles to Baron and Baroness Bunsen, 2 June 1840, Geheimes Staatsarchiv Preussischer Kulturbesitz: Familienarchiv von Bunsen, B nr. 108, Bd. 1–2.

[57] Hare, *Life and Letters of Frances Baroness Bunsen*, vol. II, p. 28. Before her visit to the Continent at this time, Lady Raffles had rented 'High Wood' to a Mrs. Howard, the tenancy agreement being dated 26 October 1840 (BL:MSS.Eur.D.742/13a).

[58] Hare, *Life and Letters of Frances Baroness Bunsen*, vol. II, p. 62.

[59] Baroness Bunsen, *Memoir of Baron Bunsen*, vol. II, p. 146.

[60] Ibid., p. 145: '20th November, 1847. We shall have Mr. Brooke (the Rajah of Borneo) to dinner, and many others; Lady Raffles comes to meet him.'

[61] *Barrow's Worcester Journal*, 25 November 1847: 'His Excellency the Prussian Minister and Madame Bunsen entertained Baron des Granges, Lord and Lady Ashley, Lady Raffles, Mr. James Brooke (Rajah of Sarawak), and a large party to dinner on Saturday, at the Prussian Legation. A small circle assembled after dinner.'

[62] Bunsen, *Memoir of Baron Bunsen*, vol. II, p. 145.

[63] Ibid., pp. 145–6. Bunsen concluded: 'An attempt proved unavailing to-day to be present at a meeting relating to the Mission to Borneo; the crowd overflowed from the large Hanover Square Rooms, and it is only to be hoped that the subscriptions may be in proportion to the zeal displayed in listening to and cheering Mr. Brooke.'

[64] Rajah Brooke to Lady Raffles, 14 January 1848, BL:MSS.Eur.D.747/7.

[65] *The Morning Post*, 6 August 1825; Hare, *Life and Letters of Frances Baroness Bunsen*, vol. II, p. 80. Four letters of Ernest von Bunsen to Lady Raffles are in BL:MSS. Eur.D.742/7.

[66] Baroness Bunsen to Lady Raffles, 2 May [1854]; Baron Bunsen to Lady Raffles, 3 May 1854, BL:MSS.Eur.D.742/7.

[67] Lady Raffles to Baron and Baroness Bunsen, 4 May 1854; Baroness Bunsen to Lady Raffles, 5 May [1854], BL:MSS.Eur.D.742/7.

[68] Hare, *Life and Letters of Frances Baroness Bunsen*, vol. II, p. 236.

[69] John Watson Hull was born on 25 July 1792 at Belvidere, County Down, and was appointed a Cadet in the Bengal Army in 1813. He was posted Ensign on (16 December 1814) 5 June 1815, and promoted Lieutenant on 30 October 1817 in the 1/10th Bengal Native Infantry. He served in the Third Mahratta War during 1817–18 and in 1822 he proceeded to Bengkulu, where he was placed by Raffles in charge of the convicts and later the spice plantations. He transferred to the 14th Regiment Bengal Native Infantry (formerly the 10th) in May 1824 and was promoted Captain on 28 February 1827. He retired from the army on 13 April 1831 and married at Pannal Church in Yorkshire on 15 October 1835 Martha, daughter of John Younghusband, a linen merchant of Ballydrain, near Belfast. He died without children at his residence Mount Ida, Dromore, Country Down, on 10 November 1842. His widow died at Mt. Ida, on 31 January 1877, aged 78, and was buried with her husband in the Magherally churchyard, County Down.

[70] Chapter Six, note 54.

[71] Chapter Six, note 11.

[72] Chapter Six, note 4.

[73] Chapter Six, note 6.

[74] Chapter Six, note 3.

[75] Lady Raffles to the Bunsens, 24 July 1840, Geheimes Staatsarchiv Preussischer Kulturbesitz: Familienarchiv von Bunsen, B nr. 108, Bd. 1–2.

[76] BL:MSS.Eur.D.742/19.

[77] Horsfield to the Revd. William Charles Raffles Flint, 15 December 1858, BL:MSS. Eur.D.742/19. Horsfield's earlier letter of condolence on the death of Raffles, dated 11 July 1826, is in BL:MSS.Eur.D.742/9.

[78] Chapter Six, note 4.

[79] Papers relating to Lady Raffles's financial affairs with her solicitors Messrs. Smith, Payne and Smiths of Lombard Street, London, between 1837 and 1850, including papers relating to loans made to a Henry Kingscote, a letter of credit for the large sum of £11,742, and notes for the purchase of Bank Stock, and Mexican Stock are in BL:MSS.Eur.D.742/13b,13c.

[80] A printed plan and advertisement for the sale of 'High Wood' in 1859 by the Auctioneers and Estate Agents S.G. Taylor of Grosvenor Street, London, and Dickson

& Bell of Lombard Street, London, are in BL:MSS.Eur.D.742/13a. An advertisement for the sale of 'High Wood' was also printed in *The Times* on 7 May 1859 and in the *Herts Guardian, Agricultural Journal, and General Advertiser* on 14 May 1859. For the advertisement of sale of 'High Wood' in April 1829, see Chapter Seven, note 23

[81] A typical memorandum of agreement by Lady Raffles for the rent of land at 'High Wood' dated 3 November 1837 is in BL:MSS.Eur.D.742/13a.

## EPILOGUE

[1] Chapter Three, note 4. A summary family tree of the Raffles Family, with some errors, is printed as Appendix V to Wurtzburg, *Raffles of the Eastern Isles*, p. 750.

[2] Chapter Three, note 5.

[3] Chapter Three, note 5.

[4] Chapter Three, note 5; Chapter Five, note 31. The family line of Susannah Julia Raffles (the sister of Captain Benjamin Raffles) and Ambrose Carter continued through their daughters.

[5] Chapter One, note 19.

[6] Chapter One, note 19.

[7] Thomas Stamford Raffles, Barrister-at-Law of the Inner Temple, and Stipendiary Magistrate for the Borough of Liverpool, was the author of *Memoirs of the Life and Ministry of the Rev. Thomas Raffles, D.D., LL.D., Etc. Etc. Etc.* (London, 1864). The book contains extracts from the 'Reminiscences' of the Revd. Dr. Thomas Raffles, which he wrote shortly before his death. The manuscript copy of these 'Reminiscences' contains a chapter on Sir Stamford Raffles, which is printed in Bastin, *Letters and Books of Sir Stamford Raffles*, pp. 223–43.

# Bibliography

# MANUSCRIPT SOURCES

## THE BODLEIAN LIBRARY, UNIVERSITY OF OXFORD

William Godwin Diary, Abinger Collection; *The Diary of William Godwin*, (eds) Victoria Myers, David O'Shaughnessy, and Mark Philp (Oxford: Oxford Digital Library, 2010). http://godwindiary.bodleian.ox.ac.uk.; William Godwin Letters, Abinger Collection Shelfmark MS Abinger c 5, fols. 64–5, 68

## THE BRITISH LIBRARY

*Raffles Family Papers*

MSS.Eur.D.742/2: Letters to Sir T.S. Raffles from William Marsden

MSS.Eur.D.742/3: Letters to Sir T.S. Raffles from a variety of persons

MSS.Eur.D.742/4: Statement of personal property belonging to Sir Stamford Raffles lost on the *Fame*

MSS.Eur.D.742/7: Letters to Lady Raffles from a variety of persons

MSS.Eur.D.742/9: Letters received on the death of Sir T.S. Raffles in 1826

MSS.Eur.D.742/10: Letters to Lady Raffles from persons who received copies of her *Memoir*

MSS.Eur.D.742/11: Letters and related material concerning Lady Raffles's visits to the Continent

MSS.Eur.D.742/13: Lady Raffles: miscellaneous legal documents

MSS.Eur.D.742/15: Letters from Lady Raffles to Mrs Mary Anne Flint

MSS.Eur.D.742/17: Letters from Sir T.S. Raffles to Mrs. Mary Anne Flint and Captain William Flint

MSS.Eur.D.742/19: Letters written on the death of Lady Sophia Raffles in 1858

MSS.Eur.D.742/20: Letters from Sir T.S. Raffles to William Brown Ramsay

MSS.Eur.D.742/21: Miscellaneous letters from Sir T.S. Raffles

MSS.Eur.D.742/22: Letters from Sir T.S. Raffles to Thomas Murdoch

MSS.Eur.D.742/24: Letters from Sir T.S. Raffles to the Duchess of Somerset

MSS.Eur.D.742/25: Letters from Sir T.S. Raffles to the Duke of Somerset

MSS.Eur.D.742/26: Letters from Lady Sophia Raffles to the Duchess of Somerset

MSS.Eur.D.742/27: Letters from the Duchess of Somerset to Sir T.S. Raffles

MSS.Eur.D.742/28: Letters from the Duke of Somerset to Sir T.S. Raffles

## THE CAMBRIDGE UNIVERSITY LIBRARY

Raffles letters to Thomas Macquoid (Add Ms 7386)

## THE NATIONAL LIBRARY OF WALES COLLECTION AND MICROFORM ACADEMIC PUBLISHERS

*The Slebech Papers*

Letter Book, 1759 May 11 to 1778 April 16 (NLW ref. 11485)

Accounts, 1770 July to 1783 April 30 (NLW ref. 11685-11791)

Diaries, 1775 Sept. 14 to 1789 July 29 (NLW ref. 9402-9404)

Papers, 1777 June 12 to 1785 Jan. 31 (NLW ref. 8792-8828)

Accounts, 1789 March 28 to 1796 Dec. 5 (NLW ref. 5358-5387)

Letters, 1789 July 7 to 1794 Dec. 10 (NLW ref. 8342-8440)

Letters, 1789 Aug. 8 to 1796 Oct. 13 (NLW ref. 9124-9200)

Bills of Lading, 1794–1795 (NLW ref. 9306-9315)

Letters, 1796 Oct. 14 to 1800 Dec. 4 (NLW ref. 11569-11616)

## THE NATIONAL ARCHIVES, KEW

Prerogative Court of Canterbury (PCC) Wills [documents online]

Thomas Raffles. Proved 3/12/1784. PROB 11/1124/104

Thomas Raffles Jr. Proved 9/2/1798. PROB 11/1302/111

Charlotte Maule. Proved 19/10/1798. PROB 11/1314/120

Thomas Bingley. Proved 23/8/1797. PROB 11/1259/205

Edward Lyde. Proved 21/7/1768. PROB 11/941/131

Ann Lyde née Salter. Proved 13/8/1770. PROB 11/959/364

Mary Cole née Lyde. Proved 17/10/1799. PROB 11/1331/163

Edward Salter. Proved 26/10/1732. PROB 11/654/202

Ann Salter née Peach. Proved 3/11/1749. PROB 11/775/39

Charles Hamond. Proved 29/10/1807. PROB 11/1468/252

Sir Thomas Stamford Raffles. Proved 10/8/1826. PROB 11/1716/42

Revd. John Lindeman. Proved 10/11/1819. PROB 11/1622/126

Dr Jacob C Tancourt [*sic*] [Fancourt]. Administration Madras
(www.findmypast.com.au image © The British Library Board)

Richard Winter [*sic*] Wynter. Proved 19/7/1832. PROB 11/1803/253

Leonora Sophia Carter. Proved 11/6/1838. PROB 11/1897/346

William Lindeman. Proved 10/11/1791. PROB 11/1211/60


**PRIVATE COLLECTIONS**

MS Journal of Captain Thomas Otho Travers


**THE UNIVERSITY OF LONDON**

Dr. Williams's Library: Autobiographical fragment of Thomas Raffles


**ADDITIONAL SOURCES**

Legacies of British Slave ownership (www.ucl.ac.uk.lbs)

Brightsolid Online Publishing Australasia Pty Limited, trading as findmypast.com.au
and findmypast.co.uk

# PRINTED SOURCES

## NEWSPAPERS

Titles as cited in the Notes

## BOOKS AND ARTICLES

Anon. *The Picture of London, for 1802; being a Correct Guide to All the Curiosities, Amusements, Exhibitions, Public Establishments, and remarkable Objects, in and near London* (London, 1805).

Anon. 'Biographical Memoir of the Late Sir Hugh Inglis', *The Asiatic Journal*, vol. IX, no. 63 (March 1921), pp. 256–8.

Anon. 'Brief Memoir of the Late Charles Grant, Esq., *The Evangelical Magazine and Missionary Chronicle*, vol. II (April 1824), pp. 133–7.

Anon. *Annals of Christ's Hospital from its foundation to the Present Time and of the Original Conventual Church of Grey Friars. By an Old Blue* (London, 1867).

Archer, Mildred and Bastin, John. *The Raffles Drawings in the India Office Library London* (Oxford University Press, Kuala Lumpur, 1978).

Armytage, Frances. *The Free Port System in the British West Indies: A Study in commercial policy, 1766–1822* (London, 1953).

Auber, P. *Rise and Progress of the British Power in India* (London, 1837), 2 vols.

Barker, Juliet. *The Brontës* (London, 1995).

Bastin, John. *The Native Policies of Sir Stamford Raffles in Java and Sumatra: An Economic Interpretation* (Oxford, 1957).

Bastin, John. *Essays on Indonesian and Malayan History* (Singapore, 1961).

Bastin, John. *The British in West Sumatra (1685–1825): A selection of documents, mainly from the East India Company records preserved in the India Office Library Commonwealth Relations Office, London* (Kuala Lumpur, 1965).

Bastin, John. 'Raffles in Marble & Bronze', *The Straits Times Annual for 1972* (Singapore, 1971), pp. 58–63.

Bastin, John. 'Dr. Joseph Arnold and the Discovery of *Rafflesia Arnoldi* in West Sumatra', *J. Soc. Biblphy nat. Hist.*, vol. 6, pt. 5 (1973), pp. 305–72.

Bastin, John (ed.). 'The Java Journal of Dr Joseph Arnold', *JMBRAS*, vol. XLVI, pt. 1 (1973), pp. 1–92.

Bastin, John (ed.). 'Letters of Sir Stamford Raffles to Nathaniel Wallich 1819–1824', *JMBRAS*, vol. XLIV, Pt. 2 (1981), pp. 1–73.

Bastin, John. *Olivia Mariamne Raffles* (Singapore, 2002).

Bastin, John. *Sophia Raffles* (Singapore, 2002).

Bastin, John. *Sir Stamford Raffles's The History of Java: A Bibliographical Essay* (Eastbourne, 2004).

Bastin, John. *Lady Raffles's Memoir of the Life and Public Services of Sir Thomas Stamford Raffles* (Eastbourne, 2004).

Bastin, John. *William Farquhar: First Resident and Commandant of Singapore* (Eastbourne, 2005).

Bastin, John. *The Natural History Researches of Dr. Thomas Horsfield (1773–1859) First American Naturalist of Indonesia* (Singapore, 1990: reprinted Eastbourne, 2005).

Bastin, John. *John Leyden and Thomas Stamford Raffles* (Eastbourne, 2006).

Bastin, John. *Letters and Books of Sir Stamford Raffles and Lady Raffles: The Tang Holdings Collection of Autograph Letters and Books of Sir Stamford Raffles and Lady Raffles* (Singapore, 2009).

Bastin, John. *The Founding of Singapore 1819: Based on the Private Letters of Sir Stamford Raffles to the Governor-General and Commander-in-Chief in India, the Marquess of Hastings, preserved in The Bute Collection at Mount Stuart, Isle of Bute, Scotland* (National Library of Singapore, 2012).

Bastin, John. *Raffles and Hastings: Private Exchanges behind the Founding of Singapore* (National Library Board, Marshall Cavendish Editions, Singapore, 2014).

Bastin, John; Bastin, Christopher. 'Some Old Penang Tombstones', *JMBRAS*, vol. XXXVII, pt. 1 (1964), pp. 126–65.

Bateson, Charles. *The Convict Ships 1787–1868* (Glasgow, 1969).

Boulger, D.C. *The Life of Sir Stamford Raffles* (London, 1897).

Brown, R. 'Account of a new Genus of Plants, named RAFFLESIA', *Trans. Linn. Soc.*, vol. XIII, pt. 1 (1821), pp. 201–34.

Brunel, Isambard. *The Life of Isambard Brunel Civil Engineer (1870) A Reprint with an introduction by L.T.C. Rolt* (Tonbridge, 1971).

Bunsen, Frances Baroness. *A Memoir of Baron Bunsen Late Minister Plenipotentiary and Envoy Extraordinary of His Majesty Frederic William IV, at the Court of St. James* (London, 1868), 2 vols.

Burke, John; Burke, John Bernard. *A Genealogical and Heraldic Dictionary of the Landed Gentry of Great Britain & Ireland* (London, 1849).

Burkill, I.H. (ed.). 'William Jack's Letters to Nathaniel Wallich, 1819–1821', *JSBRAS*, no. 73 (1916), pp. 147–268.

Chamberlaine, William. *The West-India Seaman's Medical Directory, for the Use of such Merchant-Ships trading to the West Indies as Carry no Surgeons* (London, 1785).

Cholmondeley, R.H. (ed.). *The Heber Letters 1783–1832* (London, 1950).

Coldham, Peter Wilson. *The Complete Book of Emigrants 1751–1776* (Baltimore, 1987).

Collis, Maurice. *Raffles* (London, 1966).

Cotton, Sir Evan. *East Indiamen: The East India Company's Marine Service.* (ed.) Sir Charles Fawcett (London, 1949).

Dancer, Thomas. *A Short Dissertation on the Jamaica Bath Waters: To which is prefixed, An Introduction concerning Mineral Waters in general; Shewing the Methods of examining them, and ascertaining their Contents* (Kingston, Jamaica, 1784).

Danvers, F.C. *List of Marine Records of the Late East India Company, and of Subsequent Date, Preserved in the Record Department of the India Office, London* (London, 1896).

Dempster, G.L. Hawkins. *The Manners of My Time* (London, 1920).

Denning, G. (ed.). *The Marquesan Journal of Edward Robarts 1797–1824* (Canberra, 1974).

Devenish, Robert J.; McLaughlin, Charles H. *Historical and Genealogical Records of the Devenish Families of England and Ireland With an Inquiry Into the Origins of the Family Name and Some Account of the Family Lines Founded by Them in Other Countries* (The Lakeside Press, Chicago, 1948).

Dowden, Wilfred S. (ed.). *The Letters of Thomas Moore* (Oxford, 1964), 2 vols.

Dowden, Wilfred S. (ed.). *The Journal of Thomas Moore* (Newark, 1983–8) 6 vols.

Eeles, Francis C. *The Parish Church of St. Mary, Hendon: A Short History and Description* (Hendon, 1931).

Ellerton, Nerida F.; Clements, M.A. *Rewriting the History of School Mathematics in North America 1607–1861: The Central Role of Cyphering Books* (Dordrecht, 2012).

Evans, John. *The Gentleman Usher: The Life and Times of George Dempster (1732–1818) Member of Parliament and Laird of Dunnichen and Skibo* (Barnsley, 2005).

F.E.P. *Marriages at Fort St. George Madras*, transcribed and annotated by F.E.P. (Exeter, 1907), reprinted from *The Genealogist*, vols. xix-xxiii (n.s.).

Fairweather, Maria. *Madame de Staël* (London, 2005).

Farrington, Anthony. *Catalogue of the East India Company Ships' Journals and Logs 1600–1834* (London, 1999).

Faulkner, Thomas. *The History and Antiquities of the Parish of Hammersmith, Interspersed with Biographical Notices of Illustrious and Eminent Persons, who have been born, or who have resided in the Parish, during the Three Preceding Centuries* (London, 1839).

Foster, William. *The East India House: Its History and Associations* (London, 1924).

*The Gentleman's Magazine*, vol. 54, pt. 2 (1784), p. 956.

Gibson-Hill, C.A. 'The Master Attendants at Singapore 1819–67', *JMBRAS*, vol. XXXIII, pt. 1 (1960), pp. 1–64.

Glendinning, Victoria. *Raffles and the Golden Opportunity 1781–1826* (Profile Books, London, 2012).

Haan, F. De. 'Personalia der Periode van het Engelsch Bestuur over Java 1811–1816', *BKI*, vol. 92 (1935), pp. 477–681.

Hannay, David. *Letters written by Sir Samuel Hood (Viscount Hood) in 1781-2-3*, Navy Records Society, London, vol. III (1895).

Hare, Augustus J.C. *The Life and Letters of Frances Baroness Bunsen* (London, 1879), 2 vols.

Harfield, Alan. *Christian Cemeteries of Penang & Perak* (London, 1987).

Harfield, Alan. *Bencoolen: A History of the Honourable East India Company's Garrison on the West Coast of Sumatra (1685–1825)* (Barton-on-Sea, 1995).

Higman, B.W. *Jamaica Surveyed: Plantation Maps and Plans of the Eighteenth and Nineteenth Centuries* (Jamaica, 1988).

Hill, A.H. (transl.). 'The Hikayat Abdullah: An annotated translation', *JMBRAS*, vol. XXVIII, pt. 3 (1955), pp. 1–345 + [9].

Hodson, V.C.P. *List of Officers of the Bengal Army 1758–1834* (London, 1927–47), 4 vols.

Holmes and Co. *The Bengal Obituary; or, A Record to Perpetuate the Memory of Departed Worth: Being a Compilation of Tablets and Monumental Inscriptions from various parts of the Bengal and Agra Presidencies …* (Calcutta, 1851).

[Inglis, Sir Robert Harry]. *Sketch of the Life of Sir Hugh Inglis* (London, 1821).

Irwin, Graham. 'Nineteenth-Century Borneo: A Study in Diplomatic Rivalry', *VKI*, vol. XV (1955).

*Java Government Gazette* (Batavia [Jakarta], 1812–16).

Khoo, J.C.M., Kwa, C.G., Khoo, L.Y. 'The Death of Sir Thomas Stamford Raffles (1781–1826)', *Singapore Medical Journal*, vol. 39, pt. 12 (1998), pp. 564–5.

Langdon, Marcus. *Penang: The Fourth Presidency of India 1805–1830. Volume One: Ships, Men and Mansions* (Penang, 2013).

Lee Kam Hing. *The Sultanate of Aceh: Relations with the British 1760–1824* (Kuala Lumpur, 1995).

Lentzsch, Franziska et al. *Füssli: The Wild Swiss* (Zürich, 2005).

Leyden, J. *The Malay Annals: Translated from the Malay Language, by The Late Dr. John Leyden with An Introduction by Sir Thomas Stamford Raffles, F.R.S. &c. &c.* (London, 1817).

Low, C.R. *History of the Indian Navy (1613–1863)* (London, 1877), 2 vols.

Lucas, E.V. (ed.). *The Letters of Charles Lamb to which are added those of his sister Mary Lamb* (London, 1835), 3 vols.

Macdonald, D. *A Narrative of the Early Life and Services of Capt$^n$ D. Macdonald, I.N.* (Weymouth, n.d.).

Marsden, William. *The History of Sumatra* (London, 1783, 1784, 1811, 1814).

Marsden, William. *A Brief Memoir of the Life and Writings of the Late William Marsden ... Written by Himself with Notes from His Correspondence* (London, 1830).

Marshall, Peter H. *William Godwin* (New Haven, 1984).

Marshman, J.C. *Life and Times of Carey, Marshman, and Ward embracing the History of the Serampore Mission* (London, 1859), 2 vols.

Minto, Countess of. *Lord Minto in India: Life and Letters of Gilbert Elliot, First Earl of Minto from 1807 to 1814 while Governor-General of India* (London, 1880).

Moore, Thomas. *The Poetical Works of the Late Thomas Little, Esq.* (London, 1801).

Morton, Revd. James. *The Poetical Remains of the Late Dr. John Leyden, with Memoirs of His Life* (London, 1819).

Newsome, David. *The Parting of Friends: The Wilberforces and Henry Manning* (Grand Rapids, Michigan, 1966).

Oak, Bernhard H. *Mill Hill: A History of Mill Hill and its Environment* (Durham, 1994).

Oliver, George. *The History and Antiquities of the Town and Minister of Beverley, in the County of York, ...* (Beverley, 1829).

Parkinson, C. Northcote. *Edward Pellew: Viscount Exmouth Admiral of the Red* (London, 1934).

Parkinson, C. Northcote. *War in the Eastern Seas 1793–1815* (London, 1954).

Pinkerton, Joseph Culloden. *The Hull Family of County Down,* Reprinted from *Miscellanea Genealogicae et Heraldica* (London, 1932).

Raffles, T.S. 'On the Maláyu Nation, with a translation of its Maritime Institutions', *Asiatick Researches*, vol. XII (1812), pp. 102–58.

Raffles, T.S. *The Memorial of the Hon. Thomas Stamford Raffles* (London, 1816).

Raffles, T.S. *The History of Java* (London, 1817), 2 vols.

Raffles. T.S. *Statement of the Services of Sir Stamford Raffles* (London, 1824), reprinted with an Introduction by John Bastin (Kuala Lumpur, 1978).

[Raffles, T.S.] 'The Founding of Singapore' [letter Colonel Addenbrooke, 10 June 1819], *JSBRAS*, no. 2 (1878), pp. 175–82.

Raffles, Lady. *Memoir of the Life and Public Services of Sir Thomas Stamford Raffles, F.R.S. &c. Particularly in the Government of Java, 1811–1816, and of Bencoolen and its Dependencies, 1817–1824; with Details of the Commerce and Resources of the Eastern Archipelago, and Selections from His Correspondence* (London, 1830), reprinted with an Introduction by John Bastin (Singapore, 1991).

Raffles, Revd. Thomas. *Letters, during a Tour through some parts of France, Savoy, Switzerland, Germany, and The Netherlands in the Summer of 1817* (Liverpool, 1818).

Raffles, Thomas Stamford. *Memoirs of the Life and Ministry of the Rev. Thomas Raffles, D.D., LL.D., Etc. Etc. Etc.* (London, 1864).

Ramsden, Lady Guendolen (ed.). *Correspondence of Two Brothers: Edward Adolphus, Eleventh Duke of Somerset and His Brother, Lord Webb Seymour, 1800 to 1819 and After* (London, 1906).

Reynolds, Graham. *English Portrait Miniatures* (London, 1952).

Russell, Lord John. *Memoirs, Journal and Correspondence of Thomas Moore* (London, 1860).

Sadler, Thomas (ed.). *Diary, Reminiscences, and Correspondence of Henry Crabb Robinson, Barrister-at-Law, F.S.A.* (London, 1869), 3 vols.

Scott, Sir Walter. 'Biographical Memoir of John Leyden, M.D.', *The Edinburgh Annual Register for 1811*, vol. IV, pt. 2 (1813), pp. xli–lxviii.

Sumner, Revd. George Henry. *Life of Charles Richard Sumner, D.D., Bishop of Winchester, and Prelate of the Most Noble Order of the Garter, During a Forty Years Episcopate* (London, 1876).

Thorn, Major William. *Memoir of the Conquest of Java; with the subsequent operations of The British Forces in The Oriental Archipelago. To which is subjoined, A Statistical and Historical Sketch of Java; …* (London, 1815).

Travers, Thomas Otho. 'The Journal of Thomas Otho Travers 1813–1820'. (ed.) John Bastin, *Memoirs of the Raffles Museum*, no. 4 (1957/1960), pp. 1–226.

[Watkins, John; Shoberl, Frederic]. *A Biographical Dictionary of the Living Authors of Great Britain and Ireland ...* (London, 1816).

Williamson, George. *Andrew & Nathaniel Plimer* (London, 1903).

Wood, Betty (ed.) et al. 'The Letters of Simon Taylor of Jamaica to Chaloner Arcedekne, 1765–1775', *Travel, Trade and Power in the Atlantic 1765–1884*, Camden Miscellany, vol. XXXV, Fifth Series, vol. 19 (Cambridge, 2002).

Wurtzburg, C.E. 'Who Planned the Sea Route of the Java Expedition in 1811?', *The Mariner's Mirror*, vol. 37, no. 2 (April 1951), pp. 104–8.

Wurtzburg, C.E. *Raffles of the Eastern Isles* (London, 1954).

# Index